I read this book and give it a:
(please initial and rate)

	1	2	3	4	5
_____	★	★	★	★	★
_____	★	★	★	★	★
_____	★	★	★	★	★
_____	★	★	★	★	★
_____	★	★	★	★	★
_____	★	★	★	★	★
_____	★	★	★	★	★
_____	★	★	★	★	★
_____	★	★	★	★	★
_____	★	★	★	★	★
_____	★	★	★	★	★
_____	★	★	★	★	★

Not
Your Mother's®
Microwave Cookbook

Not Your Mother's

Microwave Cookbook

Fresh, Delicious, and Wholesome
Main Dishes, Snacks, Sides,
Desserts, and More

Beth Hensperger

The Harvard Common Press
Boston, Massachusetts

THE HARVARD COMMON PRESS
535 Albany Street
Boston, Massachusetts 02118
www.harvardcommonpress.com

Printed in the United States of America
Printed on acid-free paper

Library of Congress Cataloging-in-Publication Data

Hensperger, Beth.
   Not your mother's microwave cookbook : fresh, delicious, and wholesome main dishes,
snacks, sides, desserts, and more / Beth Hensperger.
      p.   cm.
Includes index.
ISBN 978-1-55832-418-3 (hardcover : alk. paper)
ISBN 978-1-55832-419-0 (pbk. : alk. paper)
   1. Microwave cookery.   I. Title.
TX832.H45   2010
641.5'882—dc22

2009035000

Special bulk-order discounts are available on this and other Harvard Common Press books.
Companies and organizations may purchase books for premiums or resale, or may arrange
a custom edition, by contacting the Marketing Director at the address above.

Cover recipe: Salmon with Crème Fraîche and Dill in Parchment (page 200)
Spine recipe: Vegetable Kabobs (page 168)
Back cover recipes: Mixed Vegetable Risotto with Fontina (page 120), Black and White Fudge (page 288)

Book design by Ralph Fowler / rlf design
Cover photographs by Joyce Oudkerk Pool
Food styling by Jen Straus

10 9 8 7 6 5 4 3 2 1

Not Your Mother's is a registered trademark of The Harvard Common Press.

For my father,
Edward Hensperger,
microwave engineer

Acknowledgments

Writing a cookbook is not a solitary endeavor, so I would like to express my appreciation to the people who contributed to this book and shared their expertise and excellent taste. I would like to thank Peggy Fallon of Dacor Appliances, for her salad; Carolyn Jung, the talented food writer, for her dad's chicken; Robert Lambert, for his expert chocolate sauce; Jacquie Higuera McMahan, for her Mexican palate; Victoria Wise, for the idea of a microwave yogurt béchamel sauce; the generous happy cook Dolores Kostelni; Phyllis Hensperger, for sharing her knowledge about and skill with vegetables, and for her springtime strawberry jam and vanilla custard for trifle; Valerie Cimino, for the care and detail she provides that make me feel like I have my own personal editor; and copyeditor Christine Corcoran Cox.

Contents

In Praise of the Microwave

Homemade Fast Food

Microwave ovens have become an essential part of modern life—even for those people who do not consider themselves cooks. Microwave cooking, especially using the ovens sold today, is a convenient and safe method of food preparation. *Not Your Mother's Microwave Cookbook* offers more than 125 recipes with the goal of empowering you to prepare delicious, healthful meals every day.

According to a survey by Panasonic's Home Appliance Group, only one-third of people who own microwave ovens use their microwaves for cooking beyond reheating food. Since most American households have a microwave, even one-third of users equals lots of people who are turning to the microwave for more than just reheating. Let's all follow their lead! Once you learn the basics and understand both the advantages and the limitations of this method of cooking, you'll find that microwaves are incredibly versatile and an invaluable tool in your kitchen.

The microwave is famous for a few elementary kitchen tasks, such as heating up leftovers and cold coffee, boiling water for tea, rewarming take-out food, heating canned soup, making instant oatmeal, popping popcorn, and cooking frozen dinners. But the microwave can also keep up with any top-of-the-line restaurant range in turning out stylish, sophisticated dishes.

Not Your Mother's Microwave Cookbook takes a middle-of-the-road approach to meal preparation. I want to get you fed, and fed well, without spending all day in the kitchen! Save the fast food for when you really have no time to cook a proper meal. Despite today's busy lifestyles, we all want nourishing, delicious, home-cooked meals. I will teach you to take advantage of the microwave's exceptional convenience to prepare quick, tasty microwave meals from scratch in less than 30 minutes. When confronted with a recipe with too many ingredients and that seems to require fancy culinary skills, most people just give up. I wrote this cookbook with ease in mind, with recipes that are simple and centered around just a few fresh, good-tasting ingredients.

These recipes focus on what the microwave does best, from hot breakfast cereals to soups to vegetables to fish and poultry to poached fruit and jams. The microwave can simmer, steam, boil, reheat, reduce, poach, and braise. The key to producing great-tasting dishes is to use flavorful broths, juices, sauces, and herbs. Fish cooks better and with less fuss in the microwave than by any other method. Polenta and risotto can become standard fare any day of the week instead of special-occasion foods, thanks to the microwave's elimination of these dishes' traditionally long preparation times. And would you believe that the microwave can produce a homemade to-mato sauce for pasta in less than 10 minutes? Cooking vegetables is probably the best job the microwave can do. All vegetables steam well since they contain a large quantity of water. Carrots, parsnips, and asparagus become aromatic and tender in the microwave. Greens become smooth, sweet, and velvety. Broccoli keeps its bright green color. Corn on the cob retains its essential sweetness. And with the microwave, you don't need to add much (if any) fat or salt, enabling you to feed the kids wholesome food they will enjoy and can easily learn to cook for themselves one day.

Not
Your Mother's®
Microwave Cookbook

The Essentials of Microwave Cooking

You do not need to know how a microwave oven works to cook with it, according to Carl Jerome, cooking assistant to iconic chef James Beard and one of the microwave-cooking experts of the 1980s and 1990s. When I first heard this statement, it released me from worrying about whether I could be a great microwave cook without understanding the scientific principles behind the microwave-cooking process. You might feel the same way, but if you're curious about what is actually going on in the microwave once you hit the Start button, here are the basics.

How the Microwave Works

First, *micro* means small—in this case, 3 to 5 inches in length and as big as your finger. Microwaves are waves of energy, not heat. Microwaves are small electromagnetic radiations, colorless, odorless, and tasteless, entering the oven through the magnetron tube and traveling at the speed of light. These ripply waves cause water or fat molecules to vibrate at a higher frequency (billions of times per second), resulting in the generation of heat. This is the reason we cook in the microwave by time and volume rather than by temperature.

Inside each microwave is a tube called the magnetron, which is the heart of the oven, converting regular electricity into high-frequency microwaves. When the waves reach the oven, they are distributed by a stirrer fan. The moisture in food absorbs them and creates friction through the vibration of the molecules, which cooks the food. The cooking process thus begins from the outside and penetrates inward. The air in the oven doesn't get hot (although heat buildup in the food from extended cooking times does, of course, occur), so the entire oven stays cool.

Microwaves are non-ionizing radiant energy in the same family as radio waves. This is a different type of wave from X-rays, which cause a chemical change. This is an important difference, since it means microwaves do not accumulate or leave any residue in food, air, or the body. Food cooked inside a microwave oven does not present any sort of radiation risk, despite the ubiquitous use of the word "nuked" to describe microwaved food. This is because microwaves cease to exist as soon as the power is turned off. Since these radiations are non-ionizing, they are not capable of changing the basic structure of any molecule to any extent. The moment you open the microwave door, the waves are already completely gone. There are special door seals to prevent leakage, so a microwave in the process of cooking is totally safe.

Microwaves are reflected, passed through, or absorbed by food, specifically water, fats, and sugar. They are not absorbed by most plastics, glass, or ceramics. The strange powers of the microwave arise from the basic fact that it cooks indirectly with the radio energy. Conventional baking, broiling, boiling, or frying transmits a particular level of heat directly to the food's surface. The entire energy generated by microwaves is used to cook the food rather than wasted on heating up the cooking vessels as in conventional cooking on a stovetop or in an oven. The radio waves, reflected off the inner walls of the oven, penetrate food from all directions at once until the oven turns off. They penetrate food only up to 1$\frac{1}{2}$ inches. Only the outer border of the food absorbs the energy, and then the heat generated is transmitted into the rest of the food. They build up energy as they move, causing the molecules in the food to accelerate or "dance." This activation (friction) creates heat, and the food is cooked. This heat is transferred by conduction to the inner/center sections of the food. Standing time allows for the energy to slow down, and cooking continues during that time. So to cook food fully and properly in the microwave, you need to have both time in the oven and standing time.

And so are microwave ovens safe? "All cooking changes foods, otherwise we wouldn't bother with it. Microwave cooking doesn't work very well for meats or baking since the food doesn't get much hotter than the boiling point of water, but it can do a good job with many other things, and in the case of vegetables, can retain vitamins much better than boiling does," says noted food scientist Harold McGee. "Even though it uses radio waves, it simply heats foods up; it doesn't do anything unusual to food or leave anything unusual in it."

"Microwaves cause water molecules in food to vibrate, producing heat that cooks the food," according to a fact sheet from the United States Food and Drug Administration Center for Devices and Radiological Health. "The microwave energy is changed to heat as it is absorbed by food, and does not make food 'radioactive' or 'contaminated.'" Some early worries about microwaves, like possible damage to pacemakers, have long since been resolved; modern pacemakers efficiently shield against electrical interference.

All microwave manufacturers follow strict safety standards within the industry. As with any kitchen appliance, your

Microwave Ovens: An Accidental Discovery

On October 8, 1945, Percy Spencer, a self-taught engineer without a high school education, was working building magnetrons for radar sets for the Raytheon Corporation and accidentally invented the microwave. During his tests, Dr. Spencer found that a candy bar that was in his pocket had melted as he stood in front of a magnetron tube that had been switched on. This event grabbed the engineer's interest. He decided to perform another experiment by placing some popcorn kernels near the magnetron; the popcorn kernels began to pop around the magnetron and inside his lab. He then designed a metal box with an opening into which he fed the microwave power, and when food was placed in the box, it became hot very rapidly and cooked. These experiments led to more research in the usage of microwave energy in cooking food and eventually led to the invention of the first microwave oven.

In 1947, Raytheon demonstrated the world's first microwave oven, the Radarange, a name submitted by an employee in a contest. The first ovens, sold for commercial use, were housed in refrigerator-size cabinets and cost $2,000 to $3,000. Raytheon eventually acquired Amana Refrigeration, and in 1967 introduced the first countertop 100-volt microwave for home use, which sold for $495. The rest, as they say, is history.

In 1975, Amana introduced microprocessor touch controls that allowed the user to select different power levels, making for more precise cooking time. In the mid 1970s, sales of microwave ovens exceeded those of gas ranges, and by 1976, microwave ovens had already become more common in the kitchen than dishwashers. But it wasn't until the mid 1980s that the microwave really took hold as an indispensable kitchen appliance.

Today, estimates are that more than 90 million American households have a microwave and that microwaves are in over 75 percent of all workplaces. The mass manufacture of magnetrons for use in microwave ovens is now carried out in Korea, Thailand, and China. Amana is now a division of the Whirlpool Corporation, which also owns KitchenAid.

—Adapted from *The History of the Microwave Oven,*
with permission from Whirlpool Corporation

oven should always be serviced by a quali-fied professional, not a home fix-it person.

A History of the Oven, or How Did We Get Here?

In the beginning there was fire. And food was cooked over an open fire. As civiliza-tion evolved, so did fire. Man learned how to control it. Soon there were fireplaces, and lots of cooking happened there, al-though statistics show lots of women who cooked that way over the centuries lost their lives when their clothes caught fire.

Then came the closed, front-loading oven on the side of the fireplace. The Indus Valley has the first known archeological ruins of mud-brick homes each having its own oven, dating from 3,200 B.C. Then, give or take a millennium, enter the iron cookstove with the fire contained inside it. People put wood or coal into these cook-stoves, which both provided heat and en-abled people to cook food. Cooking was done inside the cookstove as well as on top. Instead of regulating the fire, people moved the pots around for various temperatures.

In modern times came the natural-gas range, smaller by far than its predecessor, and the flame could be turned off and on. Ovens had a thermostat, keeping an even temperature. Then with the advent of the electric oven, the fire was so contained within that you didn't even have to see it or deal with it anymore.

The convection oven, long favored in pro-fessional kitchens and bakeries, uses a fan to circulate electric heat more efficiently. By moving hot air quickly past the food, con-vection ovens can operate at a lower tem-perature than standard conventional ovens and yet cook food more quickly. This air circulation, or convection, tends to elimi-nate "hot spots" and create an even temper-ature, so food bakes more evenly.

But the biggest jump in the evolution of the oven since the very first stove came with the microwave oven. A microwave isn't like a standard oven, in that it doesn't cook food by heating it from the outside, as in broiling, baking, or sautéing. Instead, the food heats from within and that heat spreads throughout the food. Microwaves move in unpredictable patterns, so most ovens have a revolving turntable set in the bottom to turn food as it cooks and a fan to redistribute the microwaves and promote even cooking.

Because microwave ovens don't need to heat up before cooking, they are very en-ergy efficient.

Size, Power, Cost, and Features of Today's Microwave Ovens

Size and Wattage

The interior capacity (expressed in cubic feet) and power (or wattage) should be your first considerations when purchasing a new single-purpose microwave. You can choose among countertop models to fit your home's counter space or models with brackets for hanging over the stove or under a counter or cabinet. Please note that all microwave doors open to the left.

Microwave ovens come in three general sizes and multiple power levels (be sure to check individual models for exact dimensions). Medium-size ovens are now readily available in wattages up to 1,100. The higher the wattage, the quicker food cooks. The capacity of the oven also affects cooking time: Food will cook more quickly in a small or medium-size 1,100-watt oven than in a larger-capacity oven with the same wattage.

Small, also known as compact
(good for apartments, cooking for 1 or 2, and dorm rooms)
> Interior space: 0.7 to 0.8 cubic feet
> Dimensions: 11 inches tall × 20 inches wide × 14 inches deep
> Power level: 600 to 1,100 watts

Medium-size (cooking for 4)
> Interior space: 1.4 to 1.6 cubic feet
> Dimensions: 13 inches tall × 21 inches wide × 16 inches deep
> Power level: 900 to 1,100 watts

Large (family size)
> Interior space: 1.8 to 2.2 cubic feet
> Dimensions: 14 inches tall × 24 inches wide × 18 inches deep
> Power level: 1,000 to 1,300 watts (some ovens go as high as 1,650 watts)

Price Ranges

The price of a microwave can vary according to its size, wattage, and features—whether it is a single-purpose oven, a microwave-convection combo (which cooks and browns food along with the microwaving), or an over-the-range model (which replaces the stove's range hood and provides venting capability for both the range and the microwave). More complex combination ovens are manufactured by the major appliance dealers (such as GE, KitchenAid, and Dacor) and start at around $700.

$40 to $250: countertop models
$400 and up: simple microwave-convection ovens
$100 to $700: over-the-range models
$250 to $1,000: halogen-convection ovens, whether countertop or over-the-range models

Essential Features

Microwaves are equipped with a timer and a simple numeric keypad of buttons representing a range of power levels and pre-programmed times for the most frequently cooked foods (called shortcut keys), such as Baked Potato or Popcorn. Different oven models offer a range of extra features, and it's up to you to determine which ones complement your cooking habits. All recipes in this book were prepared in microwaves without any fancy features, such as sensor probes. Listed below are the microwave features that I consider essential.

o Childproof lock: All microwaves come with a way to keep children out, by which the keys are rendered inoperable.

o View window: Every oven has this, which gives you the ability to visually monitor cooking progress. You have to be able to see what is going on.

o Heatproof glass turntable: So that you don't have to rotate food. The turntable lifts out for ease of cleaning.

o Time of day clock: This is convenient and easy to set.

o Variable cook/defrost levels: Some microwaves offer multiple levels of defrost. You want this feature. It can be used in place of the LOW power setting for cooking or melting chocolate. Another basic feature to look for is a selection of one-touch buttons, or shortcut keys, for various specific foods. They take the guesswork out of how many minutes you need to cook canned soup or defrost a chicken.

Optional Features

Microwaves are getting smarter and faster with every year and every new model. In the early 1990s the idea of a 1,000-watt microwave oven was too incredible to imagine, but today some large ovens have 1,300 watts or more. One of the newer twenty-first-century microwaves has a space-saving, door-mounted control panel, a "vapor sensor" that knows when more than a dozen different foods are done, special features for defrosting and cooking frozen foods, and a memory box that can download recipes from the Internet, with an LED display that tells you when to add ingredients or stir so that you do not have to consult the recipe. These are just a few

of the nifty features of today's microwaves, and no doubt there will be more innovations in the future.

o Keep-warm button: Keeps food warm for up to 30 minutes after cooking is completed.

o Delay timers: These give you the ability to put food into the microwave and set a future cooking time.

o Add 30 seconds or 1 minute: Many microwaves have a button you can push to automatically cook food for 30 seconds or 1 minute. Since microwave cook times can vary based on the size and power of the oven being used, the ability to add a little more cooking time at the push of a button is wonderful.

o Shortcut keys: This allows you to simply push a preset function button to automatically cook foods commonly prepared in the microwave, such as popcorn, oatmeal, pasta, and baked potatoes.

o Humidity sensor: A recent development based on infrared light or vapor, the sensor knows when food is done by measuring the level of steam rising off cooking food, preventing overcooking. Most small ovens don't offer this feature. It's not necessary, but it is very useful.

o Multilingual capability: Many new models sold in the United States can be programmed to display information in other languages, such as Spanish or French.

- "Talking" microwaves: These ovens are very useful for people who are blind or sight-impaired. They have a computerized voice that announces the cook time, current power level, when the food needs to be stirred or rotated, when the food is done, and other functions of the oven.

Features of Newer Machines

- Inverter technology: Conventional microwave ovens operate on only one power level; the microwave energy is either on or off. For example, when set at 60 percent power, a conventional microwave cooks at full power 60 percent of the time, and remains idle the rest of the time. This on/off delivery of cooking power results in food having cold spots and overcooked edges, especially with dense foods like casseroles or lasagna. Inverter technology delivers low-, medium-, and high-power levels. This targeted "soft" penetration of microwave energy into the center of food helps prevent overcooking on the edges and surfaces, and provides more even cooking compared to conventional microwaves. Microwaves with inverter technology do a better job of even heating. It is a new feature you'll see in some models, and you'll likely see lots more in the future.

- Microwave-convection combination: Microwaves with convection technology use a small fan that circulates hot air through the interior of the oven; this helps to brown food, yielding crisp French fries, crispy-skinned baked potatoes, crunchier pizza crusts, and baked goods that normally cannot be made in a single-purpose microwave. This type of oven takes up much more counter space than a standard microwave, even though it is still compact. The Sharp R-820JS is an excellent microwave-convection oven, but most major manufacturers offer these combo models since they are so versatile.

- WaveBox: Touted as the world's first portable microwave oven, the WaveBox comes in a small carry-on case to bring the power of the kitchen to minivans, trucks, recreational vehicles, job sites, boats, or virtually anywhere else you want to carry it, such as a pregame tailgate party. The WaveBox can be powered via a standard AC outlet or by connecting it to a 12-volt vehicle power outlet rated at 20 amps or higher or to a 12-volt vehicle and boat battery. Featuring a lunchbox-style design, luggage-quality handle, electronic controls, LED display, and presets for one-touch cooking, the WaveBox measures 15 × 11 × 10 inches. It even comes with an insulated cooler that fits inside the oven so you can carry along frozen items to cook. This little microwave is so popular that it is constantly on backorder.

- Halogen-microwave combination: This oven cooks food using either microwave power or a combination of microwaves and heat generated by the built-in 1,450-watt halogen lamps at the top and bottom of the oven. The halogen bulbs make up for the microwaves' inability to brown and sear food on the outside, and these ovens can cut cooking time by up to 75 percent.

The Greening of the Microwave Oven

The new push these days is to go "green" and be more energy conscious. The kitchen is a good place to start in the effort toward energy conservation and lower utility bills. Luckily for us, kitchen appliances are more energy efficient than ever and are constantly improving. The microwave, in particular, is helping pave the way toward reducing your carbon "cookprint."

We are now encouraged to consider how we cook our food, what type of energy we use, the amount of fuel consumed, and how much water it took to do it all. The kitchen is the most energy-intensive room in the house. Although the microwave may not save much energy or money compared to a stovetop burner for a task like heating water, it can be much more energy-efficient than a traditional full-size oven when it comes to cooking food. Because their heat waves are concentrated on the food, microwaves cook and heat much faster than electric or gas ovens, which need to heat up themselves before actually heating up the food. According to the federal government's Energy Star program, which rates appliances based on their energy efficiency, cooking or reheating small portions of food in the microwave can save as much as 80 percent of the energy used to cook or warm food in a traditional oven. So using the microwave is your "greenest" option for preparing small meals or portions.

In addition to using less energy, cooking in a microwave oven keeps the kitchen cooler in the summer, which can reduce air-conditioning usage. New and better microwave ovens continue to evolve to cook food even faster, with greater convenience and using less energy, so the microwave plays an important role in the energy-efficient kitchen of today and beyond.

The website Treehugger.com reports that you can optimize your energy efficiency around the kitchen by making sure to keep the inside surfaces of your microwave oven clean; this maximizes the amount of energy reflected toward your food rather than having it be diverted to the splatters from the last cooking session. Plug your microwave into a power strip and you can save the energy that is used when your microwave is off and the LED display is still on. Be sure to use a heavy-duty power strip with a grounded UL-approved, three-prong plug, not a regular extension cord.

Basic Microwave Know-How

The following is a guide to understanding the techniques and basic principles necessary for getting the best results from your microwave.

o Read the manufacturer's manual. Give your manual at least one good read-through before using a new microwave oven. Keep the manual for reference about details for your particular oven. Install the oven according to the manufacturer's instructions, with its own electrical circuit if possible. Make sure countertop models have clearance on all sides for proper ventilation.

o Know your oven's wattage. To find out how many watts your microwave has, check the owner's manual, or look on the back plate or on the inside of the oven door, where the model and serial numbers are printed. This will make a big difference when you cook using the recipes in this book, since cook times are based on wattage. These recipes were written for ovens of between 1,100 and 1,300 watts, but there are ways to adapt if your oven has a different wattage (page 23).

o The size and shape of food affects cook time. Small pieces cook faster than large; thin food cooks faster than thick; soft vegetables, like zucchini, cook faster than hard vegetables, such as carrots. Foods of a uniform shape and thickness cook more evenly than foods that are irregularly shaped. Meatballs, apples, and beets will cook more evenly, faster, than fish and poultry, which often have thick and thin sections.

o More food equals more cooking time. Large amounts of cook more slowly in the microwave than smaller amounts.

o Food temperature affects cooking time. Food cold out of the fridge and frozen foods will take longer to cook in the microwave than room-temperature ingredients.

o Salt food after cooking. Since salt absorbs microwave energy, its flavor intensifies during cooking and can dry out the food. This also applies to garlic or onion salts.

o It's better to undercook than overcook. Always cook food for the lesser amount of cook time specified in a recipe. If the food is undercooked, you can always put it back in the microwave for a few more minutes, but you can't do anything about overcooked food. Foods cooked in the microwave continue to cook when taken out of the oven, so allow for a few minutes of standing time.

o Standing time is important. After the microwave has shut off, you can let food stand in the oven itself or on a heat-resistant surface on the counter. Each recipe in this book includes instructions about standing time. Some foods require no standing time; others that cook longer will need a longer standing time. The food is not ready to serve until after the standing time.

o For best results, cook foods at the power level directed in each recipe. Foods especially sensitive to power level include eggs, cheese, mayonnaise, and cream. Remember that fats, oils, jams, and syrups all cook faster than water. So keep close tabs on the cooking, and turn off the oven as soon as the food is done. MEDIUM and LOW oven settings are useful because they pulse the microwaves on and off and slow the heating so that it's easier to control. Power levels called for in recipes, which are written in capital letters, are based on the following percentages and are often represented by numbers on the keypad (for example, 1 equals 10 percent and 10 equals 100 percent) or by five power levels. Older microwaves may only have full power and half power (or defrost).

HIGH	100 percent
MEDIUM-HIGH	70 percent
MEDIUM	50 percent
MEDIUM-LOW	30 percent
LOW	10 percent

Microwave-Cooking Techniques

There are a few basic techniques needed for microwave cooking. Since microwaves penetrate the surfaces of food, the outside areas absorb more energy than the center. By using techniques that move around and equalize heat, you can make sure that all parts of the food are done at the same time.

o Covering. Microwaving is a moist cooking method, like steaming or braising. Using a cover holds in steam, which helps food cook faster and more efficiently. Plastic wrap, waxed or parchment paper, a lid, and plain paper towels are the recommended covers (page 18). Always vent the lid or plastic wrap to prevent intense steam buildup. When food has finished cooking, always remove the cover in a direction away from your face to avoid being burned by the steam generated during cooking.

o Arranging food in the oven. A single dish is easy to position in the center of the microwave, but when you are cooking several items at the same time, arrange them in a ring with spaces in between so that energy can penetrate from all sides.

o Arranging food on a baking dish. The center of a baking dish, whether round, oval, square, or rectangular, receives less energy than the outside. Arrange the food so that thin or delicate parts, such as the florets of broccoli or the tips of asparagus spears, are pointed into the center, with thick or tough parts near the outside edge of the dish. Circular or spoke patterns work best. Even mashed potatoes cook better in a doughnut-shaped ring than in a mound. Baked potatoes can be arranged at the four corners of a piece of paper towel. Round baking dishes are more efficient than square or rectangular dishes because they absorb microwave energy more evenly.

o Rearranging food. Since there are sections of the inside of the oven that receive more or less energy than other parts, some recipes will recommend turning over or rearranging large items, such as vegetables and pieces of meat. The repositioning helps all parts of the food cook evenly.

- Stirring. One of the most useful and important techniques in microwave cooking is stirring. As you stir and move the food, you distribute the heat and food cooks more evenly. However, you do not need to stir as much as in conventional cooking. Once or twice during the cooking time will do it for most recipes.

- Rotating. If you have an older oven model that does not have a turntable, some casserole-type dishes or baked goods that cannot be stirred will need to be given a quarter or half turn to allow for more even cooking. If your microwave has a turntable, which most current models do, you will not have to worry about this.

What to Avoid Doing in the Microwave

There are distinct techniques and equipment that will *not* work in a microwave oven.

- DO NOT turn on the oven while it is empty, as this can cause sparking and start a fire. It can also damage the magnetron.

- DO NOT use the oven if the door glass is cracked or the door does not close properly, to prevent leakage of the microwaves and to ensure even cooking.

- DO NOT use plastic storage containers such as margarine tubs, take-out containers, whipped topping bowls, Styrofoam trays, and other one-time-use containers or their lids in microwave

ovens. These containers can warp or melt, possibly causing harmful chemicals to migrate into the food. Only use cookware that is specially manufactured for use in the microwave oven. Make sure glass, ceramic, and all plastic containers are labeled as safe for microwave use.

- DO NOT use thin plastic storage bags, brown paper or plastic grocery bags, plastic produce bags, newspapers, or aluminum foil in the microwave oven, as they may generate toxic fumes and risk catching fire due to their ink or other components.

- DO NOT use delicate bone china or stemware like lead crystal in the microwave, for they are not heat resistant.

- DO NOT attempt to deep-fry in a microwave.

- DO NOT use recycled paper products in the microwave, as they may contain metal flecks that could spark and cause a fire.

- DO NOT use conventional meat or candy thermometers in the microwave. Use special thermometers designed for the microwave, or remove the food from the oven and test it with an instant-read thermometer.

- DO NOT use metal utensils, skewers, or dishes, or any plates with a metallic trim. This may cause the microwaves to reflect off the metal, causing sparks and damaging the oven. While some say a little metal in the microwave is okay, I never put metal in the microwave, not even twist ties or the staples on tea bags.

o DO NOT cook whole eggs or reheat hard-boiled eggs in the microwave. They will explode.

o DO NOT cook whole tough-skinned fruit, such as apples, or whole vegetables, such as winter squash, potatoes, and spaghetti squash, without piercing the skin all over before cooking to prevent them from bursting and splattering all over the inside of the oven.

o DO NOT heat infant formula or expressed breast milk in the microwave, as it may heat unevenly and contain "hot spots" than can burn a baby.

o DO NOT cook sausage, hot dogs, or any food covered by a natural skin without piercing first. This includes egg yolks— pierce the yolk before cooking in the microwave to prevent it from exploding and splattering all over the inside of the microwave.

o DO NOT use mugs or cups with glued handles in the microwave, as the glue will melt.

o DO NOT sterilize canning jars in the microwave, as they can break if heated when empty. Use the dishwasher or boil them on the stovetop.

o DO NOT overheat water or other liquids, a phenomenon known as superheating. Microwaved water (as for tea) and other liquids do not always bubble when they reach the boiling point and

can get superheated without bubbling at all. The superheated liquid can splash up out of the cup when it is moved or when something like a spoon or tea bag is put into it. To prevent this from happening and causing injury, do not heat any liquid for more than 2 minutes per 1 cup. After heating, let the cup stand in the microwave for 30 seconds before moving it or adding anything into it. Superheating is particularly likely to occur if the vessel that the water is heated in is new, or when heating a small amount of water (less than $1/2$ cup).

o DO NOT microwave a dry sponge to disinfect it. Microwaving a sponge on HIGH for 2 minutes can kill bacteria in the sponge, but the sponge must be wet or it can catch fire.

o DO NOT reuse microwaveable packaging from commercial foods, as it could melt or start a fire.

o DO NOT try to melt paraffin in the microwave. Paraffin has no water, sugar, or fat, so it will not melt in the microwave.

o And here's a tip from food scientist Harold McGee: DO NOT use wireless devices near the microwave when it is operating. Microwaves work in the same part of the radio spectrum as cordless phones, Bluetooth devices, and wireless networks. You can lose phone connections to oven interference.

o DO NOT use the microwave to dry fabrics, as they could catch fire.

Cooking Techniques That Do Not Work in the Microwave

For all the wonderful things that the microwave can do, like steaming and poaching, there are a few techniques that are beyond its powers. You cannot sauté, broil, roast, boil pasta (or a large pot of water), or make toast; you will have to rely on other appliances for these tasks. You cannot brown foods, so forget about steak. Whole roasts and poultry do not roast well in the microwave, and uneven cooking can lead to food safety concerns. Yeast breads toughen in the microwave, so always bake them in a conventional oven, but quick breads and bread crumbs work fine in the microwave.

Foods That the Microwave Cannot (or Should Not) Cook

There are some foods that cannot be prepared in the microwave, as they just will not cook, since the best foods for microwaving have a high water content and cook by poaching or steaming.

- Biscuits and scones.
- Pancakes from scratch; however, premade frozen pancakes reheat great.
- Pie crusts and pastries do not brown or crisp.
- Choux paste (as for cream puffs) never puffs.
- Popovers or Yorkshire pudding never expand and brown.
- Chiffon and angel food cakes never rise properly, and they toughen.
- Batter-dipped foods will not crisp or brown.
- Deep- or shallow-fried foods cannot reach the high temperature needed to cook properly and are a fire danger.
- Eggs in the shell will burst.
- Home-canned goods. The sealed jars can explode.
- Infant formula and expressed breast milk, as they can heat unevenly and cause "hot spots" that could burn the baby. Microcooking breast milk can also destroy some of its nutrients.

Microwave Cookware

Size, shape, durability, weight, and price are relevant factors when choosing cookware to use in the microwave. Use only microwave-safe, heatproof glass and ceramic dishes, and heatproof plastic (thermoplastic) designed specifically for the microwave so that the microwave energy can pass through. Look to see that vessels are labeled "for use in the microwave" or "microwave safe." This category also includes clay bakers and high-fire porcelain pottery, and new genres of sturdy heat-resistant ceramic materials are being developed by Japanese researchers just for the microwave that heat up faster and retain heat longer than conventional microwave cookware, requiring less energy.

Most of the containers needed for microwave cooking are already in your kitchen. The recipes in this book were tested with standard kitchen equipment. Any cookware we recommend in the recipes is reasonably priced and available in supermarkets, hardware stores, restaurant supply and gourmet cookware shops, and by Internet mail order.

Be sure your cookware fits in your oven with plenty of room all around for the oven to work best. In my microwave cooking, I primarily use glass measuring cups, shallow baking dishes, and round casserole dishes. All of the cookware recommended can go in the dishwasher, which makes life a great deal easier. Allocate a special section in one cupboard for your microwave cookware. It is most convenient to be able to

Food Safety in the Microwave Oven

Microwave oven cookery follows many of the standard rules for food safety. Special care must be taken when cooking or reheating meat, poultry, fish, and eggs to make sure they are prepared safely. Microwave ovens can cook unevenly and leave "cold spots" where harmful bacteria can survive. This is the reason for rotating the baking dish or using the turntable. Following are some safe microwaving tips to prevent foodborne illness and injury, adapted from the publication "Cooking Safely in the Microwave Oven" from the United States Department of Agriculture.

- Remove frozen food from its packaging before defrosting in the microwave. Do not use foam trays and plastic wrappings in the microwave because they are not heat stable at high temperatures. Melting or warping may cause harmful chemicals to migrate into food.

- Cook meat, poultry, egg casseroles, and fish immediately after defrosting in the microwave because some areas of the frozen food may begin to cook during the defrosting time. Do not set aside partially cooked food to reheat later.

- Arrange food items evenly in a baking dish and add some liquid if needed; cover with a lid or vented plastic wrap to let steam escape. The moist heat that is created will help destroy harmful bacteria and ensure uniform cooking. Microwave-cooking bags also provide safe, even cooking.

- Stir or rotate food midway through the microwaving time to eliminate cold spots where harmful bacteria can survive, and for more even cooking.

- When partially cooking food in the microwave oven that will finish cooking on the grill or in a conventional oven, it is important to transfer the microcooked food to the other heat source immediately. Never partially cook food and store it for later use.

access your cookware pieces without having to dig around for them. Always have oven mitts nearby for removing the cookware from the oven after cooking.

Essential Microwave Cookware

- 2-cup, 4-cup (1-quart), and 8-cup (2-quart) Pyrex or Anchor Hocking ovenproof glass measuring cups. Use

for sauces, eggs, liquids, and vegetables. These are indispensable, inexpensive, and easy to use with their sturdy handles. Out of all the cooking equipment I have, I use these the most when cooking in the microwave.

- 2-quart Le Creuset or Anchor Hocking batter bowl. This can take the place of the 2-quart measuring cup. This bowl

- Use an instant-read thermometer or the oven's temperature probe to verify that the food has reached a safe temperature. Place the thermometer in the thickest area of the meat or poultry—not near fat or bone—and in the innermost part of the thigh of whole poultry. Cooking times may vary because ovens vary in power and efficiency. Beef, veal, and lamb steaks, roasts, and chops should cook to 145°F; pork, ground beef, ground veal, and ground lamb should cook to 160°F; egg dishes and casseroles should cook to 160°F; and all poultry should cook to 165°F. Fish should flake with a fork. Always allow standing time, which completes the cooking, before checking the internal temperature with a food thermometer.

- Cooking whole stuffed poultry in a microwave oven is not recommended. The stuffing might not reach the temperature needed to destroy harmful bacteria. Not only is a whole chicken too large to cook evenly, it will be unappealing without the crisp skin that oven-roasting imparts. The same goes for roast beef; any food that relies on a crisp, caramelized exterior will be tough and lacking in textural contrast if cooked in the microwave; use your conventional oven instead.

- You do not have to buy all new microwave-safe dishes. Any Pyrex, Anchor Hocking glass, or ceramic dish (without metallic glazes) will work fine. Thick plastic containers marked as safe for use in the microwave are also okay, but avoid thin containers that may melt, like those from the deli or your favorite take-out restaurant. Never put metal pans or aluminum foil in the microwave. Metal reflects the microwaves and can cause sparks and/or fire.

- Do not use any metal objects, such as bowls, table forks, or decorated dishes, which can contain metal shards, in the microwave. They can cause arcing, which will damage the oven's magnetron.

has a handle and extended spout, and it is one of my favorite pieces of kitchen equipment.

- o 1-quart, 1½-quart, 2-quart, and 3-quart ovenproof Pyrex glass casserole dishes with lids. These are easily found in supermarkets. Remember that round is the most efficient shape for microwave cookware.

- o Micro-Mac polycarbonate thermoplastic cookware (www.micromac-cookware.com). This cookware, made in Canada, is exclusively for microwave cooking but can go into the freezer and dishwasher. I use the 1-quart pots with lids and the 2-quart and 3-quart Simmer Pot casserole dishes in my everyday cooking.

- o 8-inch and 9-inch square Pyrex or Anchor Hocking baking dishes or ceramic baking dishes. The straight sides and rounded corners are best for microwave cooking. The strong protruding handles are also great.

- o 2-quart rectangular (11 × 7-inch) baking dish or oval gratin dish. I love French porcelain like the elegant and functional dishes made by Pillivuyt

("Pilly-veet") Culinary Porcelain and BIA Cordon Bleu, which carries soufflé dishes, a 1½-quart covered casserole, a 2-quart oval baker, and quiche pans.

- o 8-inch, 9-inch, and 10-inch Pyrex pie plates. I also like the pie plates made by Tufty Ceramics (www.tuftyceramics.com).

- o 8-inch and 9-inch glass or Tufty Ceramics loaf pans and 6-ounce round or oval glass or ceramic custard cups.

Other handy products for microwave cooking are CorningWare's line of microwave-friendly casserole and baking dishes made of lightweight glass, called SimplyLite (www.corningware.com), that are perfect for use by children and elderly adults, and Tupperware's Heat 'N Serve round and square food containers made for use in the microwave, which have a special valve to allow steam to escape during heating and which are also freezer- and dishwasher-safe (http://order.tupperware.com/coe/app/home).

Some traditional types of cookware, such as ceramic or glass platters and roasting pans, are often overlooked for microwave use. However, if they fit in your microwave and will let the carousel turn,

In Case of Fire

If your oven begins to spark, turn it off immediately. DO NOT open the oven door. Shut off the oven, then pull the plug from the power outlet immediately. Cover the top or back vent with a heavy towel to block the flow of oxygen. Wait until the fire is completely out before opening the oven door and discarding the contents.

they are ideal for microwave cooking and can go right to the serving table, as can individual dinner plates without metal or gold borders. I also like to use the plastic bacon tray with ridges made specifically for cooking bacon in the microwave. Many people swear by their microwave popcorn maker or their microwave browning tray.

When microcooking rice, I prefer to use a Pyrex round casserole dish with a lid over the fancy made-for-the-microwave rice cookers. One popular piece of specialized cookware for the microwave is the Cook-Zen cooking pot, which is great for making Japanese-style one-dish meals (www.cook-zen.com).

There are now disposable heat-resistant plastic-coated paper products available in supermarkets that are microwave-safe and suitable for one-time-only use. Avoid using printed or recycled paper products in the microwave, as they contain dyes and other impurities that can leach into the food.

Silicone bakeware is good for use in the microwave; it is heatproof, microwave-safe, freezer-safe, and dishwasher-safe. It can be transferred directly from freezer to microwave, and it is different from other bakeware because it is totally flexible. Made predominantly with silica, or sand (just like glass), food-grade nonstick silicone bakeware will not react in any way with your food when used in the microwave. It is nonporous, so it will not retain flavors or odors to taint your next dish, and it will not crack, peel, or warp. Removing food from silicone pans is super easy—a slight twist or a gentle pull

on the sides, and you can roll out your baked goods.

Wash silicone bakeware in warm soapy water before using for the first time or if unused for a while. (Silicone cake molds can hold static and attract dust like your TV screen.) I like the 6-cup muffin pan best, but you can buy a silicone baking set that includes all sorts of shallow baking dishes.

Covering Things Up

Covering the food is a crucial component of the microwave-cooking process. By using a cover, the baking dish holds in heat and moisture so that the foods cook evenly and efficiently. The material that the cover is made of must be able to let the microwave energy pass through but keep the heat in.

In the recipes in this book "microwave uncovered" means that the food does not need to be covered and moisture is allowed to evaporate a bit. Many sauces are cooked uncovered so that they will naturally thicken and intensify in flavor.

"Cover tightly" means to use a lid or plastic wrap. However, even when a recipe says to cover a dish tightly, when using plastic wrap you need to turn a small edge of the wrap back on one side or two opposing sides, so that the wrap does not expand and split, which could give the cook a steam burn. Always remove covers by lifting the lid or wrap away from yourself to avoid being burned by the hot steam. Do not let the plastic wrap touch the food, as it could melt into the food. For the tightest seal, use a casserole dish and its fitted lid or a microwave-safe dinner plate to cover the dish.

"Cover loosely" means to use waxed paper, parchment paper, or microwave-safe paper towels so that some moisture can evaporate, as these covering agents are porous. Paper towels are good because they absorb moisture and fat. Here are some of the different types of materials that work well as covers in the microwave:

o Paper towels. Paper towels are porous and allow steam to escape, and they also prevent cooked food from splattering. Paper towels are best used for reheating baked goods, crackers, chips, sandwiches, or burritos and to prevent sogginess. Microwave-safe paper towels are labeled as such. Only use plain white paper towels without dyed borders, as the dyes may be oil-based and can ignite. Never use recycled paper towels, as they are filled with impurities and metal specks. Paper towels can be moistened to steam foods like tortillas or crepes. Paper towels can be used to create "steam bundles" for vegetables like broccoli, carrots, and cauliflower. Wrap two connecting towels around the vegetables like an envelope and moisten them under the faucet. Place the bundle, folded side down, on the turntable in the microwave. Microcook on HIGH for 1 to 2 minutes; let stand for 3 minutes and open by splitting on the perforation.

o Waxed paper and parchment paper. Waxed paper is unaffected by microwaves, so it has been used in microwave cooking for decades. It is more functional than plastic wrap since it can tolerate higher temperatures than plastic wrap. These covers work well for cooking without steaming and to prevent splatters. Waxed paper is coated with paraffin, which does not melt in the microwave, so it is moisture-proof and nonstick. Waxed paper can be wrapped around the baking dish or crumpled up and pressed on top. (A little side note: Waxed paper was invented by Thomas Edison and his assistants.) Parchment paper can be used to cook en papillote, in which food is sealed in a pouch and baked. The food essentially steams in the oven in its own juices.

o Plastic wrap. Plastic wrap is invaluable for tightly sealing cookware to cook a wide variety of foods with steam. Typically sold on rolls in boxes with a cutting edge, it clings to many smooth surfaces and can thus remain tight over the opening of a container with no adhesive or other devices. Common plastic wrap is roughly 0.01 mm thick. All brands of plastic wrap cling best to glass, china, or ceramic dishes; they do not cling well to Tupperware and the like, plastic microwave cookware, and paper plates. All plastic wraps cling better when the baking dish is dry. Plastic wrap is not heated by microwave energy, but it will become heated by contact with extremely hot foods, so always leave at least 1 inch of air space between the food and the wrap covering the dish. Certain foods with high fat content (such as butter or bacon) or with a high sugar content can become very hot in a microwave oven and should not come in contact with plastic wrap.

Despite the usefulness of plastic wrap in microwave cooking, covering foods with plastic wrap is one of the most controversial techniques in microwave cookery. Some believe that certain plasticizer residues (added to make plastic wrap flexible) may leach into the food during microcooking and are unhealthy to ingest. If you do not want to use plastic wrap, use Pyrex heat-tempered glass containers or microwave-safe casserole dishes, like the Tupperware versions made of hardened polyethylene plastic that come with their own lids; these have a steam hole designed specifically for use in the microwave.

I have spent a good deal of time researching the safest plastic wraps (see "Plastic Wrap 101"). Most plastic wraps on the grocery shelf are labeled microwave-safe. Some brands are stronger than others, since high temperatures can melt or shrink them. Extra-sturdy GladWare containers with interlocking lids have a tight seal for storing leftovers or freezing them and then going straight to the microwave. There are also microwave-safe plastic cooking bags that many people enjoy using (such as Glad SimplyCooking microwave steaming bags). Remember, never use plastic grocery or produce bags in the microwave, as they are not safe at high cooking temperatures and may contain dangerous chemicals that could leach into food.

Food safety experts agree in advising that consumers should take the following precautions when using plastic wrap or plastic containers in a microwave oven:

- Only plastic containers or packaging labeled "microwave safe" should be used in microwave ovens.

- If plastic wrap is used when cooking food in the microwave, it should not be allowed to come into direct contact with food, as it could melt into the food.

Plastic Wrap 101:
The Scoop on Plastic Wrap Brands

The current trend is toward environmentally friendly, biodegradable alternatives to some plastics. More and more countries the world over are concerned about the environmental impact of PVC, a plastic material said to be toxic and difficult to recycle. Plastic wrap was first made from PVC, but non-PVC alternatives are now being sold because of intense concerns about the risk that PVC could transfer dioxins into food. PVC needs lots more chemical additives to make it soft, since it is naturally hard and rigid.

The original cling wrap material was Saran, the commercial name for PVDC. Saran films are best known in the form of Saran Wrap, the first cling wrap designed for commercial (1949) and household (1953) use, introduced by the Dow Chemical Company. In 2004, however, the formula was changed and improved to low-density polyethylene (LDPE) due to environmental concerns about its chlorine content. The name Saran Original was changed to

Saran Premium. SC Johnson, the manufacturer, claimed that this change was a result of an initiative to look for more sustainable and environmentally acceptable plastic. The film in Saran Premium does not contain traces of potentially toxic additives. Newer production processes are closing the gap between PVC and LDPE, trading a bit of the stickiness quality for safer plasticizers. Brands like Glad Cling Wrap and Handi-Wrap have also been improved to be LDPE-based and tend to not adhere as tightly as Reynolds.

In Australia, the original cling wrap material was polyethylene (PE) with a "stickifier" in the form of edible gum. The product was introduced under the brand name Glad in 1966. Glad does not use PVC plastics in its products that comply with FDA regulations, making them very safe for microwave cooking.

The little known Diamant Food Wrap, a brand sold in Canada, is plasticizer-free, environmentally friendly, and recyclable. It is the world's first non-PVC polystyrene-based stretch film. The manufacturer claims that the wrap contains no chlorine and is noncarcinogenic.

Reynolds Corporation changed the name of its plastic wrap to Seal-Tight. Reynolds Seal-Tight plastic wrap is marketed as safe for the microwave and adheres very tightly without splitting. Do not use Reynolds's colored plastic wrap in the microwave; it is for decorative use only. Reynolds also manufactures parchment paper and Cut-Rite waxed paper.

All sources from the FDA and government health agencies do agree on one point: Consumers should protect themselves when using plastic products in the microwave by following the basic precautions listed on page 19.

Reading plastic wrap boxes can be pretty frustrating. Most brands don't say what they're made of because they don't have to. All brands are not created equal. However, some brands are catching on to consumers' concerns and are reformulating their products.

The Polymer Lingo

Consumer plastic wraps were originally made from one of three categories of polymers:

- Polyethylene (PE), used in Glad and Handi-Wrap, with a softening temperature of 195°F.
- Polyvinyl chloride (PVC), used in Reynolds Seal-Tight plastic wrap, with a softening temperature of 210°F.
- Polyvinylidene chloride (PVDC), used in Saran Wrap, with a softening temperature of 250°F. In 2004, Saran Wrap was reformulated and improved to low-density polyethylene (LDPE) such that the product no longer contains PVC or any other chlorinated substance that could release dioxin.

According to *The Green Guide's Plastic Container Report* and other sources, here are the brands of plastic wrap that are best to use since they are made of #4 LDPE plastic instead of PVC and are plasticizer-free:

- Glad Cling Wrap
- Saran Cling Plus
- Best-Yet Clear Plastic Wrap
- Diamant Food Wrap
- Natural Value Plastic Wrap (carried at Whole Foods Markets and many co-op food stores; this brand also uses recycled paper boxes)

How to Read the Recipes in This Book

The recipes in this book are all written so that you can read the recipe and get all the pertinent details you need to get cooking quickly and execute the recipe in proper order. Often the prep takes more time than the cooking. Success in cooking relies on a combination of good recipes, good ingredients, and a careful cook. Remember that since cooking in the microwave is so fast, it is not a good idea to push the button and walk away.

Each recipe features a tip box listing the recommended microwave cookware for that dish. Using the recommended cookware will ensure the best results according to the volume of ingredients being used. Also listed is the recommended wattage for the microwave being used; all the recipes in the book were tested in countertop models with 1,100

to 1,300 watts, so if your microwave has more or less power, adjust your cooking time accordingly (page 23). According to Barbara Kafka, a microwave-cooking expert, the cooking times listed for older recipes are unreliable because today's microwave ovens are over 50 percent more powerful than models from several years ago.

After the wattage, you will find listed the estimated cook time, and then the standing time, which completes the cooking. Last in the tip box is the number of servings or volume of food produced by each recipe.

The list of ingredients is presented in the order they are used, including any garnish or finishing ingredients. The recipe instructions are listed in a clear step-by-step progression. Microwave cooking involves starting and stopping the oven and stirring, so you will often see a number of steps for even a basic recipe. In the recipes, I use the term "microcook" to distinguish the microwave-cooking procedure from any conventional cooking techniques that might also be included in the recipe.

Cooking times in the recipes are either precise times or a range of time. Nevertheless, you may need to use your judgment and practice trial and error to determine the exact cooking time that works for your microwave. When you see a range of time given in a recipe, check the food at the shorter amount of time, using your sense of smell as well as your sense of sight to assess whether it needs additional cooking.

In the last step, the standing time, if applicable, is listed; this time contributes to the overall texture and flavor of the dish. Unless noted otherwise, serve immediately. After making one of the recipes, I encourage you to jot down notes in the margins about any adjustments you made to the cooking time or ingredients, which will make the recipe your own and help you achieve the best results every time you prepare the dish.

Adjusting Quantities and Cook Times

Adjusting quantities when cooking in the microwave, such as doubling or halving recipes, does not work as it does in other types of cooking. You cannot simply multiply and divide evenly as you would with a conventional oven. In conventional cooking, usually there is no change in the cook time for increased quantities unless there is the factor of thickness of the sliced vegetables or meats. If you are not an experienced microwave cook, please do not attempt to multiply recipes without careful consideration to both quantity and cook time.

Do not double a recipe that feeds more than 6 to 8 people. Generally, quantities of food serving fewer than 8 cook better in the microwave, as large amounts of food tend to cook slowly and unevenly. Do not double microwave recipes for cakes, bar cookies, or lasagna, as they do not double well. The more food you put into the oven, the more time it will take to cook, as there is only so much microwave power and it must divide itself among the food.

The general rule of thumb for increasing quantities in the microwave is a bit complex. If you want to double the quantity of something like a stew or braised meat, in-crease the original cook time by half (this means adding only 50 percent more cook time) and use a larger diameter cooking vessel with the same depth. If you are cutting a recipe in half, reduce the cook time by one-third and use a smaller diameter cooking vessel with the same depth. When adding additional cook time, check the food at 30-second intervals. You cannot double soup recipes, since the volume will likely exceed the capacity of the oven. When cooking beans, split peas, and lentils, doubling or halving the recipes will not change the cook time. Always decrease salt and seasoning proportions when multiplying. You can always add more seasoning later if desired.

When multiplying recipes that require cooking in a casserole dish with a tight lid or vented plastic wrap, do not double the liquid measure, since no evaporation occurs in the microwave. When dividing and reducing a recipe, do not decrease the amount of liquid. When cooking uncovered, there will not be enough liquid to properly cook the dish.

If you are converting a conventional recipe for the microwave, the general rule is to use half the liquid required in the original recipe, but remember that the cook time will be drastically reduced—by about 75 percent.

All this changes when cooking a single raw food, such as bacon or a vegetable. If you want to increase, say, the number of potatoes or amount of corn on the cob you're preparing, determine the cook time for one piece. To cook two, double the cook time. If you are cooking more than two items, add half of the original cook time for each additional item.

How to Use These Recipes with a Lower- or Higher-Wattage Oven

As mentioned earlier, the recipes in this book were tested using 1,100- to 1,300-watt ovens, so if your microwave's wattage does not fall into this range, your cook times will be different from those specified in the recipes. If you have a lower-wattage oven, you will have to increase the cooking time, and you will need to decrease the cooking time when using a more powerful oven. Once you are familiar with your oven, you will be able to adjust cook times with no problem.

Use the following guide for adapting the recipes in this book to lower-wattage ovens. I always err on the side of less cooking time, then add time in 30- to 60-second intervals if needed to avoid overcooking.

o 950 watts: The cook time will be about the same as what is specified in the recipes in this book.

o 750 to 850 watts: Increase the cook time by one-third (for example, if the recipe says to microcook for 3 minutes, increase that to 4 minutes).

o 500 to 700 watts: Increase the cook time by one-half.

High-Altitude Microwave Cooking

High elevations affect microwave cooking just like they do conventional cooking. In a nutshell, water boils at a lower temperature and liquids evaporate faster at high elevations than at sea level. Use the following guidelines when cooking at high altitudes:

o Increase liquid measurements by 1 to 3 tablespoons since there is more evaporation in the drier atmosphere and a lower boiling point.

o Increase cook time slightly since food does not get as hot due to the low boiling point.

o Use slightly larger cooking vessels to take into account more boilovers, expansion, and foaming during cooking due to the lower atmospheric pressure. Do not fill more than half full.

o Cover foods, especially during standing time and reheating time, as foods cool faster the higher you go.

Keeping Your Microwave Clean

The interior walls of most microwaves are made of enameled metal that does not heat up during the cooking process, so splattered food doesn't bake on like in conventional ovens. That said, you should still clean up spills and drips promptly. Clean your microwave using a damp sponge or paper towel—never with scouring pads, abrasive cleansers, or hard detergents—to avoid scratching the surface. For messier spills, place a 1-quart measuring cup full of water in the oven and microcook on HIGH for 5 to 6 minutes (stir the water carefully if it does not begin to boil on its own). Let the steam from the hot water fill the inside of the closed microwave for several minutes. Remove the water and turntable tray with oven mitts, then wipe down the walls. Use a small pastry brush to clean crumbs from the corners. Wash the turntable in the sink or dishwasher. The exterior of the microwave oven can be sprayed with a gentle kitchen cleaner and wiped with paper towels. Wipe the control panel with a damp cloth while the door is open so that the oven will not turn on.

Deodorizing the Microwave

If you pop open the door of your microwave and discover that you can still smell last night's curry sauce, add a slice of lemon or squeeze a lemon wedge into 1 cup of water in a 2-cup glass measuring cup. Microcook on HIGH for 2 to 3 minutes. Let stand for 20 minutes in the closed oven; do not open the door. The released steam will bring your microwave back to a fresh, neutral state, ready to cook the next meal. Wipe down the inside of the oven with a cloth dipped in the lemon water.

Keeping Cleanup to a Minimum

Avoid ovens with crevices and nooks inside the oven that can catch food particles. A smooth, flat surface requires nothing more than a quick wipe-down. If you have a choice of exterior color, bear in mind that black or dark-hued ovens are easier to keep looking pristine than bright white ones. Clean the microwave interior after every cooking session, as food buildup will attract microwaves the next time the microwave is used, "distracting" them from the new food you are cooking.

Avoiding Exploding Bits of Food

Any "enclosed" or "encased" food, such as hot dogs, sausage, whole winter squash, chestnuts, yams, or potatoes, *must* be pricked in several places with a fork or the tip of a knife to break the outer skin so that internal steam can escape. Otherwise, the food's internal pressure will build up as it cooks and eventually burst the food, spraying it in all directions. Also, never microcook a whole, unpricked egg or egg yolk or any food in a closed jar or narrow-necked bottle, or you'll end up with an equally explosive mess to clean up.

Handy Microwave How-To's

The microwave does a bevy of little jobs efficiently. Toasting a half cup of nuts or melting one square of chocolate isn't worth turning on your conventional oven, but these things are easily and quickly done in the microwave. The microwave has a variety of other little-known talents: It makes quick work of peeling thin-skinned tomatoes and peaches and helps ripen semisoft cheeses like Brie or Camembert, and making bread crumbs has never been so easy. And how about all those times you buy herb bunches at the supermarket but only need a few fresh leaves for a recipe? The microwave can function as a drying unit so that you don't have to throw away the leftovers.

How to Melt Chocolate

The microwave oven is as proficient at melting chocolate as the old double boiler, but much neater. The trick to melting chocolate successfully via any method is to melt it slowly, as chocolate responds quickly to changes in temperature (becoming grainy); it also burns very easily. Be sure the container in which it is melted is completely dry, as water causes chocolate to "seize," or turn into a dull, thick paste, and you will have to throw it away and start over. Different types and brands of good-quality chocolate melt at different rates and have different consistencies. Milk and white chocolates take less time than dark or unsweetened. Semisweet, bittersweet, and milk chocolates tend to hold their shape when melted and must be stirred with a whisk or rubber spatula to create a smooth consistency.

How to Melt Dark and Unsweetened Chocolate

Place coarsely chopped chocolate or unwrapped squares in a completely dry microwave-safe bowl. Microcook on MEDIUM (50 percent power) in low-wattage ovens, or on DEFROST in high-wattage ovens, depending on the amount of chocolate, until the chocolate is shiny and slightly melted. The chocolate may hold its shape but still be soft. Stir at 30-second intervals throughout the melting process until the chocolate is completely melted. For 1 ounce of chocolate, melting time should be 1 to 1$\frac{1}{2}$ minutes; for 2 ounces, 2 to 2$\frac{1}{2}$ minutes; and for 3 ounces, 3 to 3$\frac{1}{2}$ minutes.

How to Melt Chocolate Chips

Place 1 cup (6 ounces) chocolate chips in a completely dry microwave-safe bowl. Microcook on MEDIUM (50 percent power) or on DEFROST for 2 minutes, until the chips are shiny; they will still hold their shape. Stir at 30-second intervals throughout the process until the chips are completely melted. For 2 cups (12 ounces) of chips, microcook for 3 to 3$\frac{1}{2}$ minutes.

How to Melt White Chocolate

White chocolate is exceptionally heat sensitive, so take extra care when melting it to prevent it from becoming lumpy. Do not melt more than 8 ounces at one time for the best results. Place coarsely chopped white chocolate in a completely dry microwave-safe bowl. Microcook on DEFROST for 1 minute, until soft but not melted. Continue to microcook in 30-second intervals, stirring after each interval until melted.

How to Make Chocolate-Dipped Biscotti

Make homemade or store-bought biscotti even tastier by dipping them in chocolate. Heat 1$\frac{1}{4}$ cups white or semisweet chocolate chips and 1 teaspoon vegetable oil in a 1-quart Pyrex measuring cup on MEDIUM (50 percent power) for 1 to 1$\frac{1}{2}$ minutes. Stir until the chips are melted. Dip the cookies halfway into the chocolate, then set them on a parchment-lined baking sheet until the chocolate is cool and firm, or refrigerate for 15 minutes.

How to Toast Nuts in the Microwave

Toasting nuts gives them a more pronounced fragrance, richer flavor, and a crisp texture. This is the method for toasting raw pine nuts, almonds (whole, blanched, slivered, or sliced), walnuts (halves or pieces), whole macadamia nuts, whole hazelnuts, and pecans (whole or pieces). Slivered or sliced nuts and pine nuts will toast much more quickly than pieces or halves.

Spread the nuts in a single layer on a shallow paper plate, on a double layer of paper towels, or in a shallow microwave-safe bowl. Microcook on HIGH for 2½ minutes per ½ cup of nuts, stirring every 45 to 60 seconds to prevent burning and facilitate even browning. This method toasts nuts very quickly, so watch them carefully! If toasting hazelnuts, place the toasted nuts in a clean dishtowel and rub vigorously to remove the skins.

How to Make Nut Flour

Ground toasted nuts can be used as a replacement for the wheat flour in baking recipes, a substitution sometimes used in gluten-free cooking and baking. Use a European-style hand nut grater, electric blender, or food processor fitted with the metal blade to grind the nuts, and be sure the toasted nuts are dry. Add 1 to 2 tablespoons of sugar or flour (don't use flour if you wish to keep it gluten free) per each cup of nuts during the grinding to absorb the nut oil and prevent the formation of a paste during the grinding; properly ground nuts have a powdery, fluffy quality. Lightly spoon the flour into a measuring cup.

How to Blanch Almonds

Place 1 cup water in a 1-quart Pyrex measuring cup. Microcook on HIGH to bring to a boil, about 2 minutes. Add 1 cup whole raw almonds to the measuring cup and microcook on HIGH for 30 seconds. Drain the nuts and pour them onto a double layer of paper towels in a single layer. Slip off the skins by rubbing with your fingers, and let the nuts dry.

How to Roast Peanuts

Pour 1 cup raw shelled peanuts into a colander and rinse thoroughly with cold water. Sprinkle with ½ teaspoon salt. Pour the nuts into a 9-inch Pyrex pie plate and spread them in an even single layer. Microcook on HIGH for 2 minutes, stir, and then microcook on HIGH for 1½ to 2½ minutes longer. The peanuts will be crisp when cool. This method is also good for refreshing soggy or slightly stale peanuts.

How to Toast Sesame Seeds

Spread 1 to 4 tablespoons white sesame seeds on a paper towel or in a 6- to 8-inch Pyrex pie plate. Microcook on HIGH for 3 to 4 minutes, or just until the seeds turn a pale golden brown and become shiny when they exude some oil. Stop and stir the seeds every minute. Use the seeds immediately, or set them on the counter to cool. You can use the same method for sunflower seeds and pumpkin seeds.

How to Toast Coconut

The microwave is by far the easiest way to toast coconut either for sweet or savory cooking, as a garnish or ingredient. Keep in mind that sweetened coconut cooks faster than unsweetened. Spread 1 cup (4 ounces) unsweetened dried coconut or shredded sweetened coconut on a paper plate or in a 9-inch Pyrex pie plate. Microcook on HIGH for 2 to 3 minutes, stirring every minute for even toasting, until the coconut is browned to your liking.

How to Rewarm Baked Goods

Wrap a muffin, doughnut, scone, or slice of coffeecake in a microwave-safe paper towel, which will keep it moist. Microcook on LOW (10 percent power) or DEFROST at 10-second intervals until warm.

How to Steam Fresh Tortillas

To steam 4 to 6 tortillas at a time, wrap the stack in a layer of moist paper towels. Microcook on HIGH for 30 to 45 seconds to warm and soften. Use immediately, as they cool quickly.

How to Defrost Frozen Tortillas

Wrap 2 corn or flour tortillas in waxed paper, and microcook on HIGH for 1 minute to warm. This defrosting technique also works well for frozen cooked waffles and pancakes.

How to Make Toasted Bread Crumbs

Place 4 to 6 slices of day-old French bread on a layer of paper towel. Microcook on HIGH, uncovered, for $1\frac{1}{2}$ to $2\frac{1}{2}$ minutes, until the bread is dry and toasted. Cool, then break the bread into pieces and place in a food processor. Pulse to make fine or coarse bread crumbs as desired.

How to Dry Fresh Pasta

Spread up to 8 ounces of fresh pasta on a microwave-safe tray (such as a microwave bacon rack) lined with a double layer of paper towels. Microcook, uncovered, on LOW (10 percent power) or DEFROST for 3 to 5 minutes, depending on the thickness of the pasta, until dry. Rearrange the pasta on the tray after 2 minutes for even drying. Remove by lifting up the paper towel and transfer to a wire rack to cool. Store in a tightly covered tin or plastic container.

How to Peel Whole Fresh Tomatoes

Many people love peeled tomatoes on their salad or prefer to make fresh tomato sauce without the skins. The microwave provides an easy way to peel those tomatoes. Place up to 6 whole tomatoes in a ring on a double layer of paper towels. Microcook on HIGH for 15 seconds. Let stand for 10 to 15 minutes, then peel the tomatoes with a paring knife; the skins will come off easily.

How to Peel Whole Fresh Peaches

No more dipping into a vat of boiling water to peel those peaches. Place up to 4 whole firm-ripe peaches in a 2-quart microwave-safe bowl or soufflé dish with ½ cup hot tap water. Cover with a lid or plastic wrap pierced in a few places. Microcook on HIGH for 1 to 1½ minutes. Let stand for 5 to 10 minutes, then uncover, drain, and peel the peaches with a paring knife. This method also works for fresh apricots.

How to Rehydrate Dried Fruit and Vegetables for Cooking

Dried fruit, such as currants, apricots, cranberries, raisins, and prunes; dehydrated mushrooms; and sun-dried tomatoes often need rehydrating before they can be used in recipes. To do so, place the fruit or vegetables in a 1-quart Pyrex measuring cup and cover with water. Microcook on HIGH for 1 to 2 minutes, to bring to a high simmer. Let stand at room temperature until cool. They will plump up beautifully. Drain before using as directed in a recipe, or cover and refrigerate until needed.

How to Ripen an Avocado

This has to be one of the miracles of the microwave—fast-ripening. It also works with bananas you intend to use for cooking. Place an unripe avocado on a paper towel and prick the skin once or twice. Microcook on DEFROST for 2 minutes. Turn the avocado over and microcook on DEFROST for 30 to 60 seconds longer to soften. Proceed to use in recipes.

How to Bring Chilled Egg Whites to Room Temperature

Place 1 to 4 chilled or partially frozen egg whites in a microwave-safe bowl. Microcook, uncovered, on DEFROST for 15 to 30 seconds per egg white, stirring every 15 seconds. Use immediately in your recipe.

How to Soften Brown Sugar

Open the box of brown sugar and remove the inner plastic bag. Cut open one corner of the bag. Microcook the package of brown sugar on DEFROST for 15 to 30 seconds, or until soft. Do not let the sugar burn or liquefy. To soften a small amount of sugar, like you would use on your morning cereal, place it in a microwave-safe bowl and drizzle it with a few drops of water before microcooking as directed above.

How to Decrystallize Honey

Honey that has solidified can be brought back to its liquid state by uncovering the jar and heating it on MEDIUM (50 percent power) for 30 seconds to 1 minute. (If the honey is in a plastic jar, place it in a microwave-safe container before heating.) Alternatively, for a small amount of honey, place the desired amount in a custard cup before microcooking. The decrystallized honey will keep at room temperature for 5 days or more.

How to Defrost Frozen Bread Dough

Remove the loaf or dinner rolls from their package. Place the dough upside down in an 8 × 4-inch ceramic loaf pan or a 9-inch square Pyrex pan coated with nonstick cooking spray. Brush the dough with melted unsalted butter or oil. Cover the pan loosely with plastic wrap that has also been coated with nonstick cooking spray so the dough will not stick to the plastic wrap. Place a 1-cup glass measuring cup full of water in a back corner of the microwave. Microcook on HIGH for 2 minutes to boil. Place the pan of frozen dough in the microwave with the water and microcook on LOW (10 percent power) or DEFROST for 4 minutes; turn the dough over, re-cover, and microcook for 3 minutes longer. Let stand in the closed oven for 10 minutes to finish defrosting. Bake the dough in a conventional oven according to the package instructions.

How to Partially Precook Foods for the Grill

To cut the grilling time on certain ingredients, cook them partway through in the microwave before putting them over the coals. Microcook on HIGH the following: chicken legs for 3 minutes, new potatoes for 2 minutes (prick them with a fork first), bell peppers for 1 minute, and thick pork chops for 2 to 3 minutes. Immediately transfer to the grill to finish cooking.

How to Micro-Roast Green Chiles or Red Bell Peppers

Use large mild green chiles, like Anaheim or New Mexico, which have a thin, translucent, tough skin that needs to be removed by loosening. Rub 4 chiles or 2 red bell peppers all over lightly with oil. Place in a single layer on a microwave-safe plate. Pierce each a few times on both sides to allow steam to escape. Cover with waxed paper. Microcook green chiles on HIGH for 3 to 3½ minutes, or red peppers for 1½ to 2 minutes. Turn over each pepper and microcook on HIGH for 1 to 2 minutes more. The peppers will not char or blister. Wrap the peppers in a damp kitchen towel; let stand at room temperature for 10 minutes to cool. The peppers will steam and the skin will separate from the flesh. Wearing rubber gloves if you wish, rub the peppers to remove the loosened skins. Slit each pepper open on one side and pull out the seeds. Rinse in cold water. The peppers are ready to use, or store in a zipper-top plastic bag in the refrigerator until needed.

How to Bring Cold Cheese to Room Temperature

No time to let the cheese come to room temperature sitting on the counter? The microwave comes to the rescue. Place 8 ounces firm or semisoft cold cheese in one piece on a plate. Microcook on LOW (10 percent power) or DEFROST for 45 to 60 seconds. Test by touching the surface of the cheese to see if it is no longer cold. This method also works with a block of cream cheese.

How to Juice Citrus Fruits

Squeeze the maximum amount of juice from an orange, lemon, or lime by placing it in the microwave and microcooking on HIGH for 20 seconds. Roll the fruit back and forth on the counter with the palm of your hand, and juice. Lemons, limes, and oranges can be frozen whole to keep them longer. To defrost the fruit before juicing it, place the whole fruit in the microwave (there's no need to prick the skin), and microcook on DEFROST for about 1 minute, then proceed to juice or zest. A surplus of citrus? Juice the fruit and keep the juice in small freezer containers or an ice cube tray. When ready to use, microcook on DEFROST in a glass measuring cup until thawed.

How to Dry Citrus Zests

For orange, tangerine, lemon, lime, and grapefruit zests: With a paring knife, cut off strips of zest, avoiding the bitter white pith underneath. Alternatively, you can use a zester to cut off thin strips, or use a grater over a layer of paper towel. Microcook the zest on HIGH for 1 to 2 minutes, depending on how thick the zest is, until dried, checking every 30 seconds. Cool and store the zest in clean, airtight jars at

room temperature or in the freezer in zipper-top plastic freezer bags.

How to Dry Fresh Herbs

Many people buy a tidy bunch of fresh herbs from the produce aisle at the supermarket or at a farmers' market when all they need is a few tablespoons for a recipe, and they end up with lots left over just languishing in the vegetable bin. Or if you are a gardener and grow your own herbs, by the end of the season you may want to preserve your remaining herbs for use over the winter. Drying herbs in the microwave is most certainly the quickest way to do it. The natural earthy colors and aromas of the herbs' essential oils are retained by the microwave better than with any other method. This is so fast, drying even small amounts of herbs is not labor intensive. The best leafy annual herbs for drying are basil, thyme, sage, tarragon, rosemary, lavender, oregano, marjoram, dill, lemon balm, and savory. Delicate herbs, such as dill and basil, will take the shortest amount of time, while rosemary and lavender, which are sturdier, will take longer. Here's how you do it:

1. Rinse the herbs and pat dry between paper towels, pressing to remove as much water as possible. Make sure the herbs are completely dry. Remove the leaves by stripping or picking them off the stems. Place the leaves in a dry measuring cup and loosely measure no more than 1 cup fresh leaves (about 1 ounce).

2. Spread out the leaves in a single layer on a double layer of paper towels, then place in the microwave. Cover with another double layer of paper towels (the paper towels will absorb the evaporating moisture during the drying process). Place a 1-cup Pyrex measuring cup filled three-quarters full of hot water in the oven with the herbs.

3. Microcook on HIGH for 1 to 2 minutes, checking every minute for degree of dryness, since the drying time will depend on the type of herb and size of the leaves. Turn the herb-filled paper towels over after 1 minute and check for dryness. When the herbs are brittle-dry, they are done. Be careful not to overdry them. Remove the paper towels from the oven and let the herbs cool between the towel layers on the counter. When cool, leave the leaves whole or crush coarsely with your fingers and place in a clean, dry glass jar with a screw-top lid. Store in a cool, dry place for up to 1 year.

Hot Dips and More

Appetizer dips

Appetizer dips are thought of as so pedestrian by some that they are not considered "posh nosh." Either you love a little plate of snacks or you don't. But most of the people I know do love them. Sometimes these are outrageously easy-to-make delicious dips like crab or shrimp dip with French bread, just the thing with a glass of wine to assuage hunger while dinner is getting its finishing touches. Or maybe it's a little something to feed a bunch of kids who need a snack (where's the hummus?).

Or it could be something to serve at a casual get-together for people to nibble along with cold beer and good conversation. From backyard barbecues to wedding showers, hot dips have their place.

When researching recipes for this chapter, I was amazed at how difficult it was to find recipes for microwave hot dips, especially ones that seemed appealing and healthy. Well, this chapter is meant to fix that problem. This is one of the best collections of hot dips you will ever find. Take your pick from creamy cheese, vegetable-laden, vegan, seafood, and bean-based. Better yet, make them all.

The microwave makes preparing appetizers easier and faster than ever. So when time is short and social gatherings are re-laxed, it is helpful to have a few easy-to-make recipes for dips or nibbles at hand. You can serve these dips straight from the microwave, or they may be reheated and served later. Dips make everything from a simple plain cracker to raw veggies taste better. Have fun matching your dip to an appropriate dipper. Pair Mexican dips with tortilla chips, Middle Eastern dips with fresh or toasted pita triangles, and thick seafood dips with plain crisp crackers or cracker flatbread that won't break when you do the dipping. A dip of Italian marinara sauce is great with thin slices of focaccia, and almost any vegetable dip tastes wonderful slathered on thinly sliced baguettes or pumpernickel bread.

Southwest Corn and Green Chile Dip

THIS IS ONE OF THE MOST UNUSUAL HOT DIPS I've encountered: a corn dip with whole corn kernels, not pureed. And it's a quick fix right out of the cupboard when you're faced with unexpected guests. If you like Mexican cheeses, use queso cotija, a sharp, crumbly goat cheese called "the Parmesan of Mexico." This dip is quite addictive, corn-sweet and cheesy good. ○ *Makes about 3 cups*

MICROWAVE COOKWARE: 1-quart ceramic dish suitable for serving
MICROWAVE WATTAGE: 1,100 to 1,300
MICROWAVE COOK TIME: 3½ to 4½ minutes
STANDING TIME: None

One 11-ounce can Mexicorn, drained
One 4-ounce can roasted diced green chiles, drained
1 cup mayonnaise
1 cup shredded cheddar–Monterey Jack cheese combination
½ cup freshly grated Parmesan cheese or crumbled queso cotija
Smoked ground paprika (optional)
Corn tortilla chips for serving

1. Place the Mexicorn, green chiles, mayonnaise, and cheeses in a small bowl and stir with a rubber spatula to evenly combine. Scoop into the ceramic dish. Cover partially with plastic wrap.

2. Microcook on HIGH for 3½ to 4½ minutes, stirring after 2 minutes, to melt the cheese and warm the dip. Sprinkle with some smoked paprika, if desired. Serve immediately with the chips.

Preparing and Cooking Fresh Baby Artichokes

Baby artichokes are just little artichokes, not a special variety, and are picked from the lower part of the plant where there is not as much sun, so their growth has been stunted to some extent. They have not developed their choke yet, which makes for easy eating. Fresh baby artichokes are addictively tasty and are also good in vegetable combos as a side dish. ○ Makes about 16 whole artichokes

MICROWAVE COOKWARE: 2-quart casserole dish
MICROWAVE WATTAGE: 1,100 to 1,300
MICROWAVE COOK TIME: 7 to 8 minutes
STANDING TIME: None

1 pound fresh baby artichokes (about 16)
2 tablespoons freshly squeezed lemon juice
¾ cup water
1 tablespoon olive oil

1. Bend back the lower, outer petals of each artichoke until they snap off easily near the base. Continue doing this until you reach a point where the leaves are half green (at the top) and half yellow (at the bottom). Using a sharp paring knife, cut off the top third of the artichokes (the leaf tips). Pare all remaining dark green areas from the bases, then cut off the stems. Rub the surface of all the artichokes with the lemon juice.

2. Place the artichokes in the casserole dish and add any remaining lemon juice, the water, and the oil. Cover with a lid or partially cover with plastic wrap.

3. Microcook on HIGH for 5 to 6 minutes. Uncover and stir to turn the artichokes over. Re-cover and microcook on HIGH for 2 minutes. Test for tenderness by piercing with the tip of a knife. If the baby artichokes are on the larger side, they may need an extra minute or two of cooking time. Drain and cool. Leave whole, or halve or quarter as desired. Serve, or for longer storage, place the artichokes in a gallon-size zipper-top plastic freezer bag and freeze for up to 6 months; defrost before using.

Artichoke-Feta Dip

ARTICHOKE DIPS ARE WILDLY POPULAR, especially in California, where all domestic artichokes are grown. This is my mother's all-time, all-the-time favorite artichoke dip, and everyone asks for the recipe after eating it. Artichokes are a member of the thistle family and are big buds that haven't flowered yet. They are available fresh throughout the year, but try frozen or canned if you don't want to prepare fresh artichokes. My mom preps fresh baby artichokes whenever she sees them at Trader Joe's, cooking them and freezing them for later use. To make this dip, she defrosts enough artichokes to yield a bit over 1 cup chopped. The fresh artichokes make a superb dip and are really worth the little extra work. ○ *Makes about 3½ cups*

MICROWAVE COOKWARE: 8- or 9-inch Pyrex or ceramic pie plate
MICROWAVE WATTAGE: 1,100 to 1,300
MICROWAVE COOK TIME: About 4 minutes
STANDING TIME: None

**12 ounces fresh cooked baby artichokes (opposite page), or
    one 14.5-ounce can artichoke hearts packed in water, drained**
1 cup mayonnaise
½ cup freshly grated Parmesan cheese
8 ounces feta cheese, crumbled
Half of a 4-ounce jar diced pimientos
1 small clove garlic, crushed
Crackers, bread sticks, pita crisps (page 40), or baguette slices for serving

1. Coarsely chop the artichoke hearts by hand or in a food processor; you will have about 1⅔ cups. Place in a medium-size bowl. Add the mayonnaise, Parmesan, feta, pimientos, and garlic. Scrape into the pie plate. Partially cover with plastic wrap.

2. Microcook on HIGH for 3 to 4 minutes, until the dip is hot and bubbly around the edges. Serve immediately with the dipper of your choice.

Spinach-Artichoke Dip

JUST COULDN'T LEAVE a hot spinach dip out of this chapter. This dip is a delicious cross-cultural mixture of Latin influences (the chiles) and middle America (spinach, artichokes, and mayonnaise). The result is a luscious taste treat that would even be good piled on top of a baked potato. ○ *Makes about 2¾ cups*

MICROWAVE COOKWARE: 8-inch Pyrex pie plate, 1-quart ceramic dish suitable for serving
MICROWAVE WATTAGE: 1,100 to 1,300
MICROWAVE COOK TIME: About 3 minutes to thaw the spinach, 3 to 4 minutes for the dip
STANDING TIME: None

One 10-ounce box frozen chopped spinach
One 6-ounce jar marinated artichoke hearts, drained and finely chopped
One 4-ounce can roasted diced green chiles, drained
1 cup mayonnaise
1 cup freshly grated Parmesan cheese
Crackers and flatbread for serving

1. Remove the outer paper wrapping from the box of spinach and place the unopened box on the pie plate. Microcook on DEFROST for 3 to 3½ minutes. Remove from the oven and let stand for 10 minutes to finish thawing. Open the box and dump the spinach into a colander; squeeze it dry.

2. Place the artichoke hearts, chiles, mayonnaise, and Parmesan in a small bowl and stir with a rubber spatula to evenly combine. Scoop into the ceramic dish. Cover partially with plastic wrap.

3. Microcook on HIGH for 3 to 4 minutes, until hot. Serve immediately with the crackers and flatbread.

Warm Bean Dip with Green Olives

THE SIMPLEST INGREDIENTS, warmed to steaming in the microwave, make a delicious and satisfying dip for tortilla chips. This dip has no cheese (save the cheese for Queso Dip with Beans, page 42). Make sure your chips are nice and fresh. Leftover dip (if you have any) tastes great in a quesadilla.

o Makes 2¾ cups

MICROWAVE COOKWARE: 1-quart ceramic dish suitable for serving
MICROWAVE WATTAGE: 1,100 to 1,300
MICROWAVE COOK TIME: 3 to 4 minutes
STANDING TIME: None

One 16-ounce can refried beans (regular or vegetarian)
½ cup fresh tomato salsa (mild or hot)
⅓ cup sliced green olives
Corn tortilla chips for serving

1. Place the refried beans, salsa, and olives in the ceramic dish. Stir to combine, and cover partially with plastic wrap.

2. Microcook on HIGH for 3 to 4 minutes, until warm. Serve immediately with the chips.

Middle Eastern Eggplant Dip
with Pita Crisps

THERE ARE ALL KINDS OF EGGPLANT DIPS, the most famous being baba ghanoush. Eggplant is in the same family as the potato and tomato and is native to India, where it is prepared in numerous ways. While we categorize eggplant as a vegetable, in reality it is a big berry. Eggplant is never eaten raw, since it is quite bitter, but it becomes soft and flavorful when cooked. Choose smaller, immature eggplants, as large ones tend to be more bitter. To test for a ripe eggplant, press it with your thumb; the flesh should give and then bounce back. If the indentation remains, it is overripe and mushy inside. The microwave does a remarkable job of cooking whole eggplant; the interior flesh retains its lovely spring green color. Instead of or in addition to the pita crisps, you could serve this with cherry tomatoes and celery sticks. ○ *Makes about 1 cup*

MICROWAVE COOKWARE: 2-cup Pyrex measuring cup, 8-inch Pyrex pie plate, plastic microwave bacon rack
MICROWAVE WATTAGE: 1,100 to 1,300
MICROWAVE COOK TIME: About 2 minutes for the crisps, 5 to 7 minutes for the dip
STANDING TIME: None

PITA CRISPS:
¼ cup (½ stick) unsalted butter
1 clove garlic, pressed
2 white or whole-wheat pita breads
Sesame seeds for sprinkling (optional)

DIP:
1 medium-size eggplant (about 1 pound), unpeeled with ends trimmed
1 scallion (green and white parts), cut into pieces
1 clove garlic, cut into thirds
3 tablespoons chopped fresh Italian parsley
3 tablespoons chopped fresh cilantro
2 tablespoons freshly squeezed lemon juice, or more to taste
2 tablespoons olive oil

¼ teaspoon ground cumin
Salt and freshly ground black pepper
Pinch of cayenne pepper

1. Make the pita crisps: Place the butter and garlic in the measuring cup. Microcook on HIGH for 30 to 40 seconds, until the butter is melted. Set aside. Cut the pita bread into quarters, then fold each quarter back, separating the top and bottom layers to make 16 triangles.

2. With a soft pastry brush, brush each pita bread triangle with the garlic butter. Sprinkle with sesame seeds, if desired. Place the triangles in a single layer on the bacon rack or a microwave-safe paper plate (you may have to work in batches). Microcook on HIGH for 1 to 1½ minutes, just until beginning to crisp. Be careful not to overcook. Remove from the oven and let cool. Cook the remaining batches of pita triangles if necessary.

3. Make the dip: With the tines of a fork, prick the eggplant in several places. Place on the pie plate or a microwave-safe paper plate and microcook on HIGH, uncovered, for 5 to 7 minutes, until the eggplant feels extremely soft and looks deflated, and the skin has turned brownish-black, as if it were roasted. Set aside to cool.

4. When cool enough to handle, cut the eggplant in half. Place the scallion and garlic in the work bowl of a food processor and finely chop. Add the parsley and cilantro; process to chop. Scoop the eggplant flesh into the processor; discard the skin. Add the lemon juice, olive oil, cumin, a few pinches of salt and pepper, and the cayenne. Puree until smooth. Taste, adding more salt and/or lemon juice as needed. (If made in advance, refrigerate the dip in a covered container for up to 24 hours.) Serve at room temperature or chilled, with the pita crisps.

Queso Dip with Beans

DIPS MADE IN THE MICROWAVE are instant appetizers because they come together and cook so fast. Here is an all-time favorite, melted cheese with some tomato so it is not spicy. This dip also has a secret ingredient: some whole white beans for texture. Keep the cheese cubes small, about ½ inch, so that they melt faster. ○ *Serves 4 to 6*

MICROWAVE COOKWARE: 1½-quart deep ceramic bowl or gratin dish suitable for serving
MICROWAVE WATTAGE: 1,100 to 1,300
MICROWAVE COOK TIME: 2 to 3½ minutes
STANDING TIME: None

6 ounces cheddar cheese, such as Colby, cubed to make about 1½ cups
6 ounces Monterey Jack or pepper Jack cheese, cubed to make about 1½ cups
½ cup peeled, seeded, and diced fresh tomato (page 27)
3 tablespoons minced red onion
1 cup canned Great Northern or baby white beans, rinsed, drained, and well mashed
Corn tortilla chips for serving

1. Place the cheeses, tomato, and onion in the ceramic bowl or gratin dish. Toss to combine. Spoon in the beans and cover partially with plastic wrap.

2. Microcook on HIGH for 2 to 3½ minutes to melt the cheese. Stir to combine. If the cheese is not melted and bubbling, microcook in 20-second intervals until it is bubbling. Serve immediately with the chips. If the dip cools off, return the dish to the microwave and heat on MEDIUM (50 percent power) for 1 to 2 minutes.

Melted Goat Cheese in Marinara

DON'T KNOW WHICH CULINARY GENIUS got the idea to put delicious soft goat cheese in a gratin dish and pour over a jar of marinara sauce, but it works. Get some freshly baked focaccia flatbread from your supermarket bakery and cut it into ³/₄-inch-thick slices, then cut those slices in half so they won't break as you use them to scoop up the dip. If you like, you can substitute 2 cups of homemade marinara for the jarred sauce. Serve this with red wine. ○ *Serves 4*

MICROWAVE COOKWARE: 1-quart ceramic gratin dish suitable for serving
MICROWAVE WATTAGE: 1,100 to 1,300
MICROWAVE COOK TIME: 2½ to 3 minutes
STANDING TIME: None

One 14-ounce jar tomato-basil marinara sauce
Zest of ½ orange
One 6-ounce log or two 3-ounce logs soft goat cheese
Pinch of *herbes de Provence*
1 tablespoon olive oil
Focaccia slices for serving

1. Pour the marinara into the gratin dish. Add the zest. Stir to combine.

2. Cut the goat cheese into ¹/₂- to ³/₄-inch-thick rounds and arrange them in an overlapping layer down the middle of the gratin dish, nestled in the sauce. Sprinkle very lightly with the *herbes de Provence* and drizzle with the olive oil. Partially cover the dish with plastic wrap, being careful that it does not touch the cheese.

3. Microcook on HIGH, uncovered, for 2¹/₂ to 3 minutes, until the cheese is melted and the sauce is bubbling. Remove the plastic wrap. Serve immediately with the focaccia slices.

Melted Orange Brie

THE ORIGINAL VERSION OF THIS RECIPE came from a Thanksgiving flier at my supermarket. Use an already-cut wedge from a large wheel of Brie, or a whole Brie wheel. Serve with fresh baguette slices from one of those very thin baguette wands, so that they are small rounds. You can assemble this ahead and zap it in the microwave just when your guests walk in the door. ○ *Serves 4 to 6*

MICROWAVE COOKWARE: 1-quart ceramic gratin dish suitable for serving
MICROWAVE WATTAGE: 1,100 to 1,300
MICROWAVE COOK TIME: About 2½ minutes
STANDING TIME: None

½ **cup orange marmalade**
Zest of 1 orange
1 tablespoon freshly squeezed lemon juice
1 tablespoon orange liqueur (such as Grand Marnier) or orange juice
One 1½-pound wedge or wheel Brie cheese
Baguette slices for serving

1. Combine the marmalade, zest, lemon juice, and liqueur in the ceramic dish, making sure the dish will comfortably hold the cheese. Partially cover with plastic wrap and microcook on HIGH to melt the marmalade, 60 to 90 seconds.

2. Remove the plastic wrap. Set the Brie in the orange sauce. Return to the oven and microcook on HIGH, uncovered, until the cheese is hot and slightly melted at the sides, about 60 seconds. Check at 20-second intervals to avoid overcooking. Serve immediately with the bread slices.

Hot Crab Dip

C RAB DIP HAS BEEN POPULAR in the entertaining sphere for years, due to its rich and delicious flavor. It has enduring appeal because it fits every occasion, from casual to elegant. This recipe makes enough for a crowd.

○ *Makes about 4½ cups*

MICROWAVE COOKWARE: 11 × 7-inch Pyrex baking dish or ceramic casserole dish, 1-quart microwave-safe dish
MICROWAVE WATTAGE: 1,100 to 1,300
MICROWAVE COOK TIME: 3 to 4 minutes
STANDING TIME: None

16 ounces cream cheese
1 cup mayonnaise
1 clove garlic, crushed
12 ounces cooked fresh lump crabmeat
⅓ cup slivered almonds
Plain crackers of your choice for serving

1. Spray the baking dish with nonstick cooking spray. Place the cream cheese in the 1-quart microwave-safe dish. Microcook on HIGH for 30 seconds to soften. Transfer the cream cheese to a stand mixer fitted with the paddle attachment and add the mayonnaise and garlic. Beat until fluffy, 2 minutes.

2. Fold in the crabmeat. Spread the mixture into the prepared baking dish in a thin layer. Sprinkle with the slivered almonds. Partially cover with plastic wrap.

3. Microcook on HIGH for 3 to 4 minutes, until hot. Serve immediately with the crackers.

Peggy and Lonnie's
Hot Shrimp Cocktail Dip

PEGGY IS PEGGY FALLON and Lonnie is Lonnie Gandara, two of the best food professionals I know, and they can really cook and know what people want to eat. They call their microwave dips "new wave" or "zappetizers," some clever culinary lingo that Lonnie seems to be a master of. This is a real winner and couldn't be simpler to prepare. It tastes great with cold beer. You can find tomato-chili sauce next to the ketchup in the condiments aisle of your supermarket.

o *Makes about 1½ cups*

MICROWAVE COOKWARE: 1-quart ceramic dish suitable for serving
MICROWAVE WATTAGE: 1,100 to 1,300
MICROWAVE COOK TIME: 1 to 1½ minutes
STANDING TIME: None

3 ounces cream cheese
½ cup mayonnaise
2 tablespoons tomato-chili sauce
3 tablespoons minced scallions (white part and some of the green)
8 ounces cooked bay shrimp
Plain crackers of your choice for serving

1. Place the cream cheese in the ceramic dish. Microcook on HIGH for 30 seconds to soften.

2. Stir in the mayonnaise, tomato-chili sauce, 2 tablespoons of the scallions, and the shrimp with a rubber spatula. Wipe the sides of the dish for a neater presentation. Sprinkle with the remaining tablespoon of scallions. Partially cover the dish loosely with plastic wrap.

3. Microcook on HIGH for 1 to 1½ minutes, until hot. Serve immediately with the crackers.

Brown Bag Popcorn
(plus Seven Variations)

WHILE THERE ARE QUITE A FEW specialized accessories on the market for popping popcorn in the microwave, the good old brown bag method reigns supreme. Popcorn is best made in small batches in lunch-size brown bags (but do not use recycled-paper or regular grocery bags, which can contain metal flecks that can create sparks during microcooking and ignite the bag). A brown bag absorbs the wonderful natural moisture released in the popping process; in solid, nonporous cookware, the moisture stays put and toughens the popped kernels. No butter or oil is needed with this method. ⚬ *Makes about 2 quarts*

MICROWAVE COOKWARE: 1 small microwave-safe bowl or custard cup,
   1 unused lunch-size brown paper bag
MICROWAVE WATTAGE: 1,100 to 1,300
MICROWAVE COOK TIME: 15 to 20 seconds to melt the butter, 2 to 3 minutes for the popcorn
STANDING TIME: None

2 to 3 tablespoons unsalted butter, depending on how buttery you like your popcorn
⅓ cup high-quality popping corn
Salt to taste (see Popcorn Salt, page 53)

1. Place the butter in the small bowl and microcook on HIGH for 15 to 20 seconds, until melted. Set aside.

2. Place the popping corn in the brown paper bag. Fold the bag top down two times, about ½ inch deep, and firmly close so it doesn't open on its own (but do not use tape or any metal fasteners such as staples or paper clips).

3. Microcook on HIGH for 2 to 3 minutes, or until the popping sound slows down to 2 to 4 seconds between pops. Or, if your microwave has a POPCORN button, simply press the button and, when done, microcook for an additional 20 seconds. Do not overcook or your popcorn will burn. Open the bag, being careful not to get burned by any steam escaping from the bag, and drizzle the popcorn with the melted butter and sprinkle with salt; stir the popcorn or shake the bag to coat the kernels if you like. Eat the popcorn right out of the bag, or pour into a bowl and serve.

Popcorn in the Microwave

All popcorn can be popped in the microwave, not just the commercial microwave popcorn brands you see at the supermarket. In fact, the microwave oven is the true home for popcorn, evidenced by the fact that most microwaves have a special button labeled "popcorn" to pop the kernels perfectly.

And popcorn isn't just for eating in front of the TV as a quick snack with your favorite soft drink. It is also good flavored in a number of ways and served with cold beer or wine to ward off hunger before a casual group meal. It is great served in a big bowl for potlucks, too. I've offered multiple variations on the theme, but feel free to invent your own flavor combinations. Like the taste of cheese with your popcorn? Penzeys Spices' Brady Street Cheese Sprinkle is one of my favorite things to mix into a bowl of popcorn, as is the Vermont cheese powder from King Arthur Flour The Baker's Catalogue. Some other great flavors that go well with popcorn include Spanish smoked paprika, chipotle chile powder, soy sauce, Italian herb seasoning, melted butter mixed with saffron, Chinese five-spice powder and chow mein noodles, sesame salt, melted butterscotch morsels, and nutritional yeast. I've even seen popcorn dusted with green spirulina powder, a protein-rich nutritional supplement, and another version at a party sprinkled with edible gold dust. The sky's the limit.

I recommend buying popping corn in bulk or jars. And don't limit yourself to just yellow or white popcorn. There is a world of colored popping corn, such as red and black, each with its own particular flavor, as well as miniature kernels. Seek out bins of popping corn at natural foods markets to find these varieties, or search for them online. A tightly closed jar of kernels stored in a cool, dry place will keep almost indefinitely. Do not store popping corn in the refrigerator, as the kernels will dry out, and without the moisture within the kernel that makes it go pop, you won't have fluffy, delicious popcorn. As a guide, 2 heaping tablespoons of unpopped corn will yield approximately 3 to 4 cups of popped corn, depending on the size of the unpopped kernel.

Margie's Parmesan and Garlic Popcorn

If you are a fresh-garlic aficionado, crush a clove or two of garlic into 3 tablespoons of butter instead of the olive oil, microcook on HIGH for 15 to 20 seconds to melt the butter, then drizzle over the popcorn. ● *Makes about 2 quarts*

1 recipe Brown Bag Popcorn (page 47)
3 tablespoons light or extra-virgin olive oil
¼ to ½ cup freshly grated Parmesan cheese, to your taste
½ teaspoon garlic powder or garlic salt, or to taste

Open the bag of popped corn, being careful not to get burned by any steam escaping from the bag, and drizzle with the olive oil, then sprinkle in the cheese and the garlic powder. Stir, or shake the bag to coat the kernels. Eat the popcorn right out of the bag, or pour into a bowl and serve.

Nut Butter Popcorn

Here's a wonderful variation that will delight kids. You can substitute cashew or almond butter for the peanut butter. If you're a real nut lover, add a cup of salted roasted nuts, too. ● *Makes about 2 quarts*

2 to 3 tablespoons unsalted butter, to your taste
2 tablespoons smooth peanut butter
1 recipe Brown Bag Popcorn (page 47)

1. Place the butter and peanut butter in a small microwave-safe bowl or custard cup and microcook on HIGH for 15 to 20 seconds to melt; stir to combine. If the mixture is too thick, stir in a little bit of hot water. Set aside.

2. Open the bag of popped corn, being careful not to get burned by any steam escaping from the bag, and drizzle in the warm nut butter mixture; stir, or shake the bag to coat the kernels. Eat the popcorn right out of the bag, or pour into a bowl and serve.

Wasabi Popcorn

Wasabi, also called Japanese horseradish, is a condiment usually served with seafood or sushi. Due to its unique flavor, with a heat somewhat like that of chile peppers, wasabi is now used in everything from dips to mayonnaise to salad dressings, and I think it tastes great mixed into popcorn. In this recipe, you make the wasabi paste fresh and then stir it into melted butter and drizzle it over the popped kernels. If you like, you can use 2 teaspoons of prepared wasabi, which comes in a tube, instead of making it yourself. You can add more wasabi to the melted butter if you like a more pronounced hot and spicy flavor. **o** *Makes about 2 quarts*

1½ teaspoons wasabi powder
1 teaspoon water
2 to 3 tablespoons unsalted butter, to your taste
1 recipe Brown Bag Popcorn (page 47)
½ teaspoon salt, or to taste

1. In a small bowl, mix the wasabi powder and water together to form a thick paste that mounds. Invert the bowl on the counter (the wasabi will stick to the bowl) and let sit for 10 minutes. (This technique allows the powder to absorb the water better.)

2. Place the butter in a small microwave-safe bowl or custard cup and microcook on HIGH for 15 to 20 seconds to melt; stir in the knob of wasabi paste.

3. Open the bag of popped corn, being careful not to get burned by any steam escaping from the bag, and drizzle in the wasabi butter, then sprinkle with salt. Stir, or shake the bag to coat the kernels. Eat the popcorn right out of the bag, or pour into a bowl and serve.

Bombay Curried Popcorn

This recipe was inspired by a delicious dish called Bombay curried noodles, which involves lots of curry butter melted on wide noodles. ○ *Makes about 2 quarts*

2 to 3 tablespoons unsalted butter, to your taste
½ to 1 teaspoon curry powder, to your taste
1 recipe Brown Bag Popcorn (page 47)
½ to 1 teaspoon salt, to your taste
4 tablespoons dried currants
3 tablespoons toasted unsweetened coconut or sliced almonds (optional)

1. Place the butter in a small microwave-safe bowl or custard cup and microcook on HIGH for 15 to 20 seconds to melt; stir in the curry powder.

2. Open the bag of popped corn, being careful not to get burned by any steam escaping from the bag, and drizzle in the curried butter, then sprinkle with the salt. Add the currants and coconut, if desired. Stir, or shake the bag to coat the kernels. Eat the popcorn right out of the bag, or pour into a bowl and serve.

Mexican Popcorn

For this version, you can use packaged taco seasoning from the supermarket (such as McCormick's) or buy as a spice mixture in a jar; both are delicious as can be when fresh. If the taco seasoning you use does not contain salt, add some if you like. ○ *Makes about 2 quarts*

2 to 3 tablespoons unsalted butter, to your taste
1 to 1½ teaspoons taco seasoning, to your taste
1 recipe Brown Bag Popcorn (page 47)

1. Place the butter in a small microwave-safe bowl or custard cup and microcook on HIGH for 15 to 20 seconds to melt; stir in the taco seasoning.

2 Open the bag of popped corn, being careful not to get burned by any steam escaping from the bag, and drizzle in the seasoned butter. Stir, or shake the bag to coat the kernels. Eat the popcorn right out of the bag, or pour into a bowl and serve.

Popcorn with Green Chiles and Olives

This is popcorn for dinner, filling and satisfying. Get a fresh bottle of chili powder for this, or use a single ground chile powder, such as chipotle or ancho. If you like fresh chiles, roast and peel a large Anaheim chile or two, then dice and use in place of the canned chiles. ○ *Makes about 2 quarts*

1 recipe Brown Bag Popcorn (page 47)
Chili powder to taste
½ cup sliced black olives, drained
One 4-ounce can diced roasted green chiles, drained
1½ to 2 cups grated sharp cheddar cheese or cheddar–Monterey Jack blend, to your taste
3 tablespoons minced fresh cilantro
2 to 4 scallions (white part and some of the green), minced

1. Set out 2 to 4 shallow soup bowls that can be placed in the microwave. Divide the popped popcorn equally among the bowls.

2. Sprinkle each with some chili powder, then divide the olives, green chiles, and cheese equally among the bowls.

3. One bowl at a time, microcook on HIGH for 40 to 60 seconds, to melt the cheese. Sprinkle each bowl with some of the cilantro and scallions, and serve immediately, while the cheese is warm.

White Chocolate Pecan Popcorn

Popcorn drizzled with melted chocolate has become the rage, and it is easy to prepare in the microwave. This can be served for dessert and also makes a great gift. The oil is necessary to give the chocolate a pourable consistency, so don't skip it.

Makes about 2 quarts

8 ounces white chocolate chips
2 tablespoons vegetable oil
1 recipe Brown Bag Popcorn (page 47)
1 cup coarsely chopped pecans, toasted if you like, or unsalted dry-roasted peanuts

1. Place the white chocolate chips and oil in a 4-cup glass measuring cup and microcook on DEFROST for 60 seconds, and then at 15-second intervals until shiny and melted. Stir to a smooth consistency.

2. Place the popcorn on a large baking sheet lined with aluminum foil. Sprinkle with the pecans and then drizzle with the melted chocolate; stir gently with a wide spatula. Place the baking sheet in the refrigerator for 20 minutes, until chilled and the chocolate is set. Break into small clusters before eating; the popcorn can be stored in an airtight container for up to 1 week.

Popcorn Salt

Good salt makes popcorn taste better. Popcorn gourmets each have their own opinion on what type of salt to use on popcorn. When deciding which salt to use, don't just think about accenting the flavor of the popcorn but also about adding a bit of texture. There is a product called "popcorn salt," which is more finely ground than regular table salt so it can collect in the nooks of each popped kernel, but there are a number of flavored salts as well (hickory-smoked salt is one of my favorites). Look for popcorn salt by the popcorn shelf at your supermarket, not by the salt.

Websites that sell gourmet popping corn will usually offer their own recommended brand of popcorn salt. Unrefined natural sea salt, including *fleur de sel,* Maldon sea salt, unbleached gray salts, and artisan salts such as pink salt are a gourmet treat and becoming more available all the time since they are the new darling of the restaurant set. Just remember that many sea salts are quite coarse, and you want an extra-fine salt for popcorn, so use a salt grinder or mortar and pestle if necessary.

Eggs, Soups, and Sandwiches

Eggs, soups, and sandwiches are all incredibly versatile dishes that can be served at any time of day. Surprisingly, eggs are one of the foods that the microwave handles especially well, as they turn out remarkably tender and fluffy. And they are so simple to prepare in the microwave: You can make an individual egg frittata in a cereal bowl, a puffy omelet filled with onions and vegetables in a pie plate, and delightfully sumptuous scrambled eggs in a glass measuring cup. Small amounts

of egg seem to cook the most efficiently, rather than a dozen eggs at once. The only type of egg you cannot microcook is a hard-cooked egg in the shell, nor can you reheat them, as they will expand and burst the shell.

Soup—essentially vegetables, meat, and/or grains boiled in water—is one of the most ancient foods and is associated with every living cuisine. Commercial canned soup appeared in 1897, with the advent of canning, and has never lost popularity, with billions of cans of soup being sold every year. Though canned soup is very convenient, a few well-chosen recipes for homemade soup should be in everyone's kitchen, because soup made from scratch is nutritious and economical and tastes so good.

So many of our favorite soups are adaptable to the microwave. From clear, light soups to thick, hearty ones, the microwave does them all. They cook fast, most in less than 25 minutes, and evenly. You can make soup right before you want to eat it, or make it the day before. In the microwave oven, vegetable flavors stay strong and colors bright. Make soup in a 2- to 3-quart casserole dish—think large and deep—or a smaller quantity in a Pyrex measuring cup. You only need enough broth or water to cover the solid vegetables, then add more to adjust the consistency as desired. Partially cover your soups during cooking to prevent excess evaporation and help develop good flavor. Reheat your homemade soups, partially covered to prevent splattering, on HIGH for 2 minutes per cup until steaming hot; cream soups should always be reheated on MEDIUM. Do not fill the cooking container more than two-thirds full or the soup may boil over, especially if it has milk in it.

Sandwiches are often thought of as something quick to eat culled from whatever is in your pantry. But made with good filling ingredients and high-quality bread, tortillas, pita bread, or rolls, a sandwich can stop you in your tracks and slow you down long enough to pay attention to what you are eating. Burritos are essentially rolled-up sandwiches, and everyone should know how to make them. I like to use fresh whole-wheat tortillas for their sweet flavor, as well as fresh corn tortillas. If you are using one tortilla at a time, refrigerate or freeze the remaining ones to keep them fresh.

Perfect Scrambled Eggs

THE FIRST THING MY MOTHER MADE in her microwave back in the early 1980s was scrambled eggs. Prepared in a Pyrex measuring cup, they turn out remarkably fluffy and tender—but be sure not to overcook them, in which case they will become rubbery. You can make as many eggs as you like per serving, but each egg must be balanced with some butter and milk to help with cooking. **o** *Serves 1*

MICROWAVE COOKWARE: 1-quart Pyrex measuring cup
MICROWAVE WATTAGE: 1,100 to 1,300
MICROWAVE COOK TIME: 30 seconds to melt the butter, 75 seconds for the eggs
STANDING TIME: 50 to 60 seconds

1 teaspoon unsalted butter
2 large or extra-large eggs
¼ cup milk, half-and-half, or water
Salt and freshly ground black pepper to taste

1. Place the butter in the measuring cup, and microcook on HIGH for 30 seconds to melt.

2. In a small bowl, use a fork to beat the eggs with the milk and combine the yolks and whites. Pour into the measuring cup over the melted butter.

3. Microcook on HIGH, uncovered, for 40 seconds. Stir with a fork or chopsticks, mixing the set portions from the outside edge into the center, then pushing the center back out to the edge. Microcook on HIGH for another 20 seconds, stir, and resume cooking for 15 seconds more. The eggs should be just past the runny stage and look moist and glistening, and they will puff up. Let stand for 50 to 60 seconds, until the eggs get firm. Season with salt and pepper and serve immediately.

Note: If you want to scramble more or fewer than 2 eggs, here are some guidelines for cook times: 1 egg, 40 seconds; 3 eggs, 1¼ to 1¾ minutes; 4 eggs, 1¾ to 2 minutes; 6 eggs, 2½ to 3 minutes. Use 2 tablespoons milk, half-and-half, or water per egg. Stir in any herbs of your choice, diced cooked bacon, shredded or grated cheese, chopped tomatoes, chile strips, and so forth 30 seconds before the eggs are done, while they are still liquidy.

Avocado–Cream Cheese Omelet

OMELETS ARE BELOVED AS A BREAKFAST, brunch, lunch, or supper food. One of the most popular offerings when I worked at a restaurant was the avocado–cream cheese omelet. With avocados now deemed a "superfood," no one need limit their passion for this delicious, though high-fat, fruit. It is remarkable that an omelet can be made in the microwave oven and emerge with its traditional texture and shape intact. Omelets using 4 to 5 eggs are about the biggest you can make in the microwave, since any more eggs will not cook evenly. The reason an omelet can be cooked on HIGH is because the egg membranes are first broken up with a light beating. This recipe is best made in a glass, not ceramic, pie plate. Just as you slide an omelet out of a frying pan, you can fold and slide this omelet out of the pie plate and onto the serving plate. **o** *Serves 2*

MICROWAVE COOKWARE: 8- or 9-inch Pyrex pie plate
MICROWAVE WATTAGE: 1,100 to 1,300
MICROWAVE COOK TIME: About 3 minutes
STANDING TIME: None

2 to 3 teaspoons unsalted butter, cut into pieces
4 large eggs
2 tablespoons milk, light cream, soy milk, or water
½ cup cream cheese, softened and cut into 1-inch cubes
1 medium-size ripe avocado, peeled, pitted, and diced
Salt and freshly ground black pepper to taste

1. Place the butter in the pie plate. Microcook on HIGH, uncovered, for 30 to 45 seconds to melt. Lift and tilt the pie plate to swirl the butter around.

2. In a small bowl, use a fork to beat the eggs and milk together until the eggs are broken up and incorporated. Pour into the pie plate. Microcook on HIGH, uncovered, for 1 minute. Using a rubber spatula, gently push the eggs from the edges of the pie plate into the center to let the uncooked eggs flow beneath.

3. Return the pie plate to the oven and microcook on HIGH for another minute. Gently push the eggs from the edges to the center again. The omelet will be almost cooked at this point and moist in the center. Return to the oven and microcook on HIGH for another 30 seconds, until the eggs are just set but still moist and creamy, and not dry. Be careful not to overcook. You can test with the tip of a knife to check if the eggs are set.

4. Sprinkle the cream cheese and avocado on top of the eggs, along with a sprinkle of salt and a few grinds of pepper. With the rubber spatula, gently lift up and fold the omelet in half. Cut the omelet in half and slide each half onto a serving plate (warming the plates is a nice touch). Serve immediately.

VARIATIONS

Plain Cheese Omelet: In step 4, instead of the cream cheese and avocado, use ½ to ¾ cup shredded cheese, such as cheddar, Monterey Jack, Muenster, or Swiss; 2 slices of deli cheese, such as provolone or Swiss Alpine; or a soft cheese like Boursin, Brie, or crumbled feta.

Jam Omelet: Substitute ½ cup fruit jam or preserves, such as apricot, cherry, or strawberry, for the avocado and cream cheese and omit the salt and pepper. Spread the jam, using the back of a spoon, on the lower half of the omelet in step 4. Fold the omelet in half, sprinkle the top lightly with granulated sugar, portion, and serve as directed.

Cereal Bowl Vegetable Frittata

THIS FLUFFY FRITTATA for one is ready in just 2 minutes, so be sure to get your bread going in the toaster at the same time you start cooking the eggs. I love the single-serving portion, but you can also make this frittata for two by simply doubling the ingredients, using a 9-inch Pyrex pie plate, and increasing the microwave cook time by only 30 seconds or so. Frittatas are fun to experiment with, since they take to numerous variations: For example, try Muenster and fresh chives, green chiles and Jack cheese, or tomato, basil, and fresh mozzarella. My favorite combination is fresh tomato and spinach. ○ *Serves 1*

MICROWAVE COOKWARE: 6-inch microwave-safe cereal bowl
MICROWAVE WATTAGE: 1,100 to 1,300
MICROWAVE COOK TIME: 2 minutes
STANDING TIME: 15 to 20 seconds

2 teaspoons olive oil or unsalted butter
½ cup fresh baby spinach or arugula leaves, stemmed and chopped
½ small plum tomato, seeded and diced
2 to 3 tablespoons shredded or thin strips firm cheese, such as cheddar,
    Muenster, mozzarella, or provolone
Salt to taste (optional)
2 large or extra-large eggs
4 tablespoons water, milk, half-and-half, or soy milk

1. Rub the inside of the cereal bowl all over with the olive oil. Place the spinach, tomato, and cheese in the bowl, season with salt if you like, and then toss to combine.

2. In a small bowl, use a fork to lightly beat the eggs and water together. Pour the eggs over the tomatoes and cheese. Do not stir.

3. Microcook on HIGH, uncovered, for 2 minutes. At the signal, let rest for 15 to 20 seconds in the oven. Be careful not to overcook. The frittata will be puffed and then will drop as it cools. Serve immediately.

Huevos Rancheros for One: Place 1 corn tortilla between 2 pieces of paper towel and microcook on HIGH for 30 seconds to warm. Place on a microwave-safe plate and spread with 3 tablespoons canned refried beans. Microcook on HIGH for 30 seconds to heat. Make the frittata by combining 2 eggs, 2 tablespoons water or milk, 2 tablespoons salsa, and 2 to 3 tablespoons shredded Monterey Jack cheese or Mexican cheese blend in a microwave-safe cereal bowl. Microcook on HIGH as directed in step 2. Slide the frittata out of the bowl onto the tortilla and beans. Drizzle with more salsa and serve immediately.

Cup of Miso

MISO IS A TRADITIONAL JAPANESE FOOD made by fermenting soybeans, rice, or barley with salt and the yeast mold *koji,* resulting in a thick paste rich in B vitamins, protein, and health-giving live enzymes. It is most familiar in the soup that is the start to traditional Japanese meals. Miso, when dissolved in hot water, makes a flavorful, nutritious, and satisfying drink in lieu of tea or coffee. Rice and miso are usual components of a Japanese breakfast. The easiest types of miso to find are mild white miso (*shiromiso*) and the slightly stronger red miso (*akamiso,* the flavor most associated with Japanese restaurant miso soups), both delicious. I love miso soup for breakfast, or at any time during the day. You can steam a cup of vegetables or add a few tablespoons of leftover cooked vegetables to your miso; make it as simple or as complex as you have time for.

o *Serves 2*

MICROWAVE COOKWARE: 2-quart Pyrex measuring cup
MICROWAVE WATTAGE: 1,100 to 1,300
MICROWAVE COOK TIME: About 3 minutes
STANDING TIME: None

4 cups water
8 to 12 ounces firm or extra-firm tofu, cubed
2 scallions (white part and some of the green), chopped
3 to 4 tablespoons miso paste, to your taste
Juice of ½ lemon
Small handful fresh cilantro

OPTIONAL ADDITIONS:
Handful of watercress leaves or baby spinach, stems trimmed
Lightly steamed vegetables, such as shredded bok choy or napa cabbage or
    thinly sliced carrots, celery, or mushrooms
Tofu shirataki noodles, or leftover soba noodles or rice

1. Place the water in the measuring cup. Add the tofu and scallions. Microcook on HIGH, uncovered, for 3 minutes, to bring to a high simmer.

2. Pour ½ cup of the hot water into a small bowl. Whisk in 3 tablespoons of the miso paste; it will smooth and thin out. Pour the miso mixture into the measuring cup, stirring as you pour it in. Taste, and whisk in more miso paste, a bit at a time, if desired. Add a squeeze of the lemon juice. If you reheat the miso, do not boil it.

3. Divide the cilantro between two serving bowls and add any of the optional ingredients as desired. Divide the hot miso and tofu soup among the two bowls. Serve hot.

Watercress Soup

POTATO LEEK SOUP IS A WONDERFUL SOUP on its own, but many people do not know that this basic French soup, containing one potato to one leek, is the basis for many other rustic vegetable soups. Here is a delicious spring soup that contains watercress leaves, which give the soup a marvelous green hue. Do invest in a handheld immersion blender; you can puree right in the cooking vessel without the muss and fuss of ladling hot soup into a food processor or blender.

o *Serves 2 to 3*

MICROWAVE COOKWARE: 2-quart Pyrex or ceramic casserole dish with lid
MICROWAVE WATTAGE: 1,100 to 1,300
MICROWAVE COOK TIME: 12 to 14 minutes
STANDING TIME: None

1 tablespoon unsalted butter or olive oil
2 medium-size leeks (white part only), thoroughly washed and thinly sliced
2 medium-size russet potatoes, peeled and diced
Two 14-ounce cans vegetable broth
1 bunch fresh watercress, leaves only, packed to make at least 1 cup
Salt and freshly ground black or white pepper to taste
Dollop of sour cream or plain yogurt, or ½ cup milk, for serving (optional)

1. Combine the butter and leeks in the casserole dish. Partially cover with the lid or some plastic wrap. Microcook on HIGH for 3 minutes, until the leeks are tender.

2. Add the potatoes and broth. The broth should just cover the vegetables. Partially cover with plastic wrap and microcook on HIGH for 5 to 7 minutes, until the broth is steaming hot and the potatoes are tender. Add the watercress, re-cover, and microcook on MEDIUM (50 percent power) for 4 minutes.

3. Using a handheld immersion blender, puree the soup. Season with salt and pepper. Before serving, stir in a spoonful of sour cream or yogurt if desired, or the milk if you want to thin the soup a bit.

Microwave Butter Croutons

As a garnish for your soups and salads, croutons are a convenient way to use up those few last slices or heels of bread. These croutons are so fast and simple to prepare in the microwave that you can make a fresh batch every time you need them. Experiment using different types of bread, whatever is on hand, such as white, whole-wheat, challah, rye, country bread, or sandwich rolls. I keep an assortment of leftover slices of good-quality bread in the freezer just for croutons. ๏ Makes about 1 cup

MICROWAVE COOKWARE: 8-inch Pyrex pie plate
MICROWAVE WATTAGE: 1,100 to 1,300
MICROWAVE COOK TIME: About 2 minutes
STANDING TIME: None

3 tablespoons unsalted butter, or a combination of butter and olive oil
⅛ teaspoon paprika
2 slices bread (½ to ¾ inch thick), fresh or day-old, cut into ½- to 1-inch cubes, to make 1 cup
1 small clove garlic, crushed
1 tablespoon freshly grated Parmesan cheese (optional)
½ tablespoon fresh chopped Italian parsley (optional)

1. Place 2 tablespoons of the butter in the pie plate. Microcook on HIGH for about 25 seconds to melt. Stir in the paprika. Add the bread cubes and, with a fork or your fingers, toss to coat.

2. Microcook on HIGH, uncovered, for 2 minutes, stirring at the 1-minute mark, until the bread is golden and crisp. While hot, drizzle with the remaining 1 tablespoon butter; sprinkle with the garlic, Parmesan, and parsley, if using; and toss. Set aside at room temperature until needed.

Cream of Spinach Soup

CREAM OF SPINACH has to be one of the best vegetable soups, made with one of the most underrated but most consumed leafy greens in the world. Spinach has a bit of an exciting history. It is native to the high altitudes of Nepal and was around in ancient pre-Vedic India. The Persian traders carried spinach to China and the Middle East, and the Muslims planted it in Spain. By the Middle Ages, the Western world was eating spinach. Since Catherine de Medici loved spinach and had her private chef carry it to France when she married, dishes containing it started being labeled as "à la florentine," a term still being used in the food world today. Most of our domestic spinach is grown in California; when buying fresh spinach, it's a good idea buy organic whenever possible, as spinach is one of the vegetables that is often heavily sprayed with pesticides. This recipe uses frozen organic chopped spinach, so keep a few boxes in the freezer and you'll be able to make this soup in minutes. Keep whole nutmeg on your spice shelf; using freshly grated nutmeg will make a world of difference in the flavor of your soup. ○ *Serves 2 to 3*

MICROWAVE COOKWARE: 2- or 3-quart Pyrex or ceramic casserole dish with lid, 9-inch Pyrex pie plate
MICROWAVE WATTAGE: 1,100 to 1,300
MICROWAVE COOK TIME: 5 to 6 minutes to defrost the spinach, 6 to 8 minutes to cook the soup
STANDING TIME: 10 minutes when defrosting the spinach

Two 10-ounce boxes organic frozen chopped spinach

GOAT CHEESE DOLLOP:
2 ounces soft goat cheese, at room temperature
¼ cup plain Greek yogurt or sour cream

Two ¼-inch-thick slices white onion, quartered
One 14.5-ounce can chicken or vegetable broth
2 cups whole milk or soy milk
3 tablespoons all-purpose or whole-wheat pastry flour
¼ teaspoon freshly grated nutmeg
Salt and freshly ground black or white pepper to taste

1. Remove the outer wrapping from the boxes of frozen spinach and place the unopened boxes on the pie plate. Microcook on DEFROST for 5 to 6 minutes. Remove from the oven and let stand for 10 minutes to finish thawing. Open the boxes and dump the spinach into a colander; squeeze dry and set aside.

2. Make the Goat Cheese Dollop: In a small bowl, mash together the goat cheese and the yogurt until smooth and well combined. Set aside.

3. Place the thawed spinach, onion, broth, and milk in the casserole dish. Using a handheld immersion blender, puree the mixture. Sprinkle the top with the flour and nutmeg; puree until combined. You can puree the soup until smooth or leave it a bit chunky, as desired, but make sure the flour is incorporated well. (Alternatively, you can puree the soup in a food processor.)

4. Partially cover the casserole dish with the lid or plastic wrap and microcook on MEDIUM (50 percent power) for 6 to 8 minutes, until thickened, stirring every 2 minutes. Season with salt and pepper. Ladle into soup bowls and top with a spoonful of the Goat Cheese Dollop. Serve immediately.

Cream of Roasted Tomato Soup with Grilled Cheese Sandwiches

WHEN ASKING VERY GROWN-UP FRIENDS what was their favorite home-cooked meal, I was surprised by how many of them mentioned tomato soup and grilled cheese sandwiches. Have you tried canned fire-roasted tomatoes yet? If not, get ready for a taste treat in your easy-as-can-be homemade tomato soup. They can be a bit pricey, so stock up when they go on sale. Both Hunt's and Muir Glen, which is organic, are national brands that are readily available. I like cheddar in my grilled cheese sandwiches because it melts well. Use any variety you prefer, from supermarket orange Tillamook or Colby to an artisan farmstead sharp cheddar. It is essential to toast the bread before making the grilled cheese sandwiches, so don't skip this step. ○ *Serves 2*

MICROWAVE COOKWARE: 2-quart Pyrex or ceramic casserole dish with lid
MICROWAVE WATTAGE: 1,100 to 1,300
MICROWAVE COOK TIME: 8 to 10 minutes for the soup,
   15 to 40 seconds for the sandwiches
STANDING TIME: None

1 tablespoon unsalted butter or olive oil
1 cup chopped white onion
Two 14.5-ounce cans fire-roasted diced tomatoes, undrained
One 14-ounce can low-sodium chicken or vegetable broth
3 tablespoons chopped fresh cilantro leaves, basil leaves, or Italian parsley
1 teaspoon sugar
½ cup heavy cream or half-and-half (reduced-fat okay)

GRILLED CHEESE SANDWICHES:
4 slices whole-wheat or multigrain sandwich bread
Thin slices mild or sharp cheddar cheese (4 to 5 ounces total)

1. Combine the butter and onion in the casserole dish. Partially cover with the lid or plastic wrap, and microcook on HIGH for 2 minutes, until the onion is tender.

2. Add the tomatoes and their juice, broth, cilantro, and sugar. Partially cover and microcook on HIGH for 5 to 6 minutes, until steaming hot.

3. Using a handheld immersion blender, puree the soup. Add the cream; stir to combine. Let stand while making the sandwiches.

4. Toast the bread slices in a countertop toaster until golden. Place some of the cheese slices between two slices of the toasted bread. Wrap the sandwich in a paper towel and microcook on HIGH for 15 to 20 seconds, until the cheese is melted. Repeat with the remaining cheese and toasted bread. Or cook both sandwiches at once, microcooking for 30 to 40 seconds.

5. Return the soup to the oven and microcook on HIGH for 1 to 2 minutes, until very hot. Serve immediately in soup bowls with the grilled cheese sandwiches on the side, cut in half.

Out-of-the-Cupboard Black Bean Soup and Bacon Bread Sticks

HUNGRY NOW? MAKE THIS IMMEDIATELY. Use regular supermarket bacon, since thinner slices work better here. Look for the thin, fragile grissini rather than the thick ones; they usually come in a box and some are imported from Italy. Instead of or in addition to the sour cream and cilantro, you can top the soup with Greek yogurt or grated cheese. For a heartier meal, serve with a side of cornbread, tortillas, or rice if you have it. ○ *Serves 2*

MICROWAVE COOKWARE: 2-quart Pyrex or ceramic casserole dish with lid
MICROWAVE WATTAGE: 1,100 to 1,300
MICROWAVE COOK TIME: 7 to 9 minutes for the soup,
   2 to 3 minutes for the breadsticks
STANDING TIME: None

BACON BREAD STICKS:
6 thin slices bacon, left at room temperature for 10 minutes
6 whole grissini (long, thin bread sticks)

SOUP:
One 15-ounce can black beans, rinsed and drained
One 14.5-ounce can chicken or vegetable broth
1 cup canned diced tomatoes
1 cup frozen corn kernels
½ cup chunky fresh or jarred tomato salsa
1 canned chipotle in adobo, mashed (1 tablespoon)
2 teaspoons cider vinegar or 2 lime wedges
Sour cream and chopped fresh cilantro for serving

1. Make the bacon bread sticks: Place a double layer of paper towels on a paper plate, bacon tray, or rectangular Pyrex baking dish that will fit the bread sticks. Slice one piece of bacon in half lengthwise, then wrap the less fatty piece around one of the bread sticks from top to bottom in a spiral, like a barbershop pole. (Discard the fattier piece of bacon, or render it for another use.) Lay the bread stick on the paper towel. Repeat with the remaining bacon slices and bread sticks, and arrange the bread sticks side by side on the paper towel. Place a second paper towel over the bread sticks and microcook on HIGH for 2 to 3 minutes, until the bacon is crisp. Remove from the oven and cool while the soup is cooking. The bacon will get crisper and the bread sticks will become crunchy as they cool.

2. Make the soup: Place the beans, broth, tomatoes, corn, salsa, and chipotle in the casserole dish. Partially cover and microcook on HIGH for 7 to 9 minutes, until boiling hot. Remove from the oven.

3. Divide the soup between two deep soup bowls. Drizzle each with a teaspoon of the cider vinegar, which will bring out the flavor. Garnish with the sour cream and cilantro, and serve immediately with the bread sticks on the side.

VARIATIONS

Sweet-Savory Bacon Bread Sticks: Before cooking, roll the bacon bread sticks in a mixture of 1 tablespoon light brown sugar and 2 teaspoons New Mexican chili powder or regular chili powder.

Cheesy Bacon Bread Sticks: Before cooking, roll the bacon bread sticks in 2 tablespoons freshly grated Parmesan cheese.

Quickest Minestrone with
Green Beans and Garlic Toasts

N MY KITCHEN, minestrone is the catch-all term for any tomato-vegetable-bean soup. I adore white kidney beans, but you can use red ones too, especially in the winter. Serve with some Parmesan cheese on top and garlic toasts for floating. Use the thin loaves of bread for the garlic toasts. If the loaves are long, skinny baguettes, you can use 6 slices instead of 4; if the bread is a large loaf, use 2 big slices instead. ○ *Serves 2*

MICROWAVE COOKWARE: Plastic microwave bacon tray, 2- or 3-quart Pyrex or ceramic casserole dish with lid

MICROWAVE WATTAGE: 1,100 to 1,300

MICROWAVE COOK TIME: About 16 minutes

STANDING TIME: None

GARLIC TOASTS:

Four ½-inch-thick slices French baguette or sourdough bread

3 tablespoons olive oil

1 large clove garlic, halved

2 tablespoons olive oil

1 shallot, minced

¼ white onion, finely chopped

1 to 2 medium-size Yukon Gold potatoes, diced

⅓ cup thinly sliced carrots

1 stalk celery, thinly sliced

1 cup finely shredded green cabbage

Handful of green beans, cut into ½-inch pieces

1 cup diced stewed tomatoes, undrained

One 15.5-ounce can cannellini beans, rinsed and drained

1 cup low-sodium chicken broth, beef broth, vegetable broth, or water

3 to 4 tablespoons chopped fresh Italian parsley

3 to 4 tablespoons chopped fresh basil

A few grinds of black pepper

⅓ cup small pasta, such as orzo, *semi de melone,* small shells, tubettini, or stelline

1. Make the garlic toasts: Place the bread slices on the bacon tray or a double layer of paper towels. Brush one side of each slice with olive oil, then rub each slice with the cut side of the garlic. Microcook on HIGH for 1 to 2 minutes, until crisp. Day-old bread will cook faster than fresh bread. Remove from the oven and set aside.

2. Combine the oil, shallot, and onion in the casserole dish. Partially cover with the lid or some plastic wrap. Microcook on HIGH for 2 minutes.

3. Add the potato, carrot, celery, cabbage, and green beans to the casserole dish. Pour the tomatoes and their juice over the vegetables. Cover and microcook on HIGH for 5 to 6 minutes, until the vegetables are almost tender.

4. Add the beans, broth, parsley, basil, and pepper. Re-cover and microcook on HIGH for 6 to 8 minutes, until the soup is boiling and the vegetables are tender.

5. Meanwhile, on the stovetop, bring water to a boil in a small saucepan. Add the pasta and cook until al dente. Drain. Stir the cooked pasta into the soup. Divide the soup between two deep soup bowls and serve immediately.

Red Lentil Soup

THE RED LENTIL IS THE PRETTIEST MEMBER of the lentil family; it is small and delicate looking, and it cooks up to a golden hue. It is used in Middle Eastern cookery and sold hulled and split, so it cooks faster than other lentils. Although you do not need to soak red lentils, you can reduce your cooking time even more if you do. Red lentils cook up very creamy, making a great soup. It is the perfect lentil for the microwave, since it is smaller and cooks up more tender. Lentils can be stored indefinitely but are best used within 6 months, as their color will begin to fade as they dry and they will take longer to cook. Do not add salt to lentils before cooking them, since salt will toughen the lentils if added at the beginning of the cook time. ○ *Makes 3½ cups*

MICROWAVE COOKWARE: 1-quart Pyrex measuring cup, 2-quart Pyrex or ceramic casserole dish
MICROWAVE WATTAGE: 1,100 to 1,300
MICROWAVE COOK TIME: About 12 minutes
STANDING TIME: None

¾ cup dried red lentils
5 cups water
2 tablespoons unsalted butter or olive oil
½ large white onion, finely chopped
1 stalk celery, diced
⅛ teaspoon ground cumin
⅛ teaspoon turmeric
⅛ teaspoon chili powder
2 vegetable bouillon cubes
Salt and freshly ground black pepper to taste
Juice of 1 to 2 lemons, to your taste

FOR SERVING:
Hot sauce, such as Crystal or Tabasco
Extra-virgin olive oil
Plain Greek yogurt
Fresh cilantro leaves

1. Spread the lentils in a single layer on a clean white kitchen towel or a light-colored work surface. Check for and discard any dirt, tiny stones, and other debris. Place the lentils in a strainer and rinse thoroughly under cold water.

2. Add 2 cups of the water to the measuring cup. Microcook on HIGH for 3 minutes, until boiling. Add the lentils and set aside on the counter to soak for 20 minutes. Drain well.

3. In the casserole dish, combine the butter, onion, and celery. Partially cover with plastic wrap. Microcook on HIGH for 3 minutes, until the onion is tender. Add the cumin, turmeric, and chili powder and microcook on HIGH for 1 minute.

4. In a small bowl, mash the bouillon cubes in 1 cup of the water. Add the lentils, the remaining 2 cups water, and the bouillon water to the casserole dish. Partially cover with plastic wrap and microcook on HIGH for 5 to 6 minutes, until the soup is steaming hot and the lentils have disintegrated. Add more water if the soup needs thinning. Season with salt and pepper, then add the lemon juice.

5. Serve the soup in bowls with a few dashes of hot sauce, a drizzle of oil, a dollop of yogurt, and some cilantro leaves sprinkled over all.

Coconut Chicken Soup with Bok Choy

A VERSION OF THIS CREAMY WHITE SOUP is offered in most Thai restaurants, but homemade is still the best, and here's one you can make quickly in the microwave. To chop fresh lemongrass, remove the outer sheath and hard ends. Use only the bottom white part (about 6 inches) and discard the woody grass part. With the flat side of a cleaver or a heavy object, pound and bruise the lemongrass so it releases its flavor, then cut it into segments or chop. The lemongrass, lime, *nam pla* or one of its substitutes, and ginger make the flavor base, so seek these out in an Asian market or at Whole Foods Market. If you use the fish sauce, add ½ teaspoon brown sugar to balance it. For a vegetarian version, substitute 8 ounces extra-firm tofu cut into strips or cubes for the chicken and use vegetable broth instead of chicken broth. ○ *Serves 2*

MICROWAVE COOKWARE: 2-quart Pyrex or ceramic casserole dish
MICROWAVE WATTAGE: 1,100 to 1,300
MICROWAVE COOK TIME: 9 to 12 minutes
STANDING TIME: None

One 14-ounce unsweetened coconut milk
One 10.75-ounce can low-sodium chicken broth
¼ cup freshly squeezed lime juice
One 3 × 1-inch piece of lime zest or 2 kaffir lime leaves
3 tablespoons chopped fresh lemongrass
One 4-inch piece fresh ginger, peeled and grated (2 tablespoons)
2 tablespoons soy sauce, Bragg's liquid aminos, or Thai fish sauce (*nam pla*)
2 boneless, skinless chicken thighs, cut into ½-inch strips
1 baby bok choy, root bottom removed and chopped lengthwise into strips
Pinch of red pepper flakes
¼ cup finely chopped red bell pepper
¼ cup minced fresh cilantro

1. Combine the coconut milk, broth, lime juice, zest, lemongrass, ginger, soy sauce, and chicken in the casserole dish.

2. Partially cover with plastic wrap and microcook on HIGH for 9 to 12 minutes, until the chicken is cooked through and has turned all white on the outside. At the 5-minute mark, add the bok choy. Do not overcook or the chicken will dry out. The soup will be aromatic and steaming hot.

3. Discard the lime zest. Stir in the red pepper flakes, bell pepper, and cilantro. Taste for saltiness and sourness. You should get the earthy flavor of ginger, a noticeable amount of saltiness, sweetness from the coconut milk, and a fair bit of lime flavor, with a hint of chile in the background. Adjust the seasoning if necessary. Serve immediately in deep bowls.

Tokyo Clam Chowder

AN ARTICLE I ONCE READ in the *New York Times* talked about the opening of a new posh uptown Japanese restaurant, describing among other things the clam chowder, which was made with soy milk instead of cream. That was all the inspiration I needed to create this version of a classic American soup.

o *Serves 2*

MICROWAVE COOKWARE: 2-quart Pyrex or ceramic casserole dish
MICROWAVE WATTAGE: 1,100 to 1,300
MICROWAVE COOK TIME: 10 to 12 minutes
STANDING TIME: 3 minutes

3 tablespoons unsalted butter
¼ large white onion, finely chopped
½ cup finely chopped celery
1 medium-size white potato, peeled if desired, cut into ½-inch cubes
One 14-ounce can low-sodium chicken broth
1¼ cups soy milk
3 tablespoons minced fresh Italian parsley
3 tablespoons instant potato flakes
One 6.5-ounce can chopped clams, undrained
1½ tablespoons white or red miso paste

1. Place the butter in the casserole dish and microcook for 30 seconds to melt. Stir in the onion, celery, and potato. Partially cover with plastic wrap and microcook on HIGH for 5 minutes, until the potato is tender.

2. Add the broth, soy milk, parsley, and potato flakes. Re-cover with the plastic wrap and microcook on HIGH for 5 to 7 minutes, until bubbly, stirring once halfway through cooking. Add the clams and their juice and the miso paste, and stir to dissolve the miso in the hot soup. Cover and let stand for 3 minutes. Divide the soup between two soup bowls and serve immediately.

One-Minute Apple Quesadilla

THIS WONDERFUL, ÜBER-QUICK SANDWICH is suitable for lunch or break-fast. For those mornings on the run, you can grab the ingredients quickly from the refrigerator and make a sandwich to take to the office and heat in the microwave. Use your favorite firm slicing cheese, or you can use rice or soy cheese as a substitute with superb results and no loss of flavor. This is also excellent made with a firm ripe pear or Asian pear instead of the apple. ○ *Serves 1*

MICROWAVE COOKWARE: Microwave-safe plate
MICROWAVE WATTAGE: 1,100 to 1,300
MICROWAVE COOK TIME: 30 to 45 seconds
STANDING TIME: 1 minute

One 10-inch flour, whole-wheat, or spelt tortilla
2 ounces sharp Wisconsin cheddar, smoked Gouda, or Monterey Jack cheese,
    sliced or shredded
4 to 6 apple slices, ½ inch thick, peeled or unpeeled

1. Place the tortilla on a clean work surface and lay half the cheese over the lower half of the tortilla. Top with a single layer of the apple slices, then top with the remaining cheese (this will help keep the quesadilla together so that it does not fall apart while you are eating). Fold the top over the filling, making a half-moon shape.

2. Line the plate with a paper towel, place the quesadilla on it, and microcook on HIGH for 30 to 45 seconds, until the tortilla is hot and the cheese is melted. Let stand for 1 minute. Cut in half and serve immediately, while warm.

Mixed Bean and Cheese Burritos

BURRITOS ARE NOW AS COMMONPLACE AS SANDWICHES. They are a version of the sandwich, but more similar to the wrap, which was invented by four San Francisco business-school students who patterned it after the burrito but used more traditional sandwich fillings. Burrito translates as "little donkey," and what we identify as a burrito is more American than Mexican, as flour tortillas are common to the American Southwest and northern Mexico, but not the rest of Mexico. Burrito recipes go back to the nineteenth century, when they were eaten by miners and farmworker crews in the American Southwest.

Flour tortillas are a must for burritos, as they are more pliable when heated than corn tortillas. The fillings can be elaborate or simple: beans, rice, cheese, grilled or roasted vegetables, barbecued meat, fish, even shrimp or tofu. I asked my teenage friends, who are burrito lovers and make them most every day, what filling they like best. It was as plain as day: beans and cheese. No salsa, no rice, no chopped tomato, no cilantro. So here is my version of the most popular burrito, featuring four different kinds of beans. Cooking beans from scratch is not efficient in the microwave (the slow cooker does a better job), so use canned beans. You can use the beans specified in the recipe or any combination of canned beans you like. ○ *Serves 4*

MICROWAVE COOKWARE: 2-quart Pyrex measuring cup or batter bowl
MICROWAVE WATTAGE: 1,100 to 1,300
MICROWAVE COOK TIME: 3 to 4 minutes for the beans, 15 seconds for the tortillas, about 1 minute for each burrito
STANDING TIME: 20 seconds if frozen

One 15-ounce can pinto beans, drained and rinsed
One 15-ounce can black beans, drained and rinsed
One 15-ounce can red kidney beans, drained and rinsed
One 15-ounce can aduki beans, drained and rinsed
4 to 6 teaspoons chili powder (optional)
4 burrito-size flour tortillas
3 to 4 cups shredded mild or sharp cheddar cheese or Mexican cheese blend, to your taste
Salsa of your choice, sour cream, and guacamole for serving (optional)

1. Combine the beans in the measuring cup, and add the chili powder, if using. Stir, then mash about one-third of the beans with the back of a spoon. Partially cover with plastic wrap and microcook on HIGH for 3 to 4 minutes, until hot. Stir once or twice during cooking.

2. Place the stack of tortillas between two paper towels. Microcook on HIGH for 15 seconds to warm them.

3. Working quickly, spoon one-quarter of the bean mixture down the center of each tortilla; sprinkle with one-quarter of the cheese. Fold the bottom, then the sides of each tortilla over the filling, then roll up the tortillas, envelope style.

4. Place 1 burrito at a time on a paper towel and microcook, uncovered, on HIGH for 50 to 60 seconds, until warm to the touch. Serve immediately. If you want to cook all the burritos at once, arrange in a single layer side by side and microcook for 3 to 3½ minutes, until heated through. Serve with salsa, sour cream, and guacamole if desired.

5. To freeze the burritos for later use, cool them to room temperature, and wrap each one in plastic wrap, then aluminum foil. Freeze for up to 1 month. To serve the frozen burritos: Remove the foil, and place the plastic-wrapped burrito on a Pyrex pie plate. Microcook on LOW (10 percent power) or DEFROST for 2 to 3 minutes, or until soft and heated through. Let rest for 20 seconds, then remove the plastic wrap and serve.

Layered Green Enchilada Casserole

STACKED ENCHILADAS are like a savory stack of very flat chewy pancakes, made up of layers of corn tortillas with sauce and cheese in between each layer. They are essentially the same as rolled enchiladas but in a different shape that is a whole lot simpler to assemble. When shopping for tomatillos for the sauce, choose smaller ones, which are sweeter. Make the sauce ahead and store it in the refrigerator in clean olive oil bottles or Corona beer bottles, with a stylish stopper made from a whole fresh jalapeño chile. If you don't have any homemade sauce in the fridge or don't have the time to make some, in a pinch you can substitute good-quality canned green enchilada sauce. You can also use the green sauce for tacos, to pour over rice, or as a dip for tortilla chips. Ideally you should use a casserole dish that is the same diameter as or just a bit larger than the tortillas. You can also make these as individual stacks, with 3 corn tortillas per serving, on a plate. ○ *Serves 2 to 4*

MICROWAVE COOKWARE: 2-quart Pyrex measuring cup or batter bowl, shallow 8-inch round deep soufflé dish or small casserole dish
MICROWAVE WATTAGE: 1,100 to 1,300
MICROWAVE COOK TIME: About 9 minutes for the sauce, about 5 minutes for the soup
STANDING TIME: 8 minutes

MEXICAN GREEN SAUCE:
1 pound tomatillos (about 10), husked under running water, wiped with
　　a paper towel, then cut in half
½ medium-size white onion
½ cup water
2 tablespoons light olive oil
1 tablespoon champagne vinegar or apple cider vinegar
1 vegetable or chicken bouillon cube, mashed
Small handful fresh cilantro
Salt to taste

8 to 10 organic corn tortillas
12 ounces shredded Mexican blend cheese (3 cups)

FOR SERVING:
1 ripe Hass avocado
Juice of 1 lime
Salt to taste
½ cup sour cream
½ cup coarsely chopped fresh cilantro

1. To make the green sauce, place the tomatillos and onion in the measuring cup. Add the water. Partially cover with plastic wrap and microcook on HIGH for about 5 minutes, until the tomatillos are tender and the onion is translucent.

2. Pour the tomatillo mixture into a blender (not a food processor) and process until pureed. Add the olive oil, vinegar, bouillon cube, and cilantro. Process until smooth. Return the mixture to the measuring cup (you don't need to wash it), partially cover with plastic wrap, and microcook on HIGH for about 4 minutes, until simmering. Make sure the bouillon cube is dissolved. Season with salt. (The sauce can be stored in a tightly covered container in the refrigerator for up to 5 days.)

3. Spray the soufflé dish with nonstick cooking spray. Place a spoonful of sauce in the dish and place a tortilla on top. Sprinkle with ¼ cup of the cheese and drizzle with 2 tablespoons of the green sauce. Repeat the layers of tortilla, cheese, and sauce until the tortillas are used up. Pour the remaining sauce over the top of the stacked enchiladas and sprinkle with any remaining cheese. Partially cover with plastic wrap.

4. Microcook on HIGH for 5 to 6 minutes, or until all the cheese is melted and the stack is hot all the way through. Remove from the microwave and let stand on a folded kitchen towel for about 8 minutes.

5. Halve the avocado and place the flesh in a small bowl. Add the lime juice, season with salt, and mash to combine. Set aside.

6. Cut the tortillas into fat wedges and spoon each wedge and some sauce onto individual serving plates. Top with a dollop of the guacamole and some sour cream and sprinkle with the cilantro. Serve immediately. *(continued)*

Mexican Red Chile Sauce

For a different flavor, use this in place of the Mexican Green Sauce.

○ *Makes about 1½ cups*

One 8-ounce can tomato sauce
One 4-ounce can roasted chopped mild green chiles
¼ teaspoon ground cumin
¼ teaspoon chili powder
Pinch of crumbled dried oregano, savory, or marjoram

Combine all of the ingredients in a 1-quart Pyrex measuring cup; stir to dissolve the spices. Partially cover with plastic wrap and microcook on HIGH for 3 to 4 minutes, until simmering. Use immediately, or store the sauce in a tightly covered container in the refrigerator for up to 5 days.

Open-Faced Tuna Melts

TUNA MELTS MIGHT BE CONSIDERED RETRO or old-fashioned; many people probably haven't made or eaten one in years. But this sandwich is at the apex of tuna sandwich land, especially when made with summer tomatoes. Here we make a classic rémoulade sauce, the relative of tartar sauce, and then add the tuna to it. The sandwich is very filling and will soon become your favorite lunch or quick dinner. Don't be tempted to substitute fresh tuna for the canned; fresh tuna is one fish that does not cook well in the microwave. ○ *Serves 4*

MICROWAVE COOKWARE: 4 microwave-safe plates
MICROWAVE WATTAGE: 1,100 to 1,300
MICROWAVE COOK TIME: 45 to 90 seconds
STANDING TIME: None

½ cup mayonnaise, plus more for spreading on the bread
2 tablespoons drained dill or sweet pickle relish or 2 tablespoons chopped
    cornichons or dill pickles
2 tablespoons chopped celery
1 tablespoon chopped scallion or red onion
1 tablespoon nonpareil capers, rinsed and chopped
1 tablespoon chopped fresh Italian parsley
Squeeze of fresh lemon juice
1 teaspoon Dijon mustard
Two 6-ounce cans or two 6.4-ounce pouches chunk light tuna in water,
    drained and rinsed to remove some of the salt
4 slices rustic white bread or other dense white bread, toasted if desired
8 thick slices tomato
4 ounces provolone, mozzarella, or cheddar cheese, thinly sliced

1. Combine the mayonnaise, relish, celery, scallion, capers, parsley, lemon juice, and mustard in a medium-size bowl. Stir until well mixed. Refrigerate, covered, until ready to use.

2. To make the sandwiches, add the tuna to the mayonnaise mixture. Mash with a fork to flake the tuna and evenly mix the tuna salad. *(continued)*

3. Arrange the bread slices on a clean work surface. Lightly spread each slice of bread with additional mayonnaise and top with 2 slices of tomato. Divide the tuna salad evenly among the 4 bread slices, using a small spatula to spread the tuna over the tomatoes. Top each sandwich with a slice or two of cheese.

4. Line each of the plates with a paper towel and place 1 sandwich on it. One at a time, microcook the sandwiches on HIGH for 45 to 90 seconds, until the tuna is warm and the cheese is melted. Serve immediately.

Hot Turkey Meatball Sandwiches

THIS RECIPE IS FROM AN OVERSIZED MAGAZINE called *All You.* You can use your own homemade marinara or some jarred sauce out of the cupboard. These are great sandwiches, and no one will realize you made them from scratch in under 15 minutes. If you like, get some presliced provolone cheese from the deli and lay that on top of the meatballs. If you'd like a smaller sandwich, use ciabatta or French rolls instead of the big sandwich buns. You can make the meatballs ahead and freeze them if you like, then defrost them in the microwave before assembling the sandwiches. ○ *Serves 3 to 4*

MICROWAVE COOKWARE: 10-inch Pyrex pie plate, 1-quart Pyrex measuring cup
MICROWAVE WATTAGE: 1,100 to 1,300
MICROWAVE COOK TIME: 8 minutes for the meatballs, 2 to 3 minutes for the sauce
STANDING TIME: 3 minutes

1 pound ground dark turkey meat
¾ cup seasoned dried Italian bread crumbs
⅓ cup freshly grated Parmesan cheese
¼ cup ricotta cheese
1 large egg, beaten
1 tablespoon olive oil
2 to 3 cups marinara sauce
3 to 4 fresh small ciabatta rolls, small oval sub rolls, or Kaiser rolls, split

1. Place the meat, bread crumbs, Parmesan, ricotta, egg, and olive oil in a medium-size bowl. Mix with your hands or a fork to lightly combine. Divide into quarters and make 4 meatballs from each portion. Place the meatballs in a single layer around the rim of the pie plate. Partially cover with plastic wrap.

2. Microcook on HIGH for 3½ to 4 minutes. Turn the meatballs with tongs and microcook for an additional 3½ to 4 minutes. Test the insides of a meatball with an instant-read thermometer; it should read 165°F. Let stand for 3 minutes, covered. Drain any excess liquid, and set aside. (The meatballs can be frozen in zipper-top plastic freezer bags for up to 2 months and defrosted when ready to use. Thaw in the refrigerator and then rewarm in the microwave for 2 to 3 minutes on HIGH.)

(continued)

3. Place the marinara sauce in the measuring cup, partially cover, and microcook on HIGH for 2 to 3 minutes to warm. Pour the sauce over the meatballs. Warm the rolls for a minute in the oven, or toast them under the broiler, then pile on some of the meatballs and sauce. Serve immediately.

Individual Veggie Tortilla Pizzas

PIZZA IS ARGUABLY the hands-down most popular food these days. It seems incredible indeed that now we can make pizza in the microwave, but it works. With these individual pizzas, kids can make their own, and everyone can have their favorite topping. I love the toppings in this recipe, but you can use any number of topping combinations, such as just pizza sauce and mozzarella; pizza sauce, sliced mushrooms, pepperoni, and mozzarella; pesto with sliced fresh tomatoes and fresh mozzarella cheese slices; pizza sauce, black olives, and Asiago cheese; or pizza sauce with zucchini, a green pepper ring, and broccoli florets. ○ *Serves 1*

MICROWAVE COOKWARE: Microwave-safe plate
MICROWAVE WATTAGE: 1,100 to 1,300
MICROWAVE COOK TIME: 55 to 65 seconds
STANDING TIME: 1 minute

One 8-inch flour tortilla
3 tablespoons pizza sauce (page 90)
1 teaspoon olive oil
2 slices plum tomato, halved
3 thawed frozen artichoke hearts, halved
1 ounce soft goat cheese

1. Place the tortilla on a paper towel or plate. Microcook on HIGH for 30 seconds to warm.

2. Using a small metal spatula, immediately spread pizza sauce on the warm tortilla. Drizzle with the olive oil. Arrange the tomato slices and artichokes on top, and dot with the goat cheese. Microcook for 25 to 35 seconds, until the cheese melts. Let stand for 60 seconds, then cut into 4 wedges. Serve immediately. *(continued)*

No-Cook Pizza Sauce

Makes about 1 cup, enough for 4 individual tortilla pizzas

One 6-ounce can tomato paste
¾ cup water
3 tablespoons freshly grated Parmesan cheese
½ clove garlic, crushed
½ teaspoon sugar
½ teaspoon onion powder
¼ teaspoon crumbled dried oregano
¼ teaspoon crumbled dried basil
Freshly ground black pepper to taste
Pinch of cayenne pepper
Pinch of salt

In a small bowl, stir together the tomato paste, water, cheese, garlic, sugar, and all of the spices with a fork until smooth. Let stand for at least 30 minutes to blend the flavors. The sauce is now ready to use and will keep in the refrigerator for up to 2 weeks.

Cereals, Rice, and Other Grains

Grains are one of the foods the microwave excels at cooking. This chapter contains a broad selection of great recipes that will help you include a wider variety of grains in your diet with no fuss.

The microwave handles the preparation of hot breakfast cereals with a tidiness and efficiency that cannot be replicated by any other countertop appliance. In this chapter you'll find a range of options: not only oatmeal, but also wheat berries. Hot cereals are delicious topped with yogurt and dried fruit, and a fresh berry parfait cup is ready with really wonderful homemade-in-minutes granola.

All of the cereal recipes use the same basic method; only the proportions of cereal to liquid change slightly. The cereals are cooked uncovered at 50 percent power to reduce the chance of messy boilovers. It is important to use a cooking vessel that can hold at least double the volume of the ingredients. If your hot cereal comes out too soupy, microcook in 20-second intervals to thicken it; if it is too thick, add some hot water and microcook for 30 seconds. Be sure to use oven mitts when removing your hot cereal from the microwave, as the bowls get really hot. You can freeze leftover single servings of cooked oatmeal in small zipper-top plastic freezer bags; the night before you plan to eat it, transfer the bag to the refrigerator to thaw overnight. In the morning, place the oatmeal in a microwave-safe cereal bowl and microcook, covered, on DEFROST until hot, stirring once or twice.

Cooking rice and other side-dish grains, such as bulgur, wild rice, and quinoa, in the microwave is an easy alternative to using the stovetop or rice cooker. With the microwave, grains do not scorch, and will steam to perfection. Microcooking risotto shortens the traditionally long cooking time to minutes, with a minimum of stirring. Microwave risotto is not quite as creamy as risotto made in the stovetop or slow cooker, but it is certainly close enough to satisfy a craving for the Italian rice dish.

When cooking these grains, always use a container that can hold about three times the volume of the grain and water. This will prevent boilovers. Rice and other grains are usually cooked with a lid on the stovetop, which makes for a minimal amount of evaporation, but in the microwave, covering the container is optional. That is why you will see less liquid in these recipes than for other methods of cooking. The microwave is extremely efficient on this point. Every recipe will specify whether you need to stir or not; usually it will be only once, at the most twice, so as not to break the tender grains. After cooking there will often be some liquid left. Just let the dish stand, covered, in the turned-off oven or on the counter, and it will absorb the last bit of liquid. If you are not eating your cooked grains immediately, leave on the counter, tightly covered, until serving.

Cooked Wheat Berries

Of all the grains I've cooked in the microwave, wheat berries are one of the biggest challenges, and it's not easy to find a recipe for them. Look no further. This recipe makes a small batch you can use in salads or soups, add to muffin batter, or serve as a hot cereal along with a bit of honey and some chopped pecans. A fabulous way to eat wheat berries for breakfast is to stir a few tablespoonfuls of them into a cup of flavored yogurt. You may see other recipes calling for microcooking wheat berries for 1 to 5 minutes and then letting them stand, expecting to get nice *al dente* grains. But the berries take considerable time to cook properly. An overnight soak will soften the bran layer and shorten cooking time. The cooked grains freeze perfectly, making it quick and easy to use them at a moment's notice. Once you drain and rinse the cooked wheat berries, spread them out on a rimmed baking sheet to finish cooling, then pat dry with paper towels. You can store them in a covered container for up to 5 days in the refrigerator or freeze them in ⅓- to ½-cup batches. Uncooked wheat berries keep indefinitely in a tightly closed jar in a dark cupboard. Wheat berries (and their cousins, spelt, farro, and kamut) are available in bulk in natural foods stores and packaged at larger supermarkets. ❍ Makes about 1⅓ cups

MICROWAVE COOKWARE: 2-quart Pyrex measuring cup
MICROWAVE WATTAGE: 1,100 to 1,300
MICROWAVE COOK TIME: 25 minutes
STANDING TIME: 15 to 30 minutes

½ cup raw wheat berries
3 cups water

1. Pick through the wheat berries and discard any debris or stones. Set in a strainer and rinse well with cold water.

2. Place the wheat berries in a bowl filled with cold water to cover by 4 inches, cover with plastic wrap, and let soak overnight on the counter. The berries will double in volume.

3. Drain the water and place the soaked berries in the measuring cup. Add the 3 cups water.

4. Microcook on HIGH, uncovered, for 25 minutes. Stir 2 or 3 times during cooking. Add hot water or increase the cook time if needed (hard wheat berries take longer to cook than soft wheat berries, and older wheat berries take longer to cook than fresher ones). The berries are done when they are *al dente* tender and a few berries have burst open. Press a berry to feel if the starchy center is tender, or taste a few.

5. Let stand, covered, for 15 to 30 minutes. Drain and rinse under cool water.

Olive Oil Granola with Golden Raisins

GRANOLA IS OFTEN TOUTED as one of the healthiest breakfast cereals, and the microwave makes spectacular granola. The word *granola* is derived from *granula,* a toasted wheat cereal touted by the whole-grain movement of Sylvester Graham in the 1900s. It is tremendously versatile and takes to all sorts of additions and variations on the basic recipe. Do not use quick-cooking or instant oats; I buy fresh rolled oats out of the bulk foods section of my supermarket. Light olive oil is one of the best substitutes for other neutral-tasting oils, as it does not have the strong flavor regular olive oil has. Always stir in the dried fruit, along with the wheat germ and flax seed, after cooking the oats or else these items will harden. The granola can be stored in an airtight container at room temperature for up to 2 weeks. ○ *Makes about 3½ cups*

MICROWAVE COOKWARE: Wide 2-quart casserole dish or 11 × 7-inch Pyrex baking dish;
  1-cup Pyrex measuring cup
MICROWAVE WATTAGE: 1,100 to 1,300
MICROWAVE COOK TIME: About 5 minutes
STANDING TIME: 30 minutes

2 cups old-fashioned rolled oats
¼ cup raw sunflower seeds or slivered almonds
2 tablespoons light brown sugar
2 tablespoons unsweetened flaked coconut
1 tablespoon raw sesame seeds
¼ teaspoon ground cinnamon
¼ cup light olive oil
¼ cup honey or pure maple syrup
½ cup golden raisins
¼ cup toasted wheat germ (such as Kretschmer)
2 tablespoons ground flax seed

1. Line a 17 × 10-inch sheet pan with aluminum foil or parchment paper; set aside. Combine the oats, sunflower seeds, brown sugar, coconut, sesame seeds, and cinnamon in the casserole dish. Stir well.

2. Combine the oil and honey in the measuring cup. Microcook on HIGH, uncovered, for 30 seconds or until just warmed and liquefied (for easy pouring). Drizzle over the top of the oat mixture and stir with a large spoon, coating all the ingredients evenly. Smooth into an even layer in the casserole dish.

3. Microcook on HIGH for 2 minutes; stir well and smooth back into an even layer.

4. Microcook on HIGH for an additional 1½ minutes; stir well and smooth again.

5. Microcook on HIGH for about 1 minute more, until your desired degree of browning. If you need more cook time, cook at 30-second intervals. The granola will still look moist. Remove from the oven and stir in the raisins, wheat germ, and flax seed.

6. Pour the granola onto the prepared sheet pan and, with an offset spatula, spread the mixture out to the edges to make an even layer. Stir every 10 minutes until completely cooled. Alternatively, you can spread the granola in the pan to a ½-inch-thick layer, not stir it, and let it cool into a granola "bark." The granola will crisp up quickly as it cools. If you make the bark, lift the cooled granola out of the pan and break it into pieces.

Granola Berry Parfaits

Serves 4

3 cups vanilla yogurt
2½ to 3 cups mixed fresh berries (any combination of blueberries, blackberries,
raspberries, and sliced strawberries)
2 cups Olive Oil Granola with Golden Raisins

1. Spoon ¼ cup of the yogurt into the bottoms of four 12-ounce wide-mouth glass tumblers, such as French jelly jars.

2. Add a layer of berries to each glass, then sprinkle each with 2 tablespoons of the granola. Make 2 more layers of yogurt and berries, topping each with 1 tablespoon of the granola. You will use a total of ¾ cup yogurt, about ¾ cup berries, and ½ cup granola for each parfait. Serve immediately or cover loosely with plastic wrap and refrigerate for up to 4 hours.

Old-Fashioned Oatmeal

OATMEAL IN THE MICROWAVE is one of the best breakfast foods. The challenge, though, is to use the right cooking vessel so that the oatmeal does not overflow as it foams up during cooking. Using a 1-quart glass measuring cup prevents the overflow problem and makes it much easier to remove the oatmeal from the oven thanks to the measuring cup's handle. You can try different brands of oatmeal for different flavors and textures. Bob's Red Mill gluten-free oats (www.bobsredmill.com), which are grown in fields where there is no wheat or barley grown to cross-contaminate, is one of my daily standards; Holly's Au Natural Oatmeal (www.hollysoatmeal.com) and McCann's quick-cooking oatmeal (www.mccanns.ie) are also both excellent choices. Christine & Rob's oatmeal (www.christineandrobs.com) is an organic toasted oatmeal that consistently takes first prize at the International Fancy Food Show. You can also vary the liquid in which you cook the oats: Water produces a dense, chewy porridge, milk makes it creamy and tender, and fruit juices add a lot of sweetness and result in a chewy oatmeal, similar to using water. I like my oatmeal a dash thick and mounded; if you like a thinner oatmeal, increase the liquid in this recipe to 1 cup. For extra-soft oats, soak the oats overnight at room temperature, covered, and cook as directed in the morning. ○ *Serves 1*

MICROWAVE COOKWARE: 1-quart Pyrex measuring cup
MICROWAVE WATTAGE: 1,100 to 1,300
MICROWAVE COOK TIME: 2½ minutes
STANDING TIME: About 3 minutes

⅔ cup quick-cooking or old-fashioned rolled oats
¾ cup water

FOR SERVING (OPTIONAL):
Milk, half-and-half, or soy milk
1 tablespoon brown sugar, pure maple syrup, or honey
½ cup fresh berries or peaches in season, soaked and drained chopped dried fruit,
    or canned fruit

1. Place the oats and water in the measuring cup. Microcook on HIGH, uncovered, for 2 minutes. Stir and microcook on HIGH for another 30 seconds.

2. Remove from the oven and let stand for about 3 minutes; the oatmeal will thicken slightly. Transfer to a serving bowl and eat immediately with the additions of your choice.

Note: In general, you can use the same cook times for quick-cooking and old-fashioned rolled oats. However, if you use an especially thick-cut rolled oat, such as Silver Palate's Thick & Rough Oatmeal, Bob's Red Mill Extra-Thick Whole Grain Rolled Oats "Kiln Toasted," or Cream of the West Roasted Oats, you will need to microcook on LOW (10 percent power) or DEFROST for about 4 minutes, then let stand for 3 minutes, as these are not the same as regular old-fashioned rolled oats. If you like your oatmeal very soft, add 1 minute to the cook time.

VARIATIONS

Old-Fashioned Apple-Raisin Oatmeal: Substitute unsweetened apple juice for the water and add 1 to 2 tablespoons raisins before cooking. Serve topped with vanilla yogurt.

Old-Fashioned Cranberry Oatmeal: Substitute cranberry juice for the water.

Old-Fashioned Creamy Oatmeal: Substitute milk, half-and-half, rice milk, or soy milk for the water.

Old-Fashioned Oatmeal with White Chocolate: Substitute milk, half-and-half, soy milk, or rice milk for the water. After cooking, stir in 1 heaping tablespoon of white chocolate chips. Let stand for 3 minutes and stir until melted. Serve topped with Greek yogurt, chopped walnuts, and a minced dried apricot.

Old-Fashioned Oatmeal
and Wheat Berries

THIS IS ONE FABULOUS HOT BREAKFAST CEREAL. In this recipe, you cook your oatmeal in milk and then toss in some precooked wheat berries for added flavor and texture. Keep cooked wheat berries (page 93) in portioned batches in the freezer for this purpose. ○ *Serves 1*

MICROWAVE COOKWARE: 2-quart Pyrex measuring cup or a microwave-safe deep cereal bowl

MICROWAVE WATTAGE: 1,100 to 1,300

MICROWAVE COOK TIME: 3½ to 4½ minutes

STANDING TIME: About 4 minutes

½ cup quick-cooking or old-fashioned rolled oats

1 cup milk, soy milk, or rice milk

2 tablespoons raisins, dried cranberries, dried blueberries, or
    a mixture of golden raisins and tart dried cherries

⅓ cup cold cooked wheat berries (page 93)

2 teaspoons brown sugar

A few sprinkles of ground cinnamon

1 to 2 tablespoons toasted slivered almonds (page 26), for sprinkling

1. Place the oats, milk, and dried fruit in the measuring cup or cereal bowl. Microcook on HIGH, uncovered, for 2 to 3 minutes.

2. Add the wheat berries and microcook on HIGH for 90 seconds longer. Remove from the oven and let stand for about 4 minutes. Stir in the brown sugar and cinnamon, and sprinkle with the toasted almonds. Enjoy!

Family-Style Creamy Maple-Cranberry Oatmeal

COOK YOUR OATMEAL IN MILK for a really creamy consistency. Since the cranberries are cooked in the oatmeal, they plump up nicely. There is a slight difference in the cook times depending on whether you use quick-cooking or old-fashioned rolled oats. Remember that the secret to perfect microwave oatmeal is to be sure to include the standing time, as the oats will finish cooking then. ○ *Serves 4*

MICROWAVE COOKWARE: 3-quart Pyrex casserole dish
MICROWAVE WATTAGE: 1,100 to 1,300
MICROWAVE COOK TIME: 6 to 10 minutes
STANDING TIME: 5 minutes

3½ cups milk, soy milk, or rice milk
2 cups quick-cooking or old-fashioned rolled oats
½ cup dried cranberries
⅓ cup pure maple syrup, plus more for serving
¼ cup toasted wheat germ (such as Kretschmer)
Cold milk or yogurt for serving

1. Combine the milk, oats, cranberries, and maple syrup in the casserole dish and stir.

2. Microcook on HIGH, uncovered, for 6 to 7 minutes for quick-cooking oats and 9 to 10 minutes for old-fashioned oats, until most of liquid is absorbed, stirring once halfway through cooking.

3. Let stand for 5 minutes, until the desired consistency is reached. Stir in the wheat germ. Spoon the oatmeal into four cereal bowls. Serve with cold milk or topped with some yogurt and a bit more maple syrup drizzled on top.

Savory Oatmeal

WHEN MOST PEOPLE THINK OF OATMEAL, they think of it with milk and sugar, a sweet breakfast version. But for those who just don't want something sweet for breakfast, oatmeal offers lots of exciting meal opportunities when prepared with savory ingredients. Those cultures where such dishes as kedgeree, kitcharee, congee, and jook are popular for breakfast have a palate accustomed to this. There are others who eat their oatmeal with just salt and pepper or with cheese melted in, as if it were a bowl of rice. You have entered the land of BLD (Breakfast, Lunch, or Dinner) Oatmeal. Create your own savory oatmeal concoctions by cooking your oatmeal in chicken broth, water, or even canned tomatoes with their juice, adding leftover meats, good cheeses, garden-fresh vegetables, sautéed mushrooms, or whatever you happen to have on hand. You can serve savory oatmeal with a stew, in place of something like polenta, or instead of potatoes (see variations). This recipe is adapted from one in *The Quaker Oats Whole-grain Cookbook* (Quaker Oats Company, 1982). ○ *Serves 1*

MICROWAVE COOKWARE: 1-quart Pyrex casserole dish or measuring cup
MICROWAVE WATTAGE: 1,100 to 1,300
MICROWAVE COOK TIME: 2½ minutes
STANDING TIME: About 3 minutes

¾ **cup quick-cooking or old-fashioned rolled oats**
Pinch of sea salt
1 cup water, vegetable broth, or low-sodium chicken broth
1 large egg
1 scallion (green part only), chopped
A few grinds of black pepper

1. Place the oats, salt, and water in the casserole dish. Microcook on HIGH, uncovered, for 2 minutes. Stir and microcook on HIGH for another 30 seconds.

2. Remove from the oven and let stand for about 3 minutes; the oatmeal will thicken slightly. While it is standing, fry the egg on the stovetop in a sauté pan. Transfer the oatmeal to a serving bowl and top with the egg, scallion, and pepper. Serve immediately.

VARIATIONS

Exotic Oatmeal: Stir 1 tablespoon tahini, 1 tablespoon honey, and 2 teaspoons white miso paste into the hot oatmeal and let stand for 3 minutes. Top with some toasted sesame seeds, if desired.

Orient Express Oatmeal: Add 2 tablespoons low-sodium soy sauce to the water before cooking. Top with the egg and scallion.

Mediterranean Oatmeal: Drizzle 1 tablespoon extra-virgin olive oil over the cooked oatmeal and top with a few grinds of black pepper and some shaved Parmesan cheese.

Florentine Oatmeal: Serve topped with some Olive Oil–Braised Escarole (page 159) and a pat of unsalted butter.

Oatmeal Lorraine: Serve topped with a crumbled strip of cooked bacon (page 103) and ¼ cup shredded Swiss or fontina cheese.

Provençal Oatmeal: Stir ½ seeded, diced plum tomato and 1 tablespoon soft goat cheese into the hot oatmeal and let stand for 3 minutes. Top with 1 tablespoon mixed minced fresh parsley, basil, and chives.

Breakfast Steel-Cut Oats

STEEL-CUT OATS, ALSO KNOWN AS IRISH OATMEAL, are the pinnacle of oatmeal goodness. Made from chopped oat groats, they are the easiest way to eat oats as a whole grain, and they have a texture all their own. The microwave provides a quick and easy way to prepare steel-cut oats, which traditionally need a good long cooking time on the stovetop, much too long for a quick weekday breakfast. McCann's is my favorite brand of steel-cut oats; made from husked Irish-grown whole-grain oats from Counties Kildare and Meath, they have a nutty flavor that's remarkable. I also like Bob's Red Mill Original Scottish Oatmeal. Note that the amount of water used in this recipe is less than if you made the oatmeal on the stovetop, and make sure to do the overnight soak of the oats, which reduces the cook time and makes for a toothsome porridge that has just the right texture. Serve with milk, maybe a dash of maple syrup or agave nectar, some sliced banana or peach, a sprinkling of ground flax seed, or chopped dates and a pat of butter—or be adventurous and serve with milk, a few teaspoons of dark brown sugar, and ¼ teaspoon unsweetened cocoa powder sifted over the top of your oatmeal. ○ *Serves 2*

MICROWAVE COOKWARE: 1- or 2-quart Pyrex measuring cup or a large, deep microwave-safe cereal bowl
MICROWAVE WATTAGE: 1,100 to 1,300
MICROWAVE COOK TIME: 10 to 10½ minutes
STANDING TIME: About 5 minutes

1½ cups water
1 cup steel-cut oats
Milk and other toppings of your choice for serving

1. Before going to bed, place the water in the measuring cup or cereal bowl and microcook on HIGH for 2 to 2½ minutes, until almost boiling. Remove from the oven and add the oats. Cover with plastic wrap and let rest on the counter overnight or refrigerate overnight.

2. In the morning, remove the plastic wrap and microcook on HIGH, uncovered, for 5 minutes; stir.

3. Return to the oven and microcook on HIGH for 3 minutes more, stopping the oven every 30 seconds to keep it from boiling over. Remove from the oven and let rest for 5 minutes, so the cereal can thicken. Divide the oatmeal between two serving bowls, add the milk and toppings of your choice, and serve immediately.

Note: Plain cooked steel-cut oats, cooled to room temperature, can be portioned and frozen in small containers or pint-size zipper-top plastic freezer bags. To serve, transfer the frozen portion to the refrigerator and let thaw overnight. When ready to reheat, transfer the cooked oats to a deep microwave-safe cereal bowl. Microcook on HIGH, uncovered, for 2 minutes; stir, and then microcook for an additional 1 minute, until steaming hot, adding some milk if desired to help restore the creamy texture.

Bacon on the Side

Bacon cooks beautifully in the microwave: It has minimal shrinkage and crisps up nicely, excess grease is absorbed by paper towels, and there is no messy skillet to clean. You can microcook the bacon in one of two ways: between two pieces of plain paper towel, or on a flat microwave-safe ridged plastic tray called a bacon grill covered with paper towels; the fat drains away as the bacon cooks. To defrost frozen bacon before cooking it, microcook on DEFROST for 3 to 4 minutes per pound, until the slices can be separated. Cook immediately. Remember that the cook time can be affected by a number of variables: whether the bacon is at room temperature or ice cold, the thickness of the slices, how fatty the bacon is, whether it's smoked or cured (or both), the bacon's sugar and salt content, and even the size of your microwave. To cook 3 slices of bacon, fold two plain paper towels together and place in the bottom of a Pyrex baking dish that will fit the slices side by side (do not overlap). Place the bacon on the paper towels and cover with another folded paper towel. If using a bacon grill, place the bacon slices side by side on the ridges and cover with a folded piece of paper towel. Microcook on HIGH for 1½ to 2 minutes. Check for crispness and microcook on MEDIUM (50 percent power) for 20-second intervals until done to your liking. Remove the bacon from the paper towels promptly or it will stick, and let stand on a clean paper towel for 2 minutes, then serve. For 4 to 6 slices, microcook for 3 to 4 minutes. For 6 to 9 slices, microcook for 4 to 5 minutes. Always check the bacon after 2 minutes, however, and do not use this method for more than 9 slices at a time.

Microwave Wild Rice

THERE ARE TWO TYPES OF WILD RICE, which is not actually rice at all but a long-grain marsh grass. One is truly wild and is native to the upper Great Lakes area, and the other is cultivated in paddies in California, Minnesota, Idaho, and Canada. Wild rice should have a smoky-rich, nutty, earthy, flavor, and both types have this distinctive taste, with the cultivated wild rice having the milder flavor. In general, the darker the rice, the stronger the flavor.

In the microwave you can make excellent wild rice quickly and easily. The cooking vessel never gets hotter than the ingredients so the rice won't stick or burn. Expect wild rice to take two to three times longer to cook than white rice. In fact, it takes nearly as long to cook in the microwave as it does on the stovetop, as wild rice absorbs liquid slowly. Wild rice should always be cooked covered. However, you may uncover to stir the rice from time to time. Wild rice is properly cooked when kernels are tender and many have burst open to reveal a cream-colored interior. Overcooking will cause split kernels to curl, so if you see a few curls, stop cooking. Once you have invested the time in making wild rice, maximize the results by freezing leftovers in ½- to 1-cup portions in zipper-top plastic freezer bags. Then you can have wild rice whenever you want by defrosting it in the microwave.

o Makes about 2½ cups

MICROWAVE COOKWARE: 2-quart Pyrex casserole dish with lid
MICROWAVE WATTAGE: 1,100 to 1,300
MICROWAVE COOK TIME: About 30 minutes
STANDING TIME: 10 to 15 minutes

1 cup wild rice
2 cups water or low-sodium vegetable, chicken, or beef broth
2 pinches of salt
1 to 2 tablespoons unsalted butter

1. Thoroughly rinse the rice in cold water and drain. Place the rice and water in the casserole dish. Cover with the lid and microcook on HIGH for 6 to 8 minutes, to bring to a boil.

2. Microcook on MEDIUM (50 percent power) for another 24 to 28 minutes, until the rice puffs up and the inside, lighter portion of the grain begins to split and can be seen. The rice will be tender to bite, yet slightly chewy.

3. After the rice is done cooking, leave it undisturbed in the oven for 10 to 15 minutes; the rice will continue to absorb moisture and fluff as it cools. Add the salt and butter, gently fluff with a fork, and serve hot. To reheat refrigerated leftover rice, place the rice in a 4-cup microwave-safe dish and partially cover. Microcook on HIGH until hot, 2 to 3 minutes (3 to 4 minutes if the rice is frozen). Cooked wild rice can be refrigerated for up to 1 week (it seems to actually enhance the flavor), or frozen for up to 6 months.

Basmati Rice

Basmati Rice, the Queen of Rices and a staple of Indian cooking, is quick and easy to prepare in the microwave. Basmati fits into the spiritual and physical aspects of Ayurveda, the method of healthy living that includes the yogic concepts of mental, physical, social, and spiritual harmony. According to Ayurveda, basmati is *satvic* or "pure" and therefore beneficial for the body and easy to digest, while at the same time contributing to an individual's higher consciousness. All that in a grain of rice! The grain elongates up to three times its uncooked length as it cooks, looking like a needle rather than plumping out, and cooks in a very short time, depending on the freshness of the rice (older rice will take longer). The microwave shaves off only a small amount of time, but the resulting rice is really excellent and exudes a fabulous fragrance while cooking. Do not stir the rice at any time while cooking, as it breaks the grains. If using a domestic version of basmati, such as Texmati, use the same proportions specified here, but skip the washing. ● *Serves 4 to 6*

MICROWAVE COOKWARE: 2-quart Pyrex casserole dish with lid or microwave-safe ceramic casserole dish
MICROWAVE WATTAGE: 1,100 to 1,300
MICROWAVE COOK TIME: 12 to 13½ minutes
STANDING TIME: 5 to 10 minutes

1 cup basmati rice
2⅓ cups cold water
¼ teaspoon salt

1. Place the rice in a bowl and fill the bowl with cold water. Swish the rice around with your fingers. Bits of grain will float to the top, it will foam around the edges, and the water will become murky. Carefully pour off the water and wash a second time. If the rice water is still murky, wash and drain again; imported basmati usually takes 2 to 4 washings. Discard the wash water.

2. Place the wet rice, 2⅓ cups water, and salt in the casserole dish and microcook on HIGH, uncovered, for 9 to 10 minutes. Remove from the oven to check for doneness. The rice will have evaporation steam holes on the surface and the water should be almost completely absorbed.

3. Cover with the lid or partially cover with plastic wrap. Microcook on HIGH for another 3 to 3½ minutes. Remove from the oven and set on the counter. Do not uncover.

4. Let stand, covered, for 5 to 10 minutes, then gently fluff the rice with a wooden or plastic rice paddle. If the rice is too moist, re-cover and microcook on HIGH for 1-minute intervals until the desired consistency is achieved.

Thai Sticky Rice

THAI STICKY RICE (also known as "sweet rice" or "glutinous rice") is a regional specialty characteristic of the cuisine of Southeast Asia. It comes in long- and short-grain varieties, and the starchiness of raw sticky rice gives it a distinct opaque whiteness that's different from the more translucent appearance of other rice grains. When cooked properly, the grains stay whole and a dash chewy, sticking to one another in a lump (making it easier to pick up with chopsticks), but not sticky enough to stick to your hand. It is meant to be formed into small balls that can be dipped into spicy sauces. The microwave makes great sticky rice. The grains come out a little stickier than when prepared by more traditional methods, but unless you are eating with your hands, you will barely notice. This method was developed by Melissa Rubel Jacobson, senior associate recipe developer at *Food & Wine* magazine. When shopping, make sure to buy what is labeled as sticky rice (sticky rice is not the same as jasmine rice). Sticky rice is frequently served with barbecued chicken and spicy salads, and it is used in the famous Thai dessert featuring rice drenched in sweetened coconut milk with fresh mangoes.

o *Serves 6*

MICROWAVE COOKWARE: 2- or 3-quart Pyrex casserole dish with lid
MICROWAVE WATTAGE: 1,100 to 1,300
MICROWAVE COOK TIME: About 13 minutes
STANDING TIME: 5 minutes

2½ cups Thai long-grain white sticky rice, sweet rice, or glutinous rice
2¼ cups warm water

1. Place the rice in the casserole dish and cover with cold water. Let stand, uncovered, on the counter to soak for 1 hour. The rice will absorb much of the water and expand in size. It will also soften so that the grains easily break into pieces if pressed between the fingers.

2. Drain well and return the rice to the casserole dish. Add the warm water. Cover tightly with the lid or vented plastic wrap.

3. Microcook on HIGH for 5 minutes. Stir the rice around to move the rice from the top of the dish to the bottom of the dish. You will notice that some of the rice is translucent or cooked, and some still has a white center. This is okay.

4. Re-cover and microcook on HIGH for 5 minutes more. Stir again.

5. Re-cover and microcook on HIGH for 3 minutes, until soft but still firm, and fully translucent. Check to see if the rice is cooked through by mashing it between your fingers or by tasting it. Remove from the oven and let stand, still covered, for 5 minutes. Serve immediately, hot or at room temperature, portioning with a rice paddle.

Chinese Rice

I CAN'T CALL THIS CHINESE FRIED RICE, since it is cooked in the microwave and not fried, but consider this a microcooked version of that popular Chinese restaurant menu item. You can take a mix-and-match approach to the ingredients, with an aromatic of some sort (onion, scallion, garlic, shallot), leftover cooked meat or seafood (ham, pork, crumbled bacon, chicken, shrimp), and any vegetables that are quick-cooking and on hand. My favorites in this dish are napa cabbage, spinach, bok choy, mushrooms, celery, zucchini, green peas, water chestnuts, and carrots. Less is more here; choose just a few ingredients to mix with the rice, and all additions should be shredded, finely chopped, finely sliced, or julienned. Your seasoning can be as plain as a splash of soy sauce or fish sauce, or you can get a little fancier with bottled condiments such as vegetarian mushroom oyster sauce, toasted sesame oil, or hoisin sauce (page 237). You can cook the rice right before making this recipe, but I love to use leftover rice. ○ *Serves 2 to 3*

MICROWAVE COOKWARE: 2-quart Pyrex casserole dish with lid or microwave-safe ceramic casserole dish
MICROWAVE WATTAGE: 1,100 to 1,300
MICROWAVE COOK TIME: 6 to 7 minutes
STANDING TIME: None

3 tablespoons untoasted sesame oil or olive oil

2 fresh mushrooms, sliced

½ cup thin-cut strips of ham or cooked sausage

3 cups cold cooked long-grain rice, such as white or brown jasmine, converted, or basmati

¾ to 1 cup mixed green vegetables, such as finely shredded baby bok choy, spinach, and peas

¼ cup minced scallions (white part and a few inches of green)

2 tablespoons low-sodium chicken broth or water

2 to 3 tablespoons low-sodium soy sauce or tamari

1. Place the oil, mushrooms, and ham in the casserole dish. Microcook on HIGH, covered, for 2 minutes.

2. Add the rice, mixed vegetables, and scallions; stir to distribute the vegetables and break up any clumps of rice. Drizzle with the broth and soy sauce.

3. Cover and microcook on HIGH for 4 to 5 minutes, stirring at the 2-minute mark, until the rice is really hot and the vegetables are cooked. Serve immediately.

Greek Spinach Rice
(Spanakorizo)

SPANAKORIZO IS A TRADITIONAL GREEK DISH that is prepared throughout that country. If you want to make it with converted white rice, it will take about 10 minutes to cook; reduce the liquid to just 2 cups. It should be served with wedges of lemon, coarsely ground pepper, and some yummy crumbled feta cheese. ● *Serves 2 to 4*

MICROWAVE COOKWARE: 2-quart Pyrex casserole dish with lid or microwave-safe ceramic casserole dish

MICROWAVE WATTAGE: 1,100 to 1,300

MICROWAVE COOK TIME: About 26 minutes

STANDING TIME: 5 to 10 minutes

8 ounces fresh spinach (about 3 cups) or one 10-ounce package
   frozen chopped spinach, thawed

4 tablespoons olive oil

⅓ cup coarsely chopped scallion

1 cup long-grain brown rice

2¼ cups low-sodium chicken or vegetable broth

2 tablespoons tomato paste

A few pinches of sea salt, or to taste

FOR GARNISH:

4 ounces feta cheese, crumbled or diced

Freshly ground black pepper to taste

1 lemon, cut into wedges

1. If using fresh spinach, wash well, shred, and set aside to drain. If using frozen spinach that has been thawed, remove from the package and gently squeeze out excess liquid. Set aside.

2. Combine the oil and scallion in the baking dish. Microcook on HIGH, uncovered, for 30 seconds to warm. Add the rice and stir until the rice is coated. Microcook on HIGH, uncovered, for 1½ minutes.

3. Add the spinach, broth, tomato paste, and salt. Stir to liquefy the tomato paste. Cover and microcook on HIGH for 4 to 5 minutes, until bubbles appear around the edge. Stir once.

4. Re-cover, then microcook on MEDIUM (50 percent power) for 20 minutes. Do not stir during simmering; the rice will look dry on the surface and have a bit of liquid in the bottom that you can see if using the Pyrex dish. Let stand, covered, for 5 to 10 minutes, until the rest of the liquid is absorbed.

5. Fluff with a fork and portion into individual serving bowls. Top with some feta, pepper, and a squeeze of lemon juice.

Barley Pilaf with
Sun-Dried Tomatoes and Scallions

I F YOU'RE LOOKING FOR A SIDE DISH using whole grains, here is one with barley instead of the predictable rice. Barley has been deemed one of the healthiest and tastiest of the Old World grains. You see lots of barley recipes in cool-weather countries like Scotland, Russia, Canada, and Tibet. Barley is also grown in Canada and the United States. Barley can be cooked either risotto-style, uncovered, or boiled-rice-style, covered, as in this recipe. Be sure to use pearl barley with its bran layer removed, not instant barley, which is pre-steamed for fast cooking. It has a nice texture and delicious flavor, and it cooks very quickly. Serve this as a side dish to a vegetable stir-fry or meat dish. This can also be served cold the next day, drizzled with some vinaigrette. ○ *Serves 4*

MICROWAVE COOKWARE: 2-quart Pyrex casserole dish with lid or microwave-safe ceramic casserole dish

MICROWAVE WATTAGE: 1,100 to 1,300

MICROWAVE COOK TIME: About 25 minutes

STANDING TIME: 5 minutes

1 cup pearl barley

3 tablespoons unsalted butter

1 bunch scallions (white and green parts), finely chopped

1 clove garlic, crushed

3 cups low-sodium chicken broth, or 1½ cups broth and 1½ cups water

10 oil-packed sun-dried tomatoes, coarsely chopped

1 teaspoon salt

⅔ cup freshly grated Parmesan cheese or crumbled feta cheese, for serving

1. In a small bowl, thoroughly rinse the barley in several changes of water, then cover with fresh cold water by about 1 inch and soak for 1 hour. Drain well and set aside.

2. Place the butter, scallions, and garlic in the casserole dish. Partially cover and microcook on HIGH for 2 to 3 minutes, until the scallions are soft.

3. Add the drained barley, broth, sun-dried tomatoes, and salt to the scallions, and stir to combine. Partially cover and microcook on HIGH for 10 minutes, then microcook on MEDIUM (50 percent power) for 12 to 15 minutes, until the barley is chewy but tender. Let stand, covered, for 5 minutes.

4. Spoon the barley into bowls and garnish with the cheese. Serve immediately.

Not Your Mother's Risotto
with Asparagus and Mushrooms

THIS IS THE RECIPE THAT GOT ME STARTED on developing this book. Risotto purists might declare this a travesty, but when time is of the essence, risotto made in the microwave really works. The technique is precise, but very easy. The secret is, of course, to use the proper rice for risotto, Italian Arborio, which is a short-grain white rice that makes a sort of sauce while it cooks, giving the finished dish the creamy consistency that is the hallmark of a good risotto. The original recipe was created by Sam Gugino, who was my first food editor at the *San Jose Mercury News* in the late 1980s; it has become a favorite family recipe. ○ *Serves 4*

MICROWAVE COOKWARE: 2-quart Pyrex casserole dish or microwave-safe ceramic casserole dish
MICROWAVE WATTAGE: 1,100 to 1,300
MICROWAVE COOK TIME: About 19 minutes
STANDING TIME: None

2 tablespoons unsalted butter

2 tablespoons olive oil

3 tablespoons minced shallots

1½ cups Arborio or Carnaroli rice

3¾ cups hot low-sodium chicken broth, plus additional broth as needed

6 ounces mushrooms of your choice, sliced

12 ounces asparagus spears, cut into 2-inch pieces on the diagonal

Salt and freshly ground black pepper to taste

¾ cup freshly grated Parmigiano-Reggiano cheese

1. Place the butter and oil in the casserole dish. Microcook, uncovered, for 1 to 2 minutes on HIGH to melt and warm. Add the shallots and stir to coat; microcook on HIGH for 2 minutes.

2. Add the rice and stir to coat all the grains; microcook on HIGH for 2 minutes, until the rice is coated with the oil mixture and begins to turn yellow.

3. Pour in the hot broth and microcook on HIGH for 6 to 7 minutes (the rice will be undercooked and a bit soupy at this point).

4. Add the mushrooms and asparagus; microcook on HIGH for 6 minutes. Taste for texture (the risotto should be tender and creamy yet slightly chewy), and season with salt and pepper. If the rice is not yet tender, continue to microcook on HIGH in 2-minute intervals, adding a tablespoon or two of broth if necessary to adjust the consistency.

5. Remove the dish from the oven. Stir in the cheese; serve immediately.

Lemon and Parsley Risotto

PARSLEY IS AN OLD-FASHIONED HERB that is so pedestrian no one gives it much thought. Loads of savory recipes call for parsley, but does anyone know what parsley does for a dish? It does a lot, actually. There are two varieties of parsley, both bright green. One is curly and crisp and used for garnishing. The second, and my favorite, is Italian parsley, also called flat-leaf parsley. It has flat leaves with a sawtooth edge. It is more delicate in flavor and definitely easier to eat than the chewier curly type. Parsley stands up well to heat and will retain its color and flavor. It is wonderful combined with lemon to make a simple, but very flavorful, risotto. ○ *Serves 4*

MICROWAVE COOKWARE: 2-quart Pyrex casserole dish or microwave-safe ceramic casserole dish
MICROWAVE WATTAGE: 1,100 to 1,300
MICROWAVE COOK TIME: About 20 minutes
STANDING TIME: None

2 tablespoons olive oil

1 small yellow onion, finely chopped

1½ cups Arborio or Carnaroli rice

½ cup dry white wine

3¼ cups hot low-sodium chicken broth, plus additional broth as needed

⅓ cup chopped fresh Italian parsley

2 tablespoons chopped mixed fresh herbs, such as basil, thyme, chives, and sage

1 tablespoon grated lemon zest

¼ teaspoon salt

¼ teaspoon freshly ground black pepper

1 cup freshly grated Parmigiano-Reggiano cheese

1. Place the oil in the casserole dish. Microcook, uncovered, for 1 to 2 minutes on HIGH to warm. Add the onion and stir to coat; microcook on HIGH for 2 minutes.

2. Add the rice and stir to coat all the grains; microcook on HIGH for 2 minutes. Add the wine and microcook on HIGH for 2 minutes more.

3. Pour in the hot broth and microcook on HIGH for 6 to 7 minutes (the rice will be undercooked and a bit soupy at this point).

4. Add the parsley, mixed herbs, and lemon zest; microcook on HIGH for 6 minutes. Taste for texture (the risotto should be tender and creamy yet slightly chewy) and season with the salt and pepper. If the rice is not tender, continue to microcook on HIGH in 2-minute intervals, adding a tablespoon or two of broth if necessary to adjust the consistency.

5. Remove the dish from the oven. Stir in the cheese; serve immediately.

Mixed Vegetable Risotto with Fontina

RISOTTO IS ACTUALLY QUITE EASY and fast to make in the microwave, and it's very tasty. In this recipe you add some diced mixed vegetables of your choice, or you could even use frozen mixed vegetables. Italian fontina is one of the best melting cheeses for cooking and makes a very creamy risotto. **o** *Serves 4*

MICROWAVE COOKWARE: 2-quart Pyrex casserole dish or microwave-safe ceramic casserole dish

MICROWAVE WATTAGE: 1,100 to 1,300

MICROWAVE COOK TIME: About 19 minutes

STANDING TIME: None

1 tablespoon unsalted butter

1 tablespoon olive oil

½ medium-size onion, finely chopped

1 cup Arborio or Carnaroli rice

3¾ cups hot chicken or vegetable broth, plus additional broth as needed

3 cups finely chopped mixed vegetables (choose your favorites, such as red peppers, summer squash, zucchini, fresh peas, and mushrooms, or use frozen mixed vegetables)

5 ounces fontina cheese, diced

1. Place the butter and oil in the casserole dish. Microcook, uncovered, on HIGH for 1 to 2 minutes to melt and warm. Add the onion and stir to coat; microcook on HIGH for 2 minutes.

2. Add the rice and stir to coat all the grains; microcook on HIGH for 2 minutes, until the rice is coated with the oil mixture and begins to turn yellow.

3. Pour in the hot broth and microcook on HIGH for 6 to 7 minutes (the rice will be undercooked and a bit soupy at this point).

4. Add the vegetables; microcook on HIGH for 6 minutes. Taste for texture (the risotto should be tender and creamy yet slightly chewy). If the rice is not tender, continue to microcook on HIGH in 2-minute intervals, adding a tablespoon or two of broth if necessary to adjust the consistency.

5. Stir in the cheese and microcook on HIGH for 1 minute. Remove the dish from the oven; serve immediately.

Bulgur Cracked Wheat

BULGUR CRACKED WHEAT is made from whole wheat berries that have been hulled, steamed, and kiln-dried before cracking. It cooks quite fast. Bulgur cracked wheat, a favorite in the popular tabbouleh salad, is available in every supermarket and comes in three grades: fine, medium, and coarse (known as grade C), with the supermarket variety being medium unless otherwise labeled. Package directions usually call for just soaking the bulgur, but the flavor and texture is far better with a dash of cooking. I discovered bulgur wheat as a hot side dish while working on my book *The Ultimate Rice Cooker Cookbook* (The Harvard Common Press, 2003). It is deliciously rich and satisfying and great as an alternative to rice or potatoes. You can use this recipe to prepare bulgur for a cold salad or for a stuffing with vegetables added. ○ *Serves 4 to 6*

MICROWAVE COOKWARE: 2-quart Pyrex casserole dish with lid or 2-quart Pyrex measuring cup
MICROWAVE WATTAGE: 1,100 to 1,300
MICROWAVE COOK TIME: 8 to 9 minutes
STANDING TIME: 5 minutes

1 cup bulgur wheat
1¾ cups water, low-sodium chicken broth, or low-sodium beef broth
¾ teaspoon salt

1. Place the bulgur and water in the casserole dish. Cover with the lid or vented plastic wrap and microcook on HIGH for 3 to 4 minutes, until the water is simmering and bubbles appear around the edges.

2. Remove from the oven and stir, then re-cover and microcook on MEDIUM (50 percent power) for another 5 minutes, until the liquid is absorbed.

3. Let stand, covered, for 5 minutes. Fluff with a fork, season with the salt, and serve.

Perfect Quinoa

MANY HOME COOKS are finally discovering quinoa. Quinoa (pronounced KEEN-wah) is not a true grain, but the dried seeds of the goosefoot family, brightly colored herb plants related to spinach and lamb's quarters. Quinoa translates to "mother" in Quechua, the language of one of the main native Andean peoples and Incan descendants. It was one of the grains that Luther Burbank introduced to the United States as the "forgotten cereal of the ancients," but it did not catch on as a food source for North Americans. In South America it was a staple highland grain just as important as maize, and was considered the source of strength and endurance for working in the thin mountain air. It is a great alternative to rice and barley. Quinoa is a round, flat disc that looks like a cross between a sesame seed and a grain of millet. It is very mild in flavor with a gentle tangy aftertaste. It turns translucent and fluffy when cooked. A hoop-like bran layer surrounds each grain, and after cooking it looks like a crescent; an opaque dot in the center disappears when the grain is completely cooked. Quinoa is extremely digestible, with a surprising crunch despite the grains' tiny size. If left to rest after cooking, covered, the grains will swell a bit more. There are now three varieties of quinoa available: tan, black, and red. ○ *Serves 4*

MICROWAVE COOKWARE: 2-quart Pyrex casserole dish with lid or microwave-safe ceramic casserole dish

MICROWAVE WATTAGE: 1,100 to 1,300

MICROWAVE COOK TIME: About 13 minutes

STANDING TIME: 5 to 10 minutes

1 cup quinoa
2 cups water, vegetable broth, or low-sodium chicken broth
¼ teaspoon salt

1. Thoroughly rinse the quinoa in cold water and drain (see Note).

2. Place the quinoa, 2 cups water, and salt in the casserole dish. Microcook on HIGH, covered, for 5 minutes, to bring to a boil.

3. Microcook on MEDIUM (50 percent power) for 8 minutes, until the liquid is completely absorbed and you can see the little half-moon on each grain. Remove from the oven and let stand for 5 to 10 minutes. Fluff with a fork and serve hot, or spread out on a clean baking sheet to cool for use in a salad or soup.

Note: Quinoa is coated with a resiny natural compound, saponin, which gives a bitter and soapy flavor to the cooked grain. Quinoa must be rinsed before cooking, as the compound dissolves easily in cold water. Place the seeds in a deep bowl and fill with cold water to cover. Swirl the grains with your fingers; the water will foam. Drain through a fine-mesh strainer and rinse under cold running water. Repeat until there is no foam.

Polenta Casserole with Fontina and Tomato Sauce

I ADAPTED THIS WONDERFUL RECIPE from one in an old *Bon Appétit* article on a unique Tuscan farm, Spannocchia, a working farm eco-retreat. The sauce has the basic aromatic triad of onions, celery, and carrots. The freshly made polenta, which is a snap to prepare in the microwave (most commercial packages of polenta and cornmeal include microwave-cooking instructions), is layered in the pan with fontina cheese, the other great Italian melting cheese besides mozzarella, and tomato sauce. The casserole rests awhile before you cook it. *Buon appetito!* ○ *Serves 4 to 6*

MICROWAVE COOKWARE: 3-quart Pyrex or microwave-safe ceramic casserole dish for the sauce, 3-quart Pyrex or microwave-safe ceramic casserole dish for the polenta, 8-inch square Pyrex or microwave-safe ceramic baking dish for the casserole

MICROWAVE WATTAGE: 1,100 to 1,300

MICROWAVE COOK TIME: About 8 minutes for the sauce, 9 to 11 minutes for the polenta, 6 to 8 minutes for the cassserole

STANDING TIME: 1 to 2 hours

3 tablespoons olive oil

½ medium-size white onion, finely chopped

½ cup finely chopped celery

¼ cup finely chopped carrot

1 clove garlic, minced

One 28-ounce can whole tomatoes, undrained

1 tablespoon chopped fresh Italian parsley

1½ teaspoons dried oregano or 1 tablespoon fresh oregano leaves

¼ cup chopped fresh basil

Salt and freshly ground black pepper to taste

1 cup polenta or coarse-grind cornmeal

1 teaspoon salt

3½ cups water

2 cups shredded fontina cheese

1. Make the sauce: Place 2 tablespoons of the oil, the onion, celery, and carrot in the casserole dish. Cover and microcook on HIGH for about 3 minutes, until the vegetables are soft. Stir in the garlic. Microcook on HIGH for 30 seconds more.

2. Add the tomatoes and their juice (break up the tomatoes with the back of a spoon or your hands as you put them in), parsley, and oregano. Microcook on HIGH, uncovered, for 4 to 5 minutes, until steaming hot. Stir in the basil, then season with salt and pepper. Cover and set aside.

3. Place the polenta, the remaining 1 tablespoon olive oil, salt, and water in the second casserole dish; whisk to combine. Cover with vented plastic wrap. Microcook on HIGH for 5 minutes. Remove plastic wrap; stir well with a whisk or wooden spoon. Cover with a paper towel. Microcook on HIGH 4 to 6 minutes, until the polenta is very thick and the water is absorbed. Let stand, covered, for 3 minutes.

4. Brush the 8-inch baking dish with some olive oil. Spread one-third of the sauce over the bottom of the dish. Pour half of the polenta over the sauce. Sprinkle with 1 cup of the cheese. Pour another one-third of the sauce over the cheese. Pour the remaining half of the polenta over the sauce. Sprinkle with the remaining 1 cup cheese, and cover with the remaining sauce. Cover with plastic wrap. Let stand for 1 to 2 hours at room temperature. The polenta will become firm.

5. Turn back the opposite corners of the plastic wrap to vent the dish. Microcook on HIGH for 6 to 8 minutes, until completely heated through. Let stand for 10 minutes. Cut into squares and serve from the baking dish.

Overnight Cheese Lasagna

HERE'S A FAST-TO-ASSEMBLE, NO-FUSS, no-fail lasagna for the kids to eat along with you. And you know how fussy they are. While lasagna recipes I came across all called for almost the same amount of time cooking in the microwave as in the regular oven, I wanted a faster lasagna. In this recipe I achieved that goal by 1) soaking no-boil lasagna noodles (I used Barilla brand); 2) letting the uncooked lasagna rest overnight to allow the pasta to soak up more liquid from the marinara; and 3) microcooking the lasagna partially covered with plastic wrap to keep all the moisture in the casserole instead of evaporating and creating a dry lasagna. The ingredients are basic and easy to keep in the cupboard. Older microwave recipes called for covering the edges of the baking dish with aluminum foil to slow cooking in certain parts of the lasagna, which bothered me since foil reflects microwaves. But with the shorter cook time here, this is not necessary; the edges become almost browned (many people to whom I've served this especially like the chewy edges) and the casserole looks like it has been baked in a conventional oven. ○ *Serves 4 to 6*

MICROWAVE COOKWARE: 9-inch square Pyrex or microwave-safe ceramic casserole dish
MICROWAVE WATTAGE: 1,100 to 1,300
MICROWAVE COOK TIME: 18 to 22 minutes
STANDING TIME: 15 minutes

9 no-cook oven-ready lasagna noodles
One 26-ounce jar marinara of your choice, or 3 cups homemade marinara
2 cups small-curd cottage cheese
3 cups shredded mozzarella or mixed cheeses (such as a combination of mozzarella, cheddar, and Monterey Jack)
½ cup freshly grated Parmesan cheese

1. Fill the casserole dish halfway with the hottest tap water possible, and submerge the lasagna sheets in the water. Soak for 5 to 10 minutes.

2. Remove the lasagna noodles from the hot water, let any excess water drip off, and lay the noodles on a clean plate; they break easily, so handle them carefully. Discard the soaking water.

3. Using a large spoon, spread one-quarter of the marinara over the bottom of the casserole dish you used to soak the pasta (you do not need to dry it).

4. Lay 2 of the lasagna noodles over the sauce in a single layer, breaking a third sheet to fit strips around the edges and down the middle; don't worry if they overlap. You will use a bit more than 2½ sheets per layer. Spread 1 cup of the cottage cheese over the noodles to the edges of the casserole dish, then top with 1 cup of the mozzarella and 2 tablespoons of the Parmesan. Spoon another one-quarter of the sauce on top of the cheeses.

5. Repeat step 4 for a second layer. Top with the remaining noodles, and pour the remaining sauce over the top. Sprinkle with the remaining 1 cup mozzarella and the remaining ¼ cup Parmesan. Cover tightly with plastic wrap and refrigerate for 8 to 24 hours (you can assemble this in the morning or the previous night to cook at dinnertime).

6. When ready to cook, fold back two opposite corners of the plastic wrap to vent. Place the casserole in the microwave. Tuck 4 strips of paper towel under the edges of the casserole dish to catch any drips. Microcook on HIGH for 18 to 22 minutes, until the sauce is bubbly and the pasta is tender. (The amount of time will depend on how chilled the casserole is when you put it in the oven. To speed cooking, take it out of the refrigerator 45 minutes before baking.) When done, let stand for 15 minutes in the oven. Cut into pieces and serve hot.

Cottage-Style Macaroni and Cheddar Cheese with Tomatoes

WHO DOESN'T LOVE MACARONI AND CHEESE? When I was growing up, mac and cheese was the Friday night no-meat standby dinner served with stewed tomatoes and steamed spinach on the side. In this gloriously simple version of an old favorite, patterned after the quick, no-cook, stir-together sauce technique I saw in *The Well-Filled Microwave Cookbook* (Workman, 1996), sweet diced tomatoes and a pinch of fresh herbs are stirred right into the casserole. The cottage cheese and sour cream form the base of the creamy white sauce that is usually achieved by making a béchamel sauce first, making this a streamlined version that can be prepared quickly enough for lunch. You can use any type of cheddar cheese—mild, sharp, Colby, or Tillamook—or even an Italian blend of shredded cheeses. ○ *Serves 2 as a main dish or 4 as a side dish*

MICROWAVE COOKWARE: 1½- to 2-quart shallow casserole dish
MICROWAVE WATTAGE: 1,100 to 1,300
MICROWAVE COOK TIME: 8 minutes
STANDING TIME: 5 minutes

2 cups macaroni, small penne, or small shells
1 cup small-curd cottage cheese
½ cup sour cream
⅔ cup shredded mild or sharp cheddar cheese (about 3 ounces)
⅔ cup shredded Monterey Jack cheese (about 3 ounces)
⅔ cup shredded provolone cheese (about 3 ounces)
One 15.5-ounce can diced stewed tomatoes, well drained
2 teaspoons minced fresh marjoram, oregano, or flat-leaf parsley

1. Cook the macaroni according to the package directions until *al dente,* and drain well. While the pasta is draining, stir together the cottage cheese and sour cream in a deep bowl until well-combined. (If you like a very smooth sauce, use an immersion blender.) Place the pasta in a large bowl and pour the sauce over the pasta. Combine the cheeses in a small bowl. Add 1½ cups of the cheese mixture, the tomatoes, and the marjoram to the bowl with the pasta, and toss to evenly combine. Place the pasta mixture in the casserole dish.

2. Partially cover with plastic wrap and microcook on HIGH for 4 minutes, until steaming hot.

3. Remove from the microwave, stir gently, and top with the remaining ½ cup cheese.

4. Microcook, uncovered, on HIGH for another 4 minutes, or until the cheese is melted and bubbling and the casserole turns pale golden around the edges. Remove from the oven and let rest for at least 5 minutes before serving hot.

Peggy's Orzo with Peas, Parmesan, and Sun-Dried Tomatoes

HERE'S A GREAT RECIPE to bring to a potluck or summer cookout, as it serves a large number of people. Orzo, which is durum wheat pasta made in the shape of a grain of rice, cooks very well in the microwave. This recipe was created by my friend Peggy Fallon, who develops recipes for dinner demos sponsored by Dacor ovens. What did you serve this with, I asked? "Broiled pepper-crusted New York steak (thinly sliced) and a salad of roasted new potato wedges, arugula, kalamata olives, and herb vinaigrette," said Peggy, who is a wiz with all manner of vegetables, warm or cold. "You can get snazzy and add frozen artichoke hearts or whatever else to this to make it more veggie-ish, if you like." The combination of orzo cooked in chicken broth, peas, and Parmesan is reminiscent of the flavor alchemy and perennial appeal of *risi e bisi* (rice and peas). You will need a large oven to fit the cooking vessel, or you can halve the recipe (if you do, reduce the cooking time by one-third). ○ *Makes 10 cups; serves 18*

MICROWAVE COOKWARE: 1.3-gallon (20-cup) capacity microwave-safe plastic bowl with lid
MICROWAVE WATTAGE: 1,100 to 1,300
MICROWAVE COOK TIME: 28 minutes
STANDING TIME: 5 minutes

7½ cups low-sodium chicken broth, or a combination of broth and water
3 cups (about 1¼ pounds) orzo
⅓ cup chopped oil-packed sun-dried tomatoes
2 tablespoons extra-virgin olive oil
2 large cloves garlic, crushed
One 16-ounce bag frozen petite peas, thawed and drained
1 cup freshly grated Parmesan cheese
Salt and freshly ground black pepper to taste

1. In the microwave-safe plastic bowl, combine the chicken broth, orzo, sun-dried tomatoes, olive oil, and garlic. Stir to mix. Cover the container tightly; then open one corner to vent. Microcook on HIGH for 18 minutes.

2. Carefully remove the lid and gently stir with an oversized spoon. Replace the lid and microcook on HIGH for 10 minutes longer. Let stand, covered, for 5 minutes. Carefully remove the lid; fluff the orzo with a fork.

3. Add the peas and Parmesan, tossing gently to mix. Season with salt and pepper. Serve warm.

Note: In place of the 1.3-gallon container, you can use a large heatproof glass bowl or other microwave-safe container; cover with microwave-safe plastic wrap, leaving one corner uncovered to vent.

Asian Noodles

Some Asian-style noodles can be cooked in the microwave, particularly rice noodles and cellophane noodles.

Rice Stick Noodles

Dried rice stick noodles, also called *banh pho,* are made with rice flour and are especially popular throughout Southeast Asia. It's easy to find dried rice stick noodles in large supermarkets. Since they are egg-free, they are good for vegan dishes. However, check the ingredients, as usually there is some wheat starch added to the rice flour, so they are not gluten-free. There are three basic widths of rice stick noodles: thin, medium, and wide (the latter are flat noodles that can vary in width from ½ inch to 1 inch). In all cases, the noodles are soaked in warm water 15 minutes before boiling to soften them. When dry, they are whitish-silver; after soaking, they become pliable; after cooking, they become translucent and very soft. Rice stick noodles are flavorless and highly absorbent, so they pick up surrounding flavors very well. Thin rice noodles are used in soups, salads, and spring rolls. Medium-width noodles are the most versatile and can be used in soups, stir-fries, salads, under a sauce, or as a bed for meat or fish. Wide noodles are best used in soups, stir-fries, and braised dishes. ❂ Makes about 1½ cups of cooked noodles

¼ of a 14-ounce package rice noodles
4 cups water

1. Place the noodles in a bowl and cover with hot-to-the-touch warm water; let stand for 15 minutes to soften the noodles (put a plate on top to keep the noodles submerged).

2. In a 2-quart microwave-safe bowl or deep casserole dish, heat the 4 cups water on HIGH for about 4 minutes, until boiling. Add the rice stick noodles and microcook for 2½ to 4 minutes, depending on the width, until the noodles look clear. Drain in a colander and set aside. They are now ready to be used in recipes.

Asian Noodles

Cellophane Noodles

Cellophane noodles are made from mung beans and are gluten-free. They are also known as bean thread or glass noodles and are popular in Thai, Vietnamese, and Indonesian cuisine. In Hawaii they are called "long rice." Cellophane noodles should not be confused with rice stick noodles or rice vermicelli, which are made from rice and are white in color rather than opaque. Cellophane noodles are generally round, silvery gray, and available in various thicknesses, but the thin variety is most popular. They are used in stir-fries, soups, tofu salads, vegetarian dishes, and particularly hot pots. Coils of dried cellophane noodles are very brittle, and they tend to crack and shatter if roughly handled. They are really tough when dry, so don't try to break or cut them until they are softened after cooking; if using part of the package, just gently pull the coil apart. ○ Makes about 2 cups cooked noodles

One 3.75-ounce package cellophane noodles
2 cups water

1. Place the noodles in a 1-quart microwave-safe bowl or deep casserole dish. In a 2-cup measuring cup, heat the water on HIGH for 3 to 4 minutes, until boiling. Pour the water over the noodles and soak for 10 minutes.

2. Place the bowl or casserole dish in the microwave, and microcook on HIGH for 1½ to 2 minutes, stirring once halfway through to check for doneness, until the noodles look clear. Drain in a colander and set aside. They are ready to be used in recipes. Cut with kitchen shears into 2- to 4-inch pieces depending on your recipe.

Garden of Goodness: Vegetables

There are a variety of methods for cooking vegetables, but the microwave rules because of its ability to steam veggies with a minimal amount of cooking liquid. The short cooking time in the microwave allows vegetables to retain the highest percentage of nutrients and flavor.

Many people find it difficult to eat the recommended amounts of vegetables each day, but the ease of cooking them in the microwave makes it more doable. Vegetables can be cooked simply in the microwave and then

seasoned to be savory, salty, or sweet, depending on what you desire. For best results, buy the veggies that are in season and choose for freshness and bright natural colors. Avoid wilted, shriveled, brown-spotted, soft-spotted, or moldy vegetables. Buy organic if you can afford to, or just look for what is best that day.

I would like to give a nod here to microwave-cookbook author Thelma Pressman, considered a doyenne and pioneer in teaching microwave cooking. She is the author of five cookbooks, most notably *The Art of Microwave Cooking* (Contemporary Books, 1983) and *365 Quick and Easy Microwave Recipes* (HarperCollins, 1989), which have

become my go-to sources for all questions on microwave technology and cooking methods even though they were written more than 20 years ago. She also wrote one of the first columns on microwave cooking for *Bon Appétit* magazine and was host of a microwave-cooking television show in the 1980s. A few of her methods for microcooking vegetables are unique: the Italian-style artichoke cooked in a measuring cup, the green bean bundles, and wrapping broccoli stalks in wet paper towels. I had never seen these methods used anywhere else, and they ended up being the best way to prepare those vegetables, bar none.

Tips for Cooking Vegetables in the Microwave

- Take care not to overcook. Except for root vegetables and artichokes, most vegetables cook rapidly in the microwave. Keep a close watch during the cooking time and take them out of the oven as soon as they look done. Pay attention to the standing time specified in the recipe before serving, which is important for dense vegetables such as potatoes and beets.

- Check for doneness at the shortest cook time specified in the recipe. When in doubt or when making a recipe for the first time, check at the halfway point during cooking.

- Cook most vegetables on HIGH power.

- In most cases, cover vegetables during cooking to hold in moisture and promote even cooking. Whole potatoes and winter squash serve as their own covered containers, but they need to be pierced to allow for steam to escape. Turn over large vegetables partway through the cooking time to cook evenly on both sides.

- Thicker shapes and slices take longer to cook than thin ones. Position thicker sections, such as broccoli stems, toward the outside of the dish, in a spoke pattern.

- When cooking a variety of vegetables at the same time, cut them into similar-sized pieces. Start cooking the hard vegetables (such as potatoes and winter squash) first, then add the softer vegetables (such as celery and zucchini) toward the end of the cook time.

- Many vegetables, such as leafy greens, need no additional water added if they are cooked dripping wet right after washing.

- Salt vegetables after cooking. Salt attracts microwaves and may lead to uneven cooking.

- Fresh vegetables taste best in the recipes in this book, but if you have none on hand, canned or frozen veggies can be substituted (cook times are the same).

- Most every vegetable can be prepared in the microwave with great success. The most difficult one to microcook is green beans, which collapse easily, so use the following technique: Wash the beans and remove the stem ends. Do not dry them. Take a serving-size portion of beans, gather them into a bunch, and wrap the bunch in microwave-safe plastic wrap, making a pouch and twisting the ends shut. Place on a pie plate or the turntable and microcook on HIGH for 3½ minutes. Let stand for 2 minutes, then unwrap and serve immediately. This is a controversial method since the plastic wrap touches the food, but be assured that it is safe. If you love green beans and want to cook them in the microwave, this is the best method.

Steamed Artichoke
with Artichoke Hummus

WITH WHOLE ARTICHOKES, the leaves are plucked off and eaten one at a time, often after being dipped in a savory sauce, such as melted butter or mayonnaise, vinaigrette, ranch dressing, aioli, flavored olive oil, or balsamic vinegar. You pull the petal through your slightly clenched teeth to remove the soft, tender flesh at the bottom of the petal. The remaining heart is then eaten after removing the fuzzy inedible fibers of the "choke." Many home cooks are hesitant to prepare a whole artichoke in the microwave. But microcooking them one at a time in a glass measuring cup turns the job into a joy. To cook these artichokes four at a time, place the prepared artichokes in an 8- or 9-inch square Pyrex baking dish, multiply the garlic, lemon, and oil by 4, and add 3 to 4 minutes per artichoke (the amount of water used is unchanged). ● *Serves 1*

MICROWAVE COOKWARE: 1-quart or 2-quart Pyrex measuring cup
MICROWAVE WATTAGE: 1,100 to 1,300
MICROWAVE COOK TIME: 8 to 12 minutes
STANDING TIME: 5 minutes

1 large or jumbo artichoke, rinsed
¾ to 1¼ cups water, depending on the size of the artichoke
1 clove garlic, cut into 3 pieces
2 slices fresh lemon
1 tablespoon olive oil

ARTICHOKE HUMMUS:
One 15-ounce can chickpeas, drained (water reserved), then rinsed
One 14.5-ounce can artichokes packed in water, drained
½ cup mayonnaise
¼ cup mild tomato salsa
Juice of 1 lemon
1 tablespoon olive oil

Fresh whole-wheat pita breads, cut into sixths

1. Cut off the stem flush with the bottom of the artichoke and trim 1 inch off the top. You will need a very sharp knife for the top, since it is tough. If you wish, using kitchen shears, snip off the thorny tips from the leaves.

2. Place the artichoke upside-down in the measuring cup, using whichever size fits better. Add water to cover the lower one-third of the artichoke. Toss in the garlic and the lemon slices. Drizzle the oil over the artichoke. Partially cover with plastic wrap.

3. Microcook on HIGH for 8 to 12 minutes, depending on the size of the artichoke, or until the stem end is tender when pierced with the tip of a knife and some bottom leaves pull out easily. The artichoke will still be olive green. Let stand for 5 minutes, then pour off the liquid. Serve hot, or cool to room temperature and refrigerate in a zipper-top plastic bag. If you like, you can cut the artichoke in half and use a spoon to scoop out the fuzzy choke before serving.

4. Prepare the artichoke hummus: Place all of the ingredients in the work bowl of a food processor. Pulse until smooth, using the reserved chickpea water to adjust the consistency as desired. Serve as a dip for the leaves along with the pita bread.

Making Vegetable Purees for Fresh Baby Food

Prepare and cook individual vegetables according to the recipe, which usually means steaming the plain vegetable with some water. Do not add salt or butter. Let cool, and puree in a food processor until smooth. Strain if necessary. The puree can be stored in a covered container in the refrigerator for up to 3 days, or freeze the puree in small freezer containers for up to 2 months. Microcook on DEFROST for a few minutes to just warm the puree, checking to make sure there are no hot spots that could burn a baby's mouth.

Asparagus in Wine

ASPARAGUS IS THE HARBINGER OF SPRING, when the first-of-the-season young shoots are eaten. The Sanskrit name of asparagus is *shatavari* and it has been historically used in Ayurvedic medicine. Asparagus is wonderful with butter or a rich sauce like hollandaise (page 198). The stalks come in a variety of sizes, from pencil-thin (microcook in 2 minutes) to meaty, thick ones (microcook in 3 to 4 minutes). The very thick stalks will cook a minute longer. This is a deceptively simple side dish packed with plenty of flavor. ● *Serves 4*

MICROWAVE COOKWARE: 1-quart microwave-safe casserole or gratin dish, or 8-inch square Pyrex baking dish
MICROWAVE WATTAGE: 1,100 to 1,300
MICROWAVE COOK TIME: About 3½ minutes
STANDING TIME: 2 minutes

1 pound fresh medium-size asparagus spears, ends trimmed
¼ cup dry white wine
2 tablespoons unsalted butter, cut into pieces, or 2 tablespoons olive oil
2 tablespoons freshly grated Parmesan cheese

1. If using large stalks, peel the bottom one-third of the asparagus stalks with a swivel-bladed peeler or asparagus peeler. Arrange the asparagus in the casserole dish, laying the stalks side by side, so that the tips overlap in the center and the stalk ends point toward the outside of the dish like spokes. Pour in the wine and dot with the butter or drizzle with the olive oil.

2. Cover loosely with plastic wrap vented at the side and microcook on HIGH for 3 to 3½ minutes, or until tender when pierced with a knife at the thick end and still bright green. Remove from the oven and let stand for 2 minutes. Sprinkle with the Parmesan and serve.

Five-Star Sesame Broccoli

SESAME SEEDS WERE FIRST CULTIVATED in India, and they even show up in archeological evidence in the Harappa culture that flourished in the Indus Valley several thousand years ago. The Sanskrit name for sesame translates to "liquid fat," and the oil of the sesame is second only to ghee in its importance in Indian foods. The roasted seeds are known as *gomasio* in Japanese cuisine. Broccoli is one of oldest members of the cabbage family and is quite enhanced flavorwise with some sesame, not to mention ready for the table in minutes. Store your sesame seeds in the freezer for optimum freshness and flavor. ○ *Serves 2 to 4*

MICROWAVE COOKWARE: 9-inch Pyrex pie plate, a microwave-safe plate (optional)
MICROWAVE COOK TIME: 3½ to 4 minutes for the sesame seeds;
  3½ to 4 minutes for the broccoli
STANDING TIME: 3 minutes

1 heaping tablespoon sesame seeds
1 head broccoli (1½ to 2 pounds), trimmed, tough stems peeled and quartered, top cut into
  large florets and rinsed in cold water
Salt and freshly ground black or white pepper to taste

1. Spread the sesame seeds in the pie plate or on a paper towel. Microcook on HIGH for 3½ to 4 minutes, or just until the seeds turn a pale golden brown and exude some oil; stir once or twice during cooking. Remove from the oven and set aside.

2. Wrap the broccoli in a double layer of paper towels and moisten the towels under the faucet until evenly wet. Set the package on the turntable or a plate. Microcook on HIGH for 3½ to 4 minutes, until just tender when the stem end is pierced with the tip of a knife. Let stand, still wrapped in the paper towels, for 3 minutes before seasoning with salt and pepper and tossing with the sesame seeds.

Baked Beets with Anchovy Vinaigrette

BEETS ARE UNDERLOVED AND UNDERAPPRECIATED by the most people, but they are one of my favorite vegetables. A beet in the fridge is like a little money in the dinner bank. Fresh beets can be served hot like a side dish, or cooled and chilled to be used for salads. The best beets for cooking in the microwave are small or medium-size. Save the big honkers for borscht. Beets are often sold in bunches of three or four with their greens attached (the greens are also great to eat). If you use baby beets, cook them for 4 to 5 minutes. Leave a bit of the stem attached to avoid having the beets bleed during cooking, and be careful not to pierce the skin, which will cause color to bleed into the cooking water. The anchovy vinaigrette is a recipe from San Francisco Italian chef Ric O'Connell. ● *Serves 4*

MICROWAVE COOKWARE: 3-quart microwave-safe casserole dish or 9-inch square Pyrex dish
MICROWAVE WATTAGE: 1,100 to 1,300
MICROWAVE COOK TIME: 7 to 9 minutes
STANDING TIME: None

About 1½ pounds fresh beets, greens removed, each with a
    1½-inch stub of stem attached, and washed
½ cup water
1 to 2 tablespoons unsalted butter or olive oil (optional)

ANCHOVY VINAIGRETTE:
1 clove garlic, crushed
2 anchovy fillets, finely chopped
3 tablespoons red wine vinegar
3 tablespoons olive oil
A few grinds of black pepper
2 tablespoons minced fresh Italian parsley

1. Place the beets in the casserole dish and add the water. Partially cover and microcook for 7 to 9 minutes, depending on the size of the beets. Test for doneness by piercing the beets with the tip of a knife or a bamboo skewer to determine tenderness. Beets are best when tender-firm, so be careful not to overcook. Drain.

2. Place the beets on a cutting board. If you have rubber gloves, use them to avoid staining your hands and fingernails. (With gloves you can handle the beets while still hot.) Remove the remaining stem. Cut a thin sliver off the tops and root bottoms and, with a slight rubbing motion, slip off the peels. Cut the beets into slices or dice into squares. For a simple side dish, place the beets in a serving bowl and toss with the butter or olive oil, if desired.

3. Make the vinaigrette: In a medium-size bowl, whisk together the garlic, anchovies, vinegar, oil, and pepper. Add the beets and toss to lightly coat. Taste for seasoning and adjust as desired, then sprinkle with the parsley. Serve immediately, or cover and refrigerate for up to 3 days, then bring to room temperature before serving.

The Best Glazed Carrots

IT'S A BIT IFFY TO RATE any recipe "the best," since every palate is different. But everyone I know loves these; the glaze makes simple steamed carrots special. Carrots are an excellent vegetable to prepare in the microwave, as they cook without getting mushy. ○ *Serves 4*

MICROWAVE COOKWARE: 1-quart ceramic or Pyrex casserole dish,
   2-cup Pyrex measuring cup
MICROWAVE WATTAGE: 1,100 to 1,300
MICROWAVE COOK TIME: 5 to 7½ minutes
STANDING TIME: 2 minutes

2 cups sliced scrubbed carrots, cut ½ inch thick, or one 12-ounce bag baby carrots
¼ cup water
⅓ cup apricot jam
3 tablespoons unsalted butter, cut into pieces
2 teaspoons freshly squeezed lemon juice
1½ teaspoons light brown sugar
1 teaspoon grated orange zest
¼ teaspoon ground nutmeg
¼ teaspoon salt

1. Place the carrots and water in the casserole dish. Partially cover and microcook for 4 to 6 minutes, until firm-tender when pierced with a fork. Set aside to stand for 2 minutes.

2. In the measuring cup, combine the jam, butter, lemon juice, brown sugar, orange zest, nutmeg, and salt. Stir with a fork. Partially cover and microcook on HIGH for 60 to 90 seconds, until simmering.

3. Drain the carrots and place in a small serving bowl. Pour the jam mixture over the carrots and gently stir to evenly coat them. Serve immediately.

Napa Cabbage with Fresh Ginger

T IS ALWAYS A CHALLENGE to come up with new cabbage recipes beyond cole-slaw. When a big oval head of curly-edged napa cabbage showed up on the doorstep one day in my delivery box of organic produce, I knew the meal of the day was going to include fresh cabbage, so I created this recipe. Look for a ceramic grater that is made specifically for ginger, available at Asian markets. ● *Serves 4*

MICROWAVE COOKWARE: 2-quart Pyrex or microwave-safe ceramic casserole dish
MICROWAVE WATTAGE: 1,100 to 1,300
MICROWAVE COOK TIME: 3½ minutes
STANDING TIME: None

1 tablespoon light olive oil or untoasted sesame oil
1 clove garlic, minced or crushed
1 tablespoon grated fresh ginger
6 cups thinly sliced napa cabbage
¼ cup thinly sliced scallion (white part and some of the green)
1 tablespoon low-sodium soy sauce, or to taste

1. Place the oil, garlic, and ginger in the casserole dish. Microcook on HIGH, uncovered, for 30 seconds.

2. Add the cabbage and scallion. Partially cover and microcook on HIGH for 3 minutes, stirring halfway through the cook time to coat the cabbage with the ginger and garlic. Be careful not to overcook.

3. Remove from the oven and season with the soy sauce. Serve immediately.

Butter, dressings, and a variety of cold and hot sauces make vegetables taste ever so special. In addition to the recipes that follow, try topping your veggies with microwave Hollandaise (page 198), Lemon Sauce (page 202), and Yogurt Béchamel (page 226).

Shira-ae Sauce

Shira-ae is a classic tofu and sesame dressing for vegetables. It goes well with broccoli, cauliflower, carrots, spinach, chrysanthemum leaves and flowers, broccoli rabe, broccolini, shiitake or other mushrooms, and edamame. Use Chinese sesame paste, which is made from toasted sesame seeds and has a texture and flavor more like peanut butter, rather than tahini (raw sesame paste). Sesame paste comes in glass jars and needs to be refrigerated after opening. ○ Makes 1½ cups

MICROWAVE COOKWARE: None
MICROWAVE WATTAGE: 1,100 to 1,300
MICROWAVE COOK TIME: About 45 seconds
STANDING TIME: None

1 block silken tofu
1½ tablespoons toasted sesame paste
1 tablespoon sake or mirin
1 tablespoon low-sodium soy sauce
1½ teaspoons sugar
Salt to taste

1. Wrap the tofu in a paper towel and microcook on HIGH for about 45 seconds. Set aside to cool.

2. Place the cooled tofu, sesame paste, sake, soy sauce, sugar, and salt in a gallon-size zipper-top plastic freezer bag and seal it closed. Massage the bag with your hands until all of the ingredients are incorporated into a paste-like sauce. Snip off a corner of the bag and squeeze the sauce over the vegetables of your choice.

Easy Hot Peanut Sauce

Peanut sauce used to be found mainly in Thai regional cookery, but no longer. You can drizzle this sauce on practically anything. It is a great dipping sauce for egg rolls and tastes divine tossed with noodles. If you like it spicy, add a few splashes of hot sauce or some red pepper flakes before serving. ❍ Makes 1 cup

MICROWAVE COOKWARE: 1-quart Pyrex measuring cup
MICROWAVE WATTAGE: 1,100 to 1,300
MICROWAVE COOK TIME: 1½ to 2 minutes
STANDING TIME: 2 minutes

⅓ **cup vegetable broth**
1 clove garlic, crushed
One 1-inch piece ginger, peeled and grated
1 tablespoon brown sugar
½ cup smooth peanut butter, at room temperature
1 teaspoon low-sodium soy sauce
Juice of 2 limes

1. In the measuring cup, combine the broth, garlic, ginger, and brown sugar. Partially cover with plastic wrap. Microcook on HIGH for 1½ to 2 minutes, until boiling. Let stand for 2 minutes.

2. Whisk in the peanut butter, soy sauce, and lime juice. Serve immediately.

Vegetable Toppers

Better Than Butter

This dairy-and-oil-blend spreadable butter first appeared in *Laurel's Kitchen: A Handbook for Vegetarian Cookery and Nutrition* (Nilgiri Press, 1976). A favorite online culinary newsletter, Culinate, ran a story on it. Laurel's recipe was a precursor to the commercially produced spread Smart Balance. The variety of flavorful oils and healthy fats will add a full panel of nutrients to your diet. I avoid canola, corn, and soy oils since they are now made from genetically modified crops. This blend, which is naturally soft, will become loose if left at room temperature for more than 30 minutes, so keep it refrigerated until you need to use it. Use just like regular butter on any vegetable or slathered with abandon on toast, scones, and popcorn, but note that it does not work well for baking. **o** Makes 2 cups

½ cup (1 stick) unsalted butter, softened
½ cup (1 stick) salted butter, softened
⅓ cup coconut oil
⅓ cup light olive oil or grapeseed oil
⅓ cup unrefined sesame oil (not Asian toasted sesame oil)

Place the butters and coconut oil in the work bowl of a food processor; pulse a few times until smooth. With the machine running, pour in the olive and sesame oils and process just until incorporated. Pour into a covered container. You can store the mixture, covered, in the refrigerator for up to 1 month.

Cold Mustard Sauce

This sauce is simple to prepare and tastes great on vegetables. Dijon mustard is called for here, but any mustard—from grainy to hot to sweet—will work. **o** Makes 1½ cups

½ cup mayonnaise
½ cup thick plain yogurt
¼ cup Dijon mustard
Juice of 1 lemon or lime
Pinch of freshly ground white pepper

In a small bowl, stir together all of the ingredients. You can store the sauce, covered, in the refrigerator for up to 1 day.

Crème Fraîche with Tarragon

Since this topping is just crème fraîche flavored with herbs, you can devise your own variations by adding fresh dill, lemon juice and lemon zest, roasted garlic, Parmesan and a few sprinkles of nutmeg, horseradish, or whatever else you can dream up. ○ Makes ½ cup

½ cup crème fraîche
1 teaspoon minced fresh chives
1 teaspoon minced fresh tarragon
½ teaspoon freshly squeezed lemon juice
Pinch of salt

In a small bowl, stir together all of the ingredients. You can store the crème fraîche, covered, in the refrigerator for up to 1 day.

Curry Mayonnaise

This is especially delicious on microwave-steamed cauliflower. ○ Makes 1 cup

¾ cup mayonnaise
¼ cup plain yogurt or thick cream scooped off the top of canned coconut milk
1 teaspoon curry powder
1 teaspoon ground ginger
¼ teaspoon turmeric
¼ teaspoon chili powder
¼ teaspoon sweet Hungarian paprika

In a small bowl, stir together the mayonnaise and yogurt. Stir in the curry powder, ginger, turmeric, chili powder, and paprika. You can store the mayonnaise, covered, in the refrigerator for up to 1 day.

Buttered Cabbage Wedges with Caraway

SOLID-HEAD DOMESTIC GREEN CABBAGE is one of the most versatile and inexpensive vegetables to cook during the winter. When it is fresh, it is quite a delicately flavored vegetable. But there are not enough ways to prepare it simply. When contemplating this recipe, I considered adding more ingredients, but decided to keep the flavors true. Prepare cabbage within one week of purchase instead of leaving it for weeks in the veggie drawer. Store your caraway seed in the freezer for best flavor. ○ *Serves 4*

MICROWAVE COOKWARE: 10-inch Pyrex pie plate or 11 × 7-inch rectangular Pyrex baking dish; small microwave-safe glass bowl
MICROWAVE WATTAGE: 1,100 to 1,300
MICROWAVE COOK TIME: 5 to 6 minutes
STANDING TIME: 1 minute

½ medium-size head green cabbage, cut into 4 wedges
3 tablespoons water
½ teaspoon caraway seed
3 to 4 tablespoons unsalted butter

1. Arrange the cabbage wedges in the pie plate. Add the water. Sprinkle with the caraway seed, and partially cover with plastic wrap.

2. Microcook on HIGH for 5 to 6 minutes, until the cabbage is crisp-tender. Remove from the oven and let stand while melting the butter.

3. Place the butter in the glass bowl. Microcook on HIGH for 20 to 30 seconds, until melted. Drizzle the butter over the cabbage. Serve immediately.

Creamed Corn

DON'T LET THE NAME put you off if you are cutting back on dairy, as this recipe contains no cream and does not produce the heavy creamed corn casserole many people are familiar with. Instead, you grate two ears of corn (using the tool called a corn zipper, or a sharp serrated knife) to release the "milk" along with the kernels, add a little butter and seasoning, then let the microwave do its magic. ○ *Serves 1 to 2*

MICROWAVE COOKWARE: 1-quart Pyrex measuring cup
MICROWAVE WATTAGE: 1,100 to 1,300
MICROWAVE COOK TIME: 2 to 2½ minutes
STANDING TIME: None

2 medium-size ears fresh corn
2 tablespoons unsalted butter
2 teaspoons minced fresh chives
Salt and freshly ground black pepper to taste

1. Shuck the corn and remove the silk. With a serrated knife or corn zipper, cut the kernels off the cobs and place in the measuring cup, along with any liquid (the "milk") that comes off the cob. You will have ½ to ⅔ cup kernels per ear.

2. Stir the butter into the measuring cup with the corn. Partially cover with plastic wrap and microcook on HIGH for 2 to 2½ minutes, until steaming hot and thickened. Stir in the chives and season with salt and pepper. Serve hot.

VARIATIONS

Creamed Corn and Baby Limas: Microcook 1 cup of frozen baby lima beans according to the package directions. Stir the beans into the hot creamed corn along with the chives. Microcook on HIGH, covered, for 2 to 3 minutes.

Chipotle Corn: Use 1 tablespoon olive oil in place of the butter. Stir ¼ canned chipotle pepper in adobo sauce, minced, into the hot creamed corn. Sprinkle with 2 teaspoons fresh minced cilantro in place of the chives. Microcook on HIGH, covered, for 2 to 3 minutes.

Steamed Corn on the Cob

COOKING FRESH CORN ON THE COB in the microwave brings out its true flavor, making it even sweeter and more corn-like than boiling ever did. It is the best way to cook one to four ears at a time, but don't try to cook more than that (use the conventional stovetop boiling method when making corn for a crowd). This is how to cook that corn you just got from the farmers' market that was harvested in the morning and hasn't even been refrigerated yet. That is the ideal scenario, but this method also works for fresh corn from the produce section of your supermarket, as long as it's firm and not brown. You will be cooking the corn in its own packaging—the husk, which creates great natural steaming conditions and heats up the core. Exact cooking time will be determined by the size and age of the corn. You can also use this technique to partially precook corn before grilling it. Be sure to use unhusked raw corn within two days of purchase. ○ *Serves 1 to 4*

MICROWAVE COOKWARE: 1-quart Pyrex measuring cup
MICROWAVE WATTAGE: 1,100 to 1,300
MICROWAVE COOK TIME: About 2 minutes per ear
STANDING TIME: 5 minutes

1 to 4 medium-size to large ears fresh corn

1. Remove any outside soiled leaves on the ear of corn. Leave 2 layers of inner husk leaves and the silk intact. Fill a bowl with cold water. Place the corn in the cold water and soak for 3 to 5 minutes; drain. Arrange the still-moist cobs on the microwave turntable like spokes of a wheel, with the tapered ends to the center and stems pointing to the outer edge.

2. Microcook on HIGH for 2 minutes for 1 ear, until steaming hot. Microcook 2 ears for 4 to 5 minutes; 4 ears for 6 to 8 minutes. Let stand for 5 minutes in the oven or wrapped in a towel or aluminum foil.

3. To remove the husks after cooking, stand the ear on its stem, and using a paper towel or clean tea towel (the cooked corn will be very hot), pull the husks and silk down and off the ear; discard. Serve the corn immediately with butter and salt, chili powder and lime, or a flavored butter. If the corn comes to room temperature before being eaten, you can microcook on HIGH for 1 minute per ear to reheat it, and the flavor will still be wonderful.

VARIATION

Husked Corn on the Cob: If the ears are husked, wrap 1 rinsed ear in waxed paper or microwave-safe plastic wrap with both ends twisted closed like a firecracker. Microcook on HIGH for 1 minute, then turn the corn over and microcook on HIGH for another 50 seconds. Let stand for a few minutes; it comes out perfect every time.

Italian-Style Eggplant Slices

MARK BITTMAN, CHEF, COOKBOOK AUTHOR, and *New York Times* columnist, once wrote a column endorsing the microwave as a valuable kitchen tool. He unabashedly proclaimed the microwave a boon for cooking any sort of steamed vegetable, but one vegetable in particular stood out as marvelous: eggplant. While eggplant can be cooked whole for an appetizer dip (page 41), here is a technique for cooking slices. Mark did a delightful Indian version adapted from a recipe submitted by a reader named Roopa Kalyanaraman, who writes her own cooking blog (www.raspberryeggplant.blogspot.com) when she is not at work as a top-notch scientist at Johns Hopkins. Here I use the same technique, but I've given the eggplant an Italian flavor. o *Serves 4*

MICROWAVE COOKWARE: 11 × 7-inch or 13 × 9-inch Pyrex baking dish or 10-inch Pyrex pie plate

MICROWAVE WATTAGE: 1,100 to 1,300

MICROWAVE COOK TIME: 7 to 9 minutes

STANDING TIME: None

½ **bunch fresh Italian parsley**

10 fresh basil leaves

2 tablespoons capers, rinsed

1 clove garlic, crushed

½ **cup plain dried bread crumbs**

Large pinch of salt

About 3 tablespoons extra-virgin olive oil, plus more for garnish

1 large or 2 medium-size eggplant, rinsed and dried

1. In a food processor, pulse the parsley, basil, and capers. Add the garlic, bread crumbs, salt, and oil; pulse to make a thick but spreadable mixture. Add a bit more olive oil if the mixture is too dry. Set aside.

2. Trim off the ends of the eggplant and cut into 1- to 1¼-inch-thick slices to make 8 slices. With a sharp knife, score the flesh, ½ inch deep, on one side of each slice in several places to make a crisscross pattern. With a metal spreader, press the spice mixture into the gashes. Arrange the slices in a single layer (you can overlap ever so slightly) in the baking dish. You may have to cook the eggplant in two batches.

3. Partially cover the dish loosely with waxed paper. Microcook on HIGH for 5 minutes. Uncover and continue to microcook on HIGH for another 2 to 4 minutes, until the eggplant is very soft. Drizzle with some extra-virgin olive oil and serve hot or warm.

South Indian Eggplant Slices

THE SPICE MIXTURE HERE is gentle so you can really enjoy the full flavor of the eggplant. The blend of cumin, ginger, and turmeric is one of my favorite flavor combinations. You can find tamarind paste and chickpea flour at stores such as Whole Foods Market. When you see tamarind paste in a recipe, it is a tipoff that the dish is from southern India, whose cuisine makes much use of it. Asafetida powder is a digestive aid and very strong, so store it in an airtight jar. Asafetida has a pungent, garlicky smell when raw, but in cooked dishes, it delivers a smooth flavor reminiscent of sautéed leeks. ○ *Serves 4*

MICROWAVE COOKWARE: Microwave-safe small bowl; 11 × 7-inch or 13 × 9-inch Pyrex baking dish or 10-inch Pyrex pie plate

MICROWAVE WATTAGE: 1,100 to 1,300

MICROWAVE COOK TIME: 10 to 12 minutes

STANDING TIME: None

3 tablespoons olive oil

1 tablespoon plus 1½ teaspoons chickpea flour

¼ teaspoon turmeric

Pinch of ground cumin

Dash of asafetida, or 1 clove garlic, crushed

3 tablespoons finely shredded unsweetened coconut

One 2-inch piece fresh ginger, peeled and grated

¾ teaspoon salt

2 teaspoons tamarind paste

1 large or 2 medium-size eggplant

3 to 4 tablespoons chopped fresh cilantro leaves

1. Using a fork, mix together the oil, chickpea flour, turmeric, cumin, and asafetida in the small bowl. Microcook on HIGH for 90 seconds, stopping to mash the mixture together halfway through the cook time. Spread the coconut in the pie plate and microcook on HIGH for 90 seconds, stirring halfway through, until ever-so-slightly golden. Add the coconut, ginger, salt, and tamarind paste to the chickpea flour mixture. The mixture will be spreadable.

2. Trim off the ends of the eggplant and cut into 1- to $1\frac{1}{4}$-inch-thick slices to make 8 slices. With a sharp knife, score the flesh, $\frac{1}{2}$ inch deep, on one side of each slice in several places to make a crisscross pattern. With a metal spreader, press the chickpea mixture into the gashes. Arrange the slices in a single layer (you can overlap ever so slightly) in the baking dish. You may have to cook the eggplant in two batches.

3. Partially cover the dish loosely with waxed paper. Microcook on HIGH for 5 minutes. Uncover and continue to microcook on HIGH for another 2 to 4 minutes, until the eggplant is very soft. Garnish with the cilantro and serve hot or warm.

Chinese Eggplant Slices

FIRST STARTED USING jarred black bean garlic sauce, which tends to be very salty on its own, on a tip from my boss, food writer Carolyn Jung, while working at the *San Jose Mercury News*. It tastes great (with garlic, chile, ginger, and soy already in it) and is so much easier to use than plain fermented dried black beans, which need to be soaked. The sauce tastes even better in this eggplant recipe.

○ *Serves 4*

MICROWAVE COOKWARE: 11 × 7-inch or 13 × 9-inch Pyrex baking dish or
10-inch Pyrex pie plate
MICROWAVE WATTAGE: 1,100 to 1,300
MICROWAVE COOK TIME: 7 to 9 minutes
STANDING TIME: None

8 teaspoons black bean garlic sauce (such as Lee Kum Kee brand;
    find it in Chinese markets or well-stocked supermarkets)
1 tablespoon honey
1 tablespoon untoasted sesame oil
1 large or 2 medium-size eggplant
2 tablespoons slivered fresh ginger
2 to 3 scallions (white part and some of the green), shredded
2 to 3 tablespoons minced fresh cilantro, for garnish

1. In a small bowl, mash together the black bean garlic sauce, honey, and oil. Trim off the ends of the eggplant and cut into 1- to 1¼-inch-thick slices to make 8 slices. With a sharp knife, score the flesh, ½ inch deep, on one side of each slice in several places to make a crisscross pattern. With a metal spreader, spread 1 teaspoon of the garlic sauce mixture per slice into the gashes. Stuff with some of the slivered ginger and scallions.

2. Arrange the slices in a single layer (you can overlap ever so slightly) in the baking dish. You may have to cook the eggplant in two batches.

3. Partially cover the dish loosely with waxed paper. Microcook on HIGH for 5 minutes. Uncover and continue to microcook on HIGH for another 2 to 4 minutes, until the eggplant is very soft. Garnish with the cilantro and serve hot or warm.

Olive Oil–Braised Escarole

THIS RECIPE COMES FROM prolific food writer and East Coast radio talk show host Dolores Kostelni. Escarole is a member of the same botanical family, *Cichorium,* as chicory; the family also includes radicchio and curly endive (also known as frisée). It comes in a big leafy head, is far milder than other chicories, and is often served raw in salads with a hot bacon dressing, as well as being cooked and served as a side dish. When serving this recipe, be sure to have a hunk of Parmesan and a hand grater at the ready. Cooked escarole reheats well. ○ *Serves 2*

MICROWAVE COOKWARE: 2-quart microwave-safe casserole dish with lid
MICROWAVE WATTAGE: 1,100 to 1,300
MICROWAVE COOK TIME: 4 to 5 minutes
STANDING TIME: 1 minute

12 ounces to 1 pound escarole
½ cup extra-virgin olive oil
2 cloves garlic, thinly sliced
Pinch of hot pepper flakes
Salt and freshly ground black pepper to taste
Freshly grated Parmesan cheese for serving (optional)

1. Cut the root end off the escarole and trim any unsightly outside leaves. Divide the head lengthwise into halves or thirds, depending on its size. Discard the core. Cut the leaves into bite-size pieces and rinse in a bowl with several changes of cold water. Lightly spin dry, leaving the leaves a little moist but eliminating all excess water.

2. Pour ¼ cup of the olive oil in the bottom of the 2-quart casserole. Add one of the garlic cloves. Pack half of the escarole into the casserole dish. Using your hands, mix to coat the escarole with the garlic and oil. Pack the remaining escarole into the casserole dish. Sprinkle with the remaining garlic clove and pepper flakes, then pour the remaining ¼ cup oil over the top. Using your hands, mix to evenly coat the escarole. *(continued)*

3. Cover the casserole dish, and microcook on HIGH for 4 minutes for 12 ounces and for 5 minutes for 1 pound, until wilted. Allow the escarole to sit for 1 minute in the microwave. Stir the escarole. Season with salt and pepper, sprinkle with Parmesan cheese, if desired, and serve.

VARIATIONS

Braised Escarole and Cannellini Beans: In step 3, remove the escarole when it is done cooking and let stand on the counter instead of in the microwave. Place one 15-ounce can drained and rinsed cannellini beans in a 1-quart glass measuring cup. Microcook on HIGH for 2 to 3 minutes, until hot. Toss the beans with the escarole and serve immediately, with plenty of Parmesan.

Braised Escarole alla Romana: In step 3, add 2 tablespoons pine nuts and 2 tablespoons dried currants to the escarole before cooking.

Minted Peas with Feta

A BAG OF FROZEN PETITE PEAS is a boon to the creative cook. They go into a risotto as easily as into a stew or curry, and they complement other vegetables without taking over. Here is a divine incarnation of peas with a subtle Greek flair, achieved by simply adding some fresh mint and crumbled feta cheese.

o *Serves 5*

MICROWAVE COOKWARE: 2-quart microwave-safe casserole dish
MICROWAVE WATTAGE: 1,100 to 1,300
MICROWAVE COOK TIME: About 5 minutes
STANDING TIME: 3 minutes

One 16-ounce bag frozen petite peas, broken into chunks if necessary,
    or 3 cups shelled fresh peas
3 tablespoons water
1 heaping tablespoon finely chopped fresh mint leaves
½ cup crumbled feta cheese
Salt and freshly ground black pepper to taste

1. Place the peas and water in the casserole dish. Partially cover and microcook on HIGH for about 5 minutes, until tender, stirring once halfway through cooking. Drain.

2. Let stand, covered, for 3 minutes. Toss the peas with the mint and feta. Season with salt and pepper and serve hot.

Balsamic Braised Bell Peppers

SWEET BELL PEPPERS come in a rainbow of colors, although the most common are green, yellow, and red. They are a versatile ingredient, delicious served as a side dish to meats and poultry, as a condiment on sandwiches and burgers, or piled on fish. This is a great summer dish. ○ *Serves 4*

MICROWAVE COOKWARE: 2-quart microwave-safe casserole dish with lid
MICROWAVE WATTAGE: 1,100 to 1,300
MICROWAVE COOK TIME: 4 to 5 minutes
STANDING TIME: None

1 large red bell pepper, stemmed, seeded, and cut into strips
1 large green bell pepper, stemmed, seeded, and cut into strips
1 large yellow bell pepper, stemmed, seeded, and cut into strips
2 tablespoons olive oil
1 clove garlic, minced
2 tablespoons minced fresh basil
1 tablespoon balsamic vinegar, or to taste
Salt and freshly ground black pepper to taste

1. Place the peppers, oil, and garlic in the casserole dish. Partially cover with plastic wrap and microcook on HIGH for 3 to 4 minutes, until the peppers are tender but not mushy (if you accidentally cook the peppers too long and they become soft, you can puree them and make a sauce or dip).

2. Add the basil and balsamic vinegar, and sprinkle with a bit of salt and pepper. Re-cover and microcook on HIGH for 1 minute. Stir and serve.

Rustic Spinach Soufflé

SPINACH IS A LEAFY GREEN that grows best in temperate climates with cooler temperatures. It is a wildly popular green for its agreeable, healthy flavor, showing up in many cuisines from Indian to Italian. A true soufflé would have a flour and milk béchamel base, but this is not that giant eggy puff; it's a more rustic version that is mixed right in its baking dish. This is great as a side dish, and can also serve as a bed for a poached egg. Or, pile it onto a piece of toasted country bread, top with some cheese, and broil until the cheese melts. ❍ *Serves 4*

MICROWAVE COOKWARE: 6 × 3-inch deep ceramic soufflé dish or 1½-quart microwave-safe casserole dish
MICROWAVE WATTAGE: 1,100 to 1,300
MICROWAVE COOK TIME: 7 minutes
STANDING TIME: 5 minutes

One 16-ounce bag frozen chopped spinach, thawed
1 large egg
½ cup milk
½ cup freshly grated Parmesan, Asiago, or Manchego cheese, plus more for serving if desired
Pinch of onion powder
Pinch of salt and freshly ground black pepper
Pinch of ground nutmeg
Freshly squeezed lemon juice for sprinkling (optional)

1. Drain the spinach in a colander and squeeze out the excess liquid with your hands.

2. Place the egg and milk in the soufflé dish; beat well with a fork. Stir in the cheese, onion powder, salt, pepper, and nutmeg. With a spatula, fold in the spinach, evenly moistening with the egg mixture; the spinach will soak it up.

3. Partially cover with plastic wrap and microcook on HIGH for 3½ minutes.

4. Pull back the plastic wrap to release the steam, re-cover, and microcook on HIGH for another 3½ minutes. When done, the edges will be firm and slightly pull away from the sides of the dish, and the center will still be moist. Let stand, covered, for 5 minutes, then divide the hot soufflé between four serving dishes. Sprinkle with some additional cheese or a squeeze of lemon juice, if you like.

Braised Peas, Celery, and Onion

ONE OF THE VEGETABLE DISHES I inherited from my mother is this very simple combination of frozen baby peas, crunchy celery, and mild white onion. For some reason, the sum total of these ordinary vegetables is way more than the individual parts. We used to just devour big bowls of this at family dinners. It was a nice, simple green vegetable to complement other, stronger vegetables. I made it for a catering job for 100, piling it in a chafing dish, and guests came back for seconds and thirds. You can whip this up in minutes, and it goes as a side dish with everything from fish and poultry to pasta and eggs. ○ *Serves 4*

MICROWAVE COOKWARE: 2- or 3-quart microwave-safe casserole or gratin dish with lid
MICROWAVE WATTAGE: 1,100 to 1,300
MICROWAVE COOK TIME: 7 to 9 minutes
STANDING TIME: 5 minutes

6 to 8 ribs celery, sliced ½ inch thick
⅓ cup finely chopped white onion
2 tablespoons water
⅛ teaspoon salt
One 10-ounce package frozen petite peas, broken into chunks

1. Place the celery, onion, water, and salt in the casserole dish. Partially cover with the casserole lid or plastic wrap. Microcook on HIGH for 4 minutes.

2. Add the peas and re-cover with the lid or plastic wrap. Microcook on HIGH for 3 to 5 minutes longer, until the vegetables are tender, stirring once. Let stand, covered, 5 minutes, and serve hot.

Beet Greens and Scallions

D ON'T WASTE THE BEET GREENS when you cook beets. They are delicious. Add some other greens, like spinach, if you wish. Cooked beet greens are also great added to vegetable soups. ○ *Serves 2*

MICROWAVE COOKWARE: 3-quart microwave-safe casserole dish
MICROWAVE WATTAGE: 1,100 to 1,300
MICROWAVE COOK TIME: 2 minutes
STANDING TIME: None

3 cups packed chopped beet greens
⅓ cup chopped scallions (white and green parts)
1 tablespoon olive oil
Salt

1. Place the beet greens in the casserole dish and add enough water to come ½ inch up the side of the casserole dish. Partially cover with the lid or plastic wrap.

2. Microcook on HIGH for 2 minutes, until wilted and tender. Drain the excess liquid. Toss with the scallions and olive oil, then season with salt to taste. Serve warm.

Mixed Garden Vegetables with Tomatoes and Fresh Herbs

W HEN COOKING A VARIETY OF VEGETABLES in the microwave, use vegetables that have a similar density so that they take the same amount of time to cook. Take care to cut them into similar-size pieces, too. Below is the method for arranging the vegetables in concentric circles, which maximizes the oven's potential for even cooking. The vegetable mélange has a Southern touch with the addition of chayote. Chayote, also known as mirliton or vegetable pear, is a fruit that's a member of the gourd family with squash and cucumbers; it does not need to be peeled and has a texture like a raw potato. It's also high in potassium. After the hard vegetables are mostly cooked, they are sprinkled with some fresh tomato wedges (use only fresh here) then drizzled with an herb butter and cheese. This is really a good way to get everyone to eat a variety of vegetables at one sitting. ○ *Serves 4*

MICROWAVE COOKWARE: 10-inch Pyrex pie plate,
  5-ounce microwave-safe custard cup
MICROWAVE WATTAGE: 1,100 to 1,300
MICROWAVE COOK TIME: 4 to 4½ minutes for the chayote, 1 minute to melt the butter,
  7 to 9 minutes for the other vegetables
STANDING TIME: 2 minutes

1 whole chayote (about 12 ounces)
1 to 2 cups broccoli, cut into ¼-inch-thick pieces, including stems cut in half
½ medium-size head cauliflower, broken into small florets
2 to 3 medium-size carrots, scrubbed and sliced on the diagonal ¼ inch thick
3 tablespoons unsalted butter
½ teaspoon onion powder
1 tablespoon chopped fresh thyme, cilantro, savory, or marjoram
2 medium-size plum tomatoes, cut into wedges
⅓ cup freshly grated Parmesan, Romano, or Asiago cheese

1. Prick the chayote in half a dozen places with a fork. Place on a paper towel. Microcook on HIGH for 4 to 4½ minutes, until firm-tender when pierced with a knife. Set aside.

2. Arrange the broccoli, cauliflower, and carrots in circles on the pie plate, with the broccoli around the outside, the cauliflower the next ring in, and the carrots piled in the center. Partially cover with plastic wrap.

3. Microcook on HIGH for 6 to 8 minutes, until crisp-tender when pierced with the tip of a knife. Let stand for 2 minutes.

4. In the custard cup, microcook the butter, onion powder, and herbs on HIGH for 1 minute, to melt the butter and warm the herbs to take the raw edge off them.

5. Cut the chayote in half lengthwise; remove the pit with a spoon and then cut each half crosswise into ½-inch slices. Lift the plastic wrap on the pie plate. Arrange the chayote slices over the carrots, then sprinkle the tomato wedges in a single layer over the top. Drizzle the butter mixture over the vegetables, then sprinkle with the cheese. Microcook on HIGH for 60 to 80 seconds, just until heated and the cheese melts slightly. Serve immediately.

Vegetable Kabobs

SPEAK OF KABOBS and the vision is one of outdoor cooking and backyard picnics. But the microwave does a great job with kabob cuisine and, whether vegetable, fruit, or seafood, kabobs are one of the great dishes that can be prepared in minutes for an indoor picnic. Kabobs are convenient since they can be assembled ahead of time and cooked when you're ready. You can add large chunks of fresh pineapple to the skewers if you like; they taste quite good with the peanut sauce. Serve with basmati or jasmine rice and a green salad. Alternatively, remove the vegetables from the skewers and stuff them into pita bread halves, or serve them picnic-style with potato salad, steamed corn on the cob (page 152), and cold melon wedges. ○ *Serves 4*

MICROWAVE COOKWARE: 10-inch microwave-safe plate
MICROWAVE WATTAGE: 1,100 to 1,300
MICROWAVE COOK TIME: 5 to 7 minutes
STANDING TIME: None

¼ cup olive oil
¼ cup freshly squeezed lime juice
¼ teaspoon garlic powder
1 large red or green bell pepper
3 medium-size zucchini
2 small yellow summer squash
1 large sweet white onion, quartered
12 large white or brown mushrooms
1 recipe Easy Hot Peanut Sauce (page 147)

1. Soak 8 large bamboo skewers in cold water for 20 minutes. In a small bowl, whisk the oil, lime juice, and garlic powder together; set aside.

2. Cut the bell pepper into twelve 1-inch pieces; it is okay if they are unevenly shaped. Cut the zucchini and yellow squash crosswise into twelve 1- to 1¼-inch chunks. Cut each of the onion quarters in half so you have a total of 8 wedges. Thread the vegetables securely onto the skewers (they need not all be identical). The longer-cooking vegetables, like the peppers and onions, are best on the outer ends of the skewers and the softer ones, like the mushrooms and squash, in the middle. Place the assembled kabobs in a shallow baking dish and pour the marinade over the kabobs. Marinate for 15 minutes.

3. Prepare the peanut sauce. Set aside.

4. Remove the skewers from the marinade; discard the marinade. Place the kabobs on the plate, side by side. Microcook on HIGH, uncovered, for 2 minutes. Turn over the kabobs and shift their positions on the plate so that the outside kabobs are now on the inside.

5. Microcook on HIGH, uncovered, for 3 to 5 minutes, until the vegetables are crisp-tender. Serve immediately with the peanut sauce for dipping.

Sugar Pie Pumpkin Puree
with Curry

USE THE SMALL SUGAR PIE PUMPKINS, with dark orange flesh, here, and not the decorative jack-o-lantern pumpkins, which cook up watery, stringy, and flavorless. Canned pumpkin can be a combination of cooking pumpkin' and Blue Hubbard squash for flavor and texture; you can mix your own pumpkin puree with more than one variety if you like. Cooking the pumpkin whole allows the flavor in the seeds to permeate the flesh for a richer flavor. Besides serving this as a side dish, you can use it in pies, cookies, or cakes. ○ *Makes 2 cups; serves 4*

MICROWAVE COOKWARE: Microwave-safe plate (optional), 10-inch Pyrex pie plate, 1-quart microwave-safe serving bowl or gratin dish
MICROWAVE WATTAGE: 1,100 to 1,300
MICROWAVE COOK TIME: 11 to 15 minutes
STANDING TIME: 10 minutes

1 sugar pie pumpkin (about 2 pounds), washed and dried,
    then pierced 3 times with the tip of a paring knife
2 to 3 tablespoons unsalted butter
2 to 3 tablespoons pure maple syrup
1 to 2 teaspoons mild or hot curry powder, to your taste
Salt and freshly ground black or white pepper to taste

1. Place the pumpkin on the turntable or a plate. Microcook on HIGH for 5 minutes. Cool for 10 minutes, then cut in half and scoop out the fibrous pulp and seeds. Place the halves in the pie plate and partially cover with plastic wrap.

2. Microcook on HIGH for 5 to 8 minutes, until a knife goes in and out easily. If your pumpkin is larger, cook for 5 minutes per pound. Remove from the oven and cool.

3. Scoop out the flesh with an oversized spoon all the way to the skin. Place the flesh in the work bowl of a food processor and process until smooth. (Homemade pumpkin puree is more watery than canned, so strain if you are going to use it in baking. Line a large strainer with a double thickness of cheesecloth. Place the strainer in a bowl, then pour the puree into the lined strainer. Lay a piece of plastic wrap directly on top of the pumpkin and place into the refrigerator to drain overnight. This puree can be used just like canned pumpkin in recipes.) You can store the puree in the refrigerator, covered, for up to 5 days, or freeze for up to 3 months.

4. Scrape the puree into the serving bowl. Stir in the butter, maple syrup, and curry powder, and season with salt and pepper. Partially cover and microcook on HIGH for 1 to 2 minutes before serving.

Pumpkin and Winter Squash

To prepare winter squash such as pumpkin and acorn squash for cutting, be sure to select a squash that will fit in your microwave with lots of room around it on all sides. Pierce the whole squash a few times with a fork. Place on the turntable and microcook on HIGH for 1 minute. This will soften the squash and make cutting much easier. Cut off the stem end and cut in half or quarters lengthwise, or in thick slices. Scoop out the seeds and fiber with a spoon.

Spaghetti Squash with Creamy Crab and Mushroom Sauce

S PAGHETTI SQUASH is the one in the pile of winter squash at the grocery store that looks like a yellow football. When you buy squash, be sure it will fit into your microwave oven with room around the sides for the turntable to rotate. Oddly enough, spaghetti squash cooks better in a microwave than in a conventional oven. It gets its name from the fact that its insides, when cooked, separate into a tangle of long spaghetti-like strands, which can be used in exactly the same way you would use spaghetti. Serve it just like pasta with a rich, homemade sauce, or all by itself, dressed with some butter and a few Indian or Italian herbs and spices. Be sure to pierce the squash before cooking to prevent it from bursting.

o *Serves 2*

MICROWAVE COOKWARE: 2-quart Pyrex measuring cup or batter bowl
MICROWAVE WATTAGE: 1,100 to 1,300
MICROWAVE COOK TIME: 17 to 20 minutes
STANDING TIME: 10 minutes

1 whole spaghetti squash (3¼ to 4 pounds), washed, dried, and
    pierced 8 to 10 times with the tip of a knife
4 ounces white mushrooms, sliced
3 tablespoons unsalted butter
1 cup frozen artichoke hearts, thawed
4 to 5 ounces flaked crabmeat
⅔ cup heavy cream
Salt and freshly ground black pepper to taste
Chopped fresh parsley for garnish (optional)

1. Place the squash on a paper towel on the turntable in the microwave. Microcook on HIGH for 6 minutes.

2. Turn the squash over, which helps for even cooking, and microcook on HIGH for 6 to 8 minutes more. When cooked, the squash will still be firm but will give slightly when pressed with your finger. Remove from the oven with oven mitts. Wrap in a clean kitchen towel and let stand for 10 minutes to cool slightly.

3. In the measuring cup or batter bowl, combine the mushrooms and butter. Microcook on HIGH, uncovered, for 2 minutes. Add the artichoke hearts, crabmeat, and cream; stir to combine. Microcook on LOW (10 percent power) or DEFROST for 3 to 4 minutes, until steaming hot. Do not overcook. Cover and set aside.

4. Test the squash by piercing with the tip of a sharp knife; the squash should be tender. If not, return to the microwave and microcook on HIGH in 1-minute intervals. Cut the squash in half lengthwise. Remove the seeds with a spoon and discard. Be careful, as the squash will be hot and will emit steam.

5. Working over a bowl, scrape out the squash flesh with a dinner fork, loosening and separating the strands. Season with salt and pepper, then pour the artichoke-crab mixture over the squash. Serve immediately, sprinkled with parsley, if you like.

Acorn Squash with
Maple Brown Sugar

WHEN THE CHILL OF FALL hits the air, you'll see lots of fresh winter squash in the produce section. Acorn squash looks like an oversized green acorn with ridges running parallel down the surface, and it has tasty yellow-orange flesh. Store your winter squash at room temperature for up to a month; if you have a cool, dark place it will keep longer. When you make this recipe, you can sprinkle some ground cinnamon and nutmeg on top or drizzle with soy sauce instead of the salt. You can also scoop the flesh out of its shell and mash it.

o *Serves 2*

MICROWAVE COOKWARE: 9- or 10-inch Pyrex pie plate
MICROWAVE WATTAGE: 1,100 to 1,300
MICROWAVE COOK TIME: About 12 minutes
STANDING TIME: 3 minutes

**1 acorn squash (1 to 1½ pounds), washed and dried, then pierced all over with
  the tip of a paring knife**
3 to 4 tablespoons brown sugar
4 to 6 teaspoons unsalted butter
2 to 3 teaspoons pure maple syrup
Salt and freshly ground black or white pepper to taste

1. Place the squash directly on the turntable. Microcook on HIGH for 4 minutes. Turn over and microcook on HIGH for 4 minutes more. Let stand for 3 minutes.

2. With a chef's knife, cut the squash in half and remove the seeds and fiber with a spoon. Sprinkle each half with 1½ to 2 tablespoons brown sugar to lightly coat, then add 2 to 3 teaspoons butter and 1 to 1½ teaspoons maple syrup to the cavity of each squash half. Season lightly with salt and pepper. Place the halves in the pie plate, cut side up.

3. Microcook on HIGH, uncovered, for 3 to 4 minutes, until the squash is tender when pierced with a fork and the brown sugar is bubbly. Serve hot.

Potatoes and Onions

ONE OF MY FAVORITE ADDITIONS to a weekend breakfast is fried potatoes and onions with either eggs or scrambled tofu. The microwave does an amazing job cooking the onions. ○ *Serves 2*

MICROWAVE COOKWARE: 2-quart Pyrex casserole dish or microwave-safe ceramic casserole dish
MICROWAVE WATTAGE: 1,100 to 1,300
MICROWAVE COOK TIME: 13 to 17 minutes
STANDING TIME: 10 minutes

2 large russet potatoes (about 8 ounces each), scrubbed
2 tablespoons unsalted butter or olive oil
1 medium-size yellow or white onion, sliced
½ teaspoon salt
A few grinds of freshly ground black pepper
A few shakes of paprika or smoked paprika
A few shakes of dried Italian herb blend

1. Pierce each potato all over with the tip of a sharp knife; it is okay if the potatoes are wet. Place the potatoes on a layer of paper towel or directly on the turntable in the microwave. Microcook on HIGH until slightly soft when squeezed, 8 to 9 minutes, turning the potatoes halfway through the cooking time. Pierce each potato with a fork when you turn it over to let steam escape. Remove from the oven and let stand for at least 10 minutes. Peel and slice.

2. Place the butter and onion in the casserole dish. Partially cover and microcook on HIGH for 3 to 5 minutes, until the onions start to brown.

3. Add the potato slices, salt, pepper, paprika, and Italian herb blend to the casserole dish and toss to combine. Cover with a piece of parchment paper and microcook on HIGH for 2 to 3 minutes, until hot. Serve immediately.

Roasted Potatoes with Garlic and Rosemary

W**HEN YOU SEE CREAMER RED POTATOES,** those really tiny, cute new potatoes, in the supermarket, you can make this recipe, one of my absolute favorites. Serve with beef stew or roasted or grilled meat or fish.

o *Serves 4*

MICROWAVE COOKWARE: 9-inch square or 11 × 7-inch rectangular Pyrex baking dish
MICROWAVE WATTAGE: 1,100 to 1,300
MICROWAVE COOK TIME: 8 to 10 minutes
STANDING TIME: 3 minutes

2 to 3 tablespoons olive oil
2 cloves garlic, crushed
1½ pounds small creamer red potatoes, left whole, or medium-size red potatoes, quartered, to make about 4 cups
1 teaspoon dried rosemary, crushed
¼ to ½ teaspoon sea salt, to your taste
Freshly ground black pepper to taste

1. Place the oil and garlic in the baking dish. Microcook on HIGH, uncovered, for 20 seconds to warm.

2. Add the potatoes, then toss with the rosemary, salt, and pepper.

3. Partially cover with plastic wrap and microcook on HIGH for 8 to 10 minutes, or until the potatoes are tender. Let stand for 3 minutes. Serve immediately.

Gold and White Potato Gratin

ADORE SCALLOPED POTATOES, and this version combines russets and sweet potatoes with Swiss cheese. This one is so delicious and a real treat for potato lovers. It's a great dish for the holidays. ● *Serves 6*

MICROWAVE COOKWARE: 8-inch square Pyrex baking dish
MICROWAVE WATTAGE: 1,100 to 1,300
MICROWAVE COOK TIME: 18 to 21 minutes
STANDING TIME: 10 minutes

2 large russet potatoes (about 1¼ pounds), peeled and thinly sliced
Salt and freshly ground black pepper to taste
1 tablespoon minced fresh thyme
2 large orange-fleshed sweet potatoes or yams (about 1 pound), peeled and thinly sliced
1½ cups heavy cream
1 cup shredded Swiss cheese
⅓ cup freshly grated Parmesan cheese

1. Arrange half of the russet potatoes in the baking dish. Season lightly with salt and pepper. Sprinkle with one-quarter of the thyme. Make another layer with half of the sweet potatoes. Season again with salt and pepper and sprinkle with one-quarter of the thyme. Repeat the layering of the remaining russets and sweet potatoes, seasoning each layer with salt, pepper, and thyme. Pour the cream over the top. Partially cover with plastic wrap.

2. Microcook on HIGH until the potatoes are tender when pierced with the tip of a knife, 16 to 18 minutes.

3. Remove from the oven and sprinkle with the Swiss and Parmesan cheeses. Microcook, uncovered, on HIGH until the cheeses are melted and bubbly, 2 to 3 minutes. Remove from the oven and let rest for 10 minutes, then cut pieces out of the baking dish and serve.

Scalloped Potatoes

GOOD OLD SCALLOPED POTATOES are an important part of the American "comfort food" repertoire. Scalloped potatoes are generally made with russets for their low moisture and high starch content, which let them hold their shape and cook up oh so tender. Scalloped potatoes need to be assembled right before baking (you can store the raw sliced potatoes in water after slicing, which will prevent them from browning), so gather the ingredients ahead of time so that you can put the dish together assembly-line style. You can bake this hours or even a day ahead, and then rewarm it at serving time. It will taste just as good as when freshly made. ○ *Serves 6*

MICROWAVE COOKWARE: 1½-quart microwave-safe baking dish or 11 × 7-inch Pyrex baking dish; 2-cup Pyrex measuring cup

MICROWAVE WATTAGE: 1,100 to 1,300

MICROWAVE COOK TIME: About 12 minutes

STANDING TIME: 5 to 10 minutes

4 medium-size russet potatoes, peeled and sliced ⅛ inch thick

2 tablespoons all-purpose flour or potato flour

¾ teaspoon salt

2 tablespoons unsalted butter

1 cup whole milk, half-and-half, or heavy cream

½ cup freshly grated Parmesan cheese

1. Grease the baking dish with butter or nonstick cooking spray. Arrange half of the potatoes in the bottom of the baking dish in an overlapping layer. Combine the flour and salt in a small bowl, then sprinkle half of the mixture evenly over the potatoes. Top with several small dots of the butter.

2. Arrange the remaining potatoes in a second overlapping layer and sprinkle with the remaining flour-salt mixture and dot with the remaining butter.

3. Place the milk in the measuring cup. Microcook on HIGH, uncovered, for $1\frac{1}{2}$ to 2 minutes to scald. Pour the milk over the potatoes.

4. Cover the baking dish with a lid or plastic wrap, folding back two corners of the plastic wrap to vent. Microcook on HIGH for 5 minutes. Uncover, sprinkle with the Parmesan, and microcook on HIGH for another 5 minutes, or until the milk is boiling and the potatoes are becoming soft. Test for doneness by piercing the potatoes with the tip of a knife. If they are not quite done, microcook on HIGH for another 1 to 2 minutes.

5. Remove the baking dish from the oven and let rest on a folded kitchen towel for 5 to 10 minutes. Serve hot, cutting servings right out of the pan.

Microwave Mashed Potatoes

HERE'S AMERICA'S FAVORITE VEGETABLE prepared Americans' favorite way. This is a great way to make mashed potatoes without heating up the kitchen when the weather is steamy. If you like, you can make them ahead; reheat on HIGH, covered, for 2 to 4 minutes, stirring once. ○ *Serves 4 to 6*

MICROWAVE COOKWARE: 2-quart Pyrex casserole dish with lid,
   1-cup Pyrex measuring cup
MICROWAVE WATTAGE: 1,100 to 1,300
MICROWAVE COOK TIME: 8 to 10 minutes
STANDING TIME: 5 minutes

2 pounds (4 to 5 medium-size) russet potatoes, peeled and quartered
¼ cup water
½ to ¾ cup milk, half-and-half, plain soy milk, or plain rice milk
¼ cup (½ stick) unsalted butter, softened
Salt and freshly ground black or white pepper to taste

1. Place the potatoes and water in the casserole dish. Partially cover with the lid or plastic wrap. Microcook on HIGH for 8 to 10 minutes, until very tender, stirring once halfway through cooking. Let stand for 5 minutes. Drain.

2. During the standing time, place the milk in the measuring cup. Microcook on HIGH, uncovered, for 45 seconds to warm.

3. Mash the potatoes with a hand potato masher or a ricer to remove the lumps. Add the butter and ½ cup warm milk while mashing. Add more milk as needed to achieve the desired consistency. Season with salt and pepper and serve immediately.

VARIATIONS

Miracle Mashers: Use 2 medium-size russet potatoes, peeled and quartered, and 1 head cauliflower, cored and broken into florets, in place of the 2 pounds russet potatoes. Steam the potatoes and cauliflower with the water as directed in step 1. Let stand as directed, drain and mash with the milk and butter until smooth, season with salt and pepper, and serve.

Mashed Carrots and Potatoes: This combo is great for holiday dinners. Use 3 medium-size russet potatoes, peeled and quartered, and 3 medium-size carrots, scrubbed and cut into 1-inch chunks, in place of the 2 pounds russet potatoes. You want slightly less carrots than potatoes. Steam the potatoes and carrots with the water as directed in step 1. Let stand as directed, drain and mash with the milk and butter until smooth, season with salt and pepper, and serve.

Stuffed Potatoes

Although there are a few steps involved in making stuffed potatoes, it is time well spent. People of all ages adore them. Stuffing potatoes is an enjoyable way to showcase them. Also called twice-baked, or in this case, twice-microwaved, potatoes, they can be prepared in nearly unlimited varieties. You cook the potatoes whole, cool them, and then scoop out the centers. They soak up cheese of any type, and can be embellished with vegetables, crab, chicken, or any already-cooked filling. You can make them ahead and then do the final heating right before serving as a side or entrée. See pages 183 and 184 for my recipe suggestions.

Shredding the cheese can be a chore, but don't even think about using preshredded cheese unless you really have to. Freshly shredded cheese has a fuller flavor and won't be dry, which results in a better-tasting dish. Shredding your own is usually more economical, too. Just make sure you have the right kitchen utensil for the job and you are ready to go. Use the old-fashioned box grater, just like at Grandma's house, which has fine holes on one side for grating hard cheeses, such as Parmesan, manchego, and aged (dry) Jack, and extra-coarse holes on the other side for semi-firm cheeses like cheddar and Swiss. The Microplane box grater comes with a finger protector so you grate only cheese, not your knuckles. There's also the handheld grater with medium-size holes and the food processor fitted with the shredding attachment. Another handy tool is Tupperware's Grate 'N Measure, which is a really clean way to grate; it has a 2½-cup measuring cup attached to the back to catch the cheese as you grate it. Some cooks spray the grater with nonstick cooking spray before shredding since it prevents any cheese buildup and makes the grater easier to clean. For an easier time grating, use cheese that is cold.

Yogurt Smashed Potatoes

THERE HAVE BEEN VOLUMES WRITTEN on the best way to make rustic, chunky smashed potatoes, with different advice on how long you should cook them, whether you should peel them or not, whether you should mash them with some of the cooking liquid, what kind of potatoes to use, whether to use a potato ricer or handheld wire masher, and so on. Whichever way you go on these issues, the secret to heavenly smashed potatoes is to make them with a medium-starch waxy potato, such as red potatoes with skins left on, since they hold their shape and don't absorb water. Look for bigger new potatoes for this recipe.

o *Serves 4*

MICROWAVE COOKWARE: 2- or 3-quart Pyrex casserole dish with lid
MICROWAVE WATTAGE: 1,100 to 1,300
MICROWAVE COOK TIME: 6 to 9 minutes
STANDING TIME: None

2 pounds red potatoes, peeled or unpeeled, cut into eighths
¼ cup milk
1¼ cups thick plain yogurt, such as Greek yogurt
4 scallions (white part and some of the green), sliced
Salt and freshly ground black pepper to taste
Chopped fresh Italian parsley for garnish

1. Place the potatoes in the casserole dish and add the milk. Cover and microcook on HIGH for 6 to 9 minutes, until the potatoes are tender but not mushy.

2. Remove from the oven and add the yogurt and scallions; mash coarsely in the dish. Season with salt and pepper. Transfer to a serving bowl or portion onto serving plates. Sprinkle liberally with parsley. Serve immediately.

Pesto Potatoes in Their Jackets

S TUFFED BAKED POTATOES are one of the great standby dinners, as well as a tasty side dish. If you make pesto and keep it stashed in your freezer, here is a fabulous way of using it with something other than pasta. There are two methods of stuffing potatoes: In one, you scrape the flesh from the baked potatoes, combine it with additional ingredients, and pile the mixture inside the potato shells; in the other, you cut open the potatoes and stuff a topping down inside. Here is the second method, and it's ever so delicious. ● *Serves 4*

MICROWAVE COOKWARE: 10-inch Pyrex pie plate
MICROWAVE WATTAGE: 1,100 to 1,300
MICROWAVE COOK TIME: About 11 minutes
STANDING TIME: None

4 large russet potatoes (8 to 12 ounces each), scrubbed
2 to 3 plum tomatoes, seeded and diced
¼ cup store-bought or homemade basil pesto
2 cups shredded mozzarella or fontina cheese (about 8 ounces)

1. Pierce the potatoes all over with the tip of a sharp knife; it is okay if they are wet. Place a potato at each of the four corners of a layer of paper towel, or place the potatoes in a circle on the pie plate. Microcook on HIGH for 5 to 6 minutes; pierce the potatoes with a fork to let steam escape, turn them over, and microcook on HIGH for an additional 5 to 6 minutes, until the potatoes are slightly soft when squeezed.

2. In a small bowl, combine the tomatoes and pesto. Gently stir to coat the tomatoes. Add the cheese and toss to combine.

3. Cut a large X into the top of each potato and squeeze the potato to push it open. Stuff one-quarter of the pesto-cheese mixture into the opening of each potato.

4. Microcook on HIGH for 30 to 60 seconds, until the filling is heated and the cheese is melted. Serve immediately.

Chili Bean–Stuffed
Twice-Microwaved Potatoes

WHEN A BAKED POTATO IS STUFFED with beans and cheese, it becomes a hearty, filling lunch or dinner. After the potatoes are cooked, they need to cool for a bit before being stuffed. This makes it easy to scoop out the insides efficiently without tearing/collapsing the shell, which is softer when cooked in the microwave than when oven-roasted. Make the simple Fast Chili Beans in the microwave while the potatoes are cooling, or use two cans of your favorite commercial chili beans. I have also seen baked potatoes stuffed with canned baked beans, a British favorite along with beans on toast. ○ *Serves 4*

MICROWAVE COOKWARE: 10-inch Pyrex pie plate, 1-quart Pyrex measuring cup
MICROWAVE WATTAGE: 1,100 to 1,300
COOK TIME: 17 to 20 minutes
STANDING TIME: 10 to 15 minutes

4 large baking potatoes (8 to 12 ounces each), scrubbed

FAST CHILI BEANS:
One 15-ounce can red kidney beans, rinsed and drained
One 15-ounce can white cannellini beans, rinsed and drained
¾ cup tomato sauce
2 to 3 teaspoons chili powder, to your taste
¼ teaspoon dried oregano
Salt to taste

2 cups shredded sharp cheddar or Colby cheese (about 8 ounces)
1 cup sour cream, for serving
⅓ cup chopped fresh cilantro, for garnish

1. Pierce the potatoes all over with the tip of a sharp knife; it is okay if they are wet. Place a potato at each of the four corners of a layer of paper towel, or place the potatoes in a circle on the pie plate. Microcook the potatoes on HIGH for 5 to 6 minutes; pierce the potatoes with a fork to let steam escape, turn the potatoes over, and microcook on HIGH for an additional 5 to 6 minutes, until slightly soft when squeezed. Remove the potatoes from the oven and let stand for 10 to 15 minutes.

2. While the potatoes are cooling, make the chili beans. Place the beans, tomato sauce, chili powder, and oregano in the measuring cup; stir to combine. Microcook on HIGH for about 5 minutes, stirring once halfway through cooking, until steaming hot. Taste and season with salt.

3. When the potatoes are cool enough to handle, carefully slice each potato in half lengthwise using a serrated knife. Scoop out the inside of each potato half, leaving a shell about ½ inch thick all around; place the insides of the potatoes in a medium-size mixing bowl and coarsely mash. Add the chili beans and 1 cup of the cheese; stir to combine.

4. Spoon the mixture back into the potato shells and arrange the potato halves like the spokes of a wheel on the pie plate. If your oven is small, you will need to cook the stuffed potatoes in two batches. Sprinkle 2 tablespoons of the remaining cheese on top of each potato half.

5. Microcook on HIGH for 2 to 3 minutes, until the potatoes and filling are hot and the cheese is melted. Place a spoonful of sour cream on top of each potato half, sprinkle with some chopped cilantro, and serve immediately.

Steamed Seasonal Vegetables

It has been established that vegetables are more nutritious and flavorful, and retain their texture better, when cooked in the microwave than by other methods. The microwave provides the easiest way to eat more vegetables, so experiment with cooking different mixed seasonal vegetables as you like. A combination of two or three different vegetables tastes the best; be sure to chop or slice them into similar sizes for even cooking. Plan on 1½ to 2 cups raw prepped vegetables per person, and follow these general guidelines for preparing some common vegetables.

MICROWAVE COOKWARE: 2-quart Pyrex casserole dish
MICROWAVE WATTAGE: 1,100 to 1,300
MICROWAVE COOK TIME: As directed per vegetable type
STANDING TIME: None

1. Place the vegetables in the casserole dish with a small amount of water and partially cover with plastic wrap or the lid of the casserole dish. For winter squash, place halves or quarters, cut side down, in a shallow dish; add water.

2. Microcook on HIGH as directed below, until crisp-tender or wilted. If not tender enough for your taste, continue to cook in 30-second intervals, checking for tenderness. Drain off the accumulated water and serve hot.

- **Leafy vegetables and small vegetables** require 2 tablespoons of water per pound and take 3 to 4 minutes to cook: spinach, bok choy, Swiss chard, beet greens, frozen petite peas, frozen artichoke hearts, edamame, canned hearts of palm, napa cabbage, whole baby vegetables.

- **Green vegetables and soft vegetables** require about 4 tablespoons of water per pound and take 5 to 8 minutes to cook, depending on the size of the pieces: green or wax beans; broccolini; red, green, or yellow bell peppers; zucchini; crookneck or pattypan squash; mushrooms, sliced or quartered; celery; fresh corn off the cob; fennel; kale and collards; green and red cabbage; asparagus.

Steamed Seasonal Vegetables

- **Flower head vegetables** require about 4 tablespoons of water per pound and take 5 to 8 minutes to cook, depending on the size of the florets: broccoli, cauliflower, romanesco broccoli, Brussels sprouts. To cook a whole cauliflower or romanesco head, break off the outer leaves and trim the stem close to the base of the head. Wash in cool water, then shake off the excess. Wrap the head loosely in plastic wrap and place on a paper plate with the sealed edges down. Alternatively, place in a deep 2- or 3-quart casserole dish with a lid and 2 tablespoons water. Microcook on HIGH for 3 minutes. If the head is on a paper plate, turn the head over; you do not have to do this if it is in the casserole dish. Microcook on HIGH for an additional 4 to 6 minutes, until the head is flexible and the floret stems are almost fork-tender. Let stand for 3 minutes. Cut in wedges to serve hot or cold.

- **Aromatic root vegetables** require about 4 tablespoons of water per pound and take 5 to 8 minutes to cook, depending on the size and whether they are whole, chopped, or in wedges: shallots and scallions; yellow, white, and red onions; white boiling onions; whole white, red, or gold pearl onions; leeks.

- **Dense vegetables** require about 6 tablespoons of water per pound and take 7 to 8 minutes to cook, depending on the size of the dice or thickness of the slices: carrots and parsnips, beets, fresh water chestnuts, rutabagas and turnips, all potatoes, sweet potatoes and yams.

- **Dense winter squashes** require 4 tablespoons of water per pound and take 6 to 7 minutes to cook, depending on the size of the peeled chunks or the thickness of the slices or halves: acorn, butternut, kabocha, baby pumpkin, sugar pumpkin, banana squash, buttercup, delicata, gold nugget, hubbard, turban, spaghetti squash. They can also be cooked whole without any water if they fit in your oven. Poke whole squash all over with a fork to break the skin, and place on the turntable. Microwave the squash on HIGH for 5 to 8 minutes (depending on the size of the squash) per pound. Because the rind makes most squash difficult to peel, it's easier to cook unpeeled squash, and then cut it in half and scoop out the cooked flesh.

In-a-Flash Fish and Poultry

Microcooking fish is not merely a good way to prepare fish; of all of the techniques available, it has become the best way to cook fish. It is so fast and simple, and since the microwave is a moist cooking environment where nothing evaporates, the fish stays succulent, tender, and sea-sweet. It cooks fish so quickly that you'd better be ready with the rest of the meal when you put the fish in the oven.

Fillets are the easiest cuts of fish to cook in the microwave, so that is the bulk of what you will find in this chapter, but fillets can be thick or thin. There are also steaks, whole fish, fish pieces, and stuffed fish, but the focus here is on some of the easiest and most convenient recipes.

How much you put in the baking dish, the size of the dish (always a shallow dish unless a soup), the thickness of the fish, the freshness of the fish (fresh cooks the fastest), and the type of fish are all variables that will affect your cooking time. The average serving is 5 to 6 ounces per person; don't cook more than 2½ to 3 pounds at one time. Smaller amounts cook more efficiently; with larger amounts, you must rearrange the fish in the middle of the cooking time for even cooking. You will know when the fish is done when it looks opaque and almost flakes easily when lifted with a fork. Undercooked fish looks translucent, while overcooked fish looks dry and falls apart. It is best to check the fish at the earliest recommended time.

If you need to cook it longer than the time specified in the recipe, microcook at 20- to 60-second intervals. Never salt fish before cooking to maintain optimum tenderness. A general rule is to cook thin fillets like sole on HIGH, but thicker fillets on MEDIUM (50 percent power), giving them time to cook slowly.

Never attempt to micro-fry fish in the microwave, as the deep fats can ignite. Also, do not cook whole lobster or crab in the microwave; they should be done one by one and will cook unevenly anyway. The exception is little rock lobster tails and crab legs.

The poultry recipes in this chapter are for chicken and turkey. Both are terrifically versatile, being as delicious plain as with a wide variety of sauces, and both cook very quickly. Boneless, skinless chicken breasts are the best type of chicken to cook in the microwave. One breast takes a mere 2 minutes to cook. You can keep a stash of individually wrapped frozen breasts for quick, no-brainer dinners. When placing the breasts on the baking dish, make sure to put the thicker section toward the outside of the dish. If in doubt whether poultry is fully cooked, use an instant-read thermometer. The safe minimum internal temperature is 165° to 175°F in the thickest part of the breast.

Fish Fillets with Buttered Crumb Coating

WHEN AT THE SEAFOOD COUNTER, look for the freshest boneless white fish fillets of the day: cod, halibut, perch, orange roughy, red snapper, or sea bass. Then grind up your favorite crackers in the food processor or by hand—whether saltines, gluten-free crackers, Ritz, artisan crackers, or Waverly Wafers. This recipe is adapted from a lovely little book titled *Easy Livin' Microwave Cooking* by Karen Kangas Dwyer (St. Martin's Press, 1989), one of those microwave cookbooks written by a microwave-cooking instructor for an oven manufacturer back in the 1980s. Serve with your own tartar sauce (page 194), of course. ○ *Serves 4*

MICROWAVE COOKWARE: 11 × 7-inch Pyrex or microwave-safe ceramic baking dish
MICROWAVE WATTAGE: 1,100 to 1,300
MICROWAVE COOK TIME: About 4 minutes
STANDING TIME: 2 minutes

5 tablespoons unsalted butter, cut into pieces
1¼ cups cracker crumbs
1¼ pounds fish fillets, ¾ inch thick, cut into 4 equal pieces
¼ teaspoon fine sea salt if crackers are unsalted, or salt-free herb blend
4 tablespoons milk

1. Place the butter in the baking dish. Microcook on HIGH for 30 seconds to melt the butter. Stir in the cracker crumbs until evenly moistened with the butter; remove half of the crumbs to a small bowl.

2. Place the fish fillets side by side in the baking dish; touching each other is okay. Sprinkle with the sea salt. Sprinkle evenly with the remaining cracker crumbs, then drizzle the fillets with the milk.

3. Cover with waxed paper. Microcook on HIGH for 4 minutes, until the fish flakes when lifted gently with a fork, checking for doneness at the 2½- to 3-minute mark. Let stand, covered, for 2 minutes. Serve immediately, removing the individual fillets with a spatula to plates.

Halibut with Lemon and Parsley

THIS IS A RECIPE from a flier tucked into an old 1983 cookbook from the Alaska Seafood Marketing Institute. Halibut is a mild-flavored fish that takes easily to all types of sauces and toppings. The most important thing is not to overcook it, for it will get really chewy if you do. The sea salt is an integral part of the dish. I have been using Himalayan pink sea salt that comes in a salt shaker; the taste is delicious. Serve with your own tartar sauce (page 194) or Papaya Salsa (page 195). **o** *Serves 4*

MICROWAVE COOKWARE: 11 x 7-inch Pyrex or microwave-safe ceramic baking dish
MICROWAVE WATTAGE: 1,100 to 1,300
MICROWAVE COOK TIME: About 4 minutes
STANDING TIME: 3 minutes

Four 4-ounce halibut steaks, ¾ inch thick
¼ teaspoon fine sea salt
Juice and grated zest of 1 lemon (about 2 tablespoons juice)
Freshly ground black pepper to taste
4½ teaspoons melted unsalted butter
2 tablespoons minced fresh Italian parsley

1. Spray the baking dish with nonstick cooking spray. Place the halibut steaks side by side in the baking dish; touching each other is okay.

2. Sprinkle first with the salt, then the lemon zest, then the pepper. Drizzle with the lemon juice and butter; sprinkle with the parsley.

3. Partially cover with plastic wrap. Microcook on HIGH for 4 minutes, until barely firm and the fish flakes when lifted gently with a fork. Let stand, covered, for 3 minutes. Serve immediately.

My Mom's Halibut with Garden Herbs

MY MOTHER KEEPS a little container garden of basic herbs outside her kitchen and is constantly snipping a little of this and a little of that to use in her cooking. Getting her to give exact measurements when using herbs in recipes is hard because she says, "You know, just cut off a bit and toss it in." This is her all-purpose basic coating for firm fish, whether a steak or a fillet, and it makes the fish very flavorful and moist. It's another foolproof and delicious recipe done in the time it takes for you to toss a salad and heat up some leftover rice in the microwave. This preparation also works well with salmon. ○ *Serves 2*

MICROWAVE COOKWARE: 8-inch Pyrex pie plate
MICROWAVE WATTAGE: 1,100 to 1,300
MICROWAVE COOK TIME: 3 to 4 minutes
STANDING TIME: 2 minutes

Two 6-ounce halibut fillets, skin on, ¾ to 1 inch thick
1½ teaspoons olive oil
⅓ cup mayonnaise
2 teaspoons minced fresh Italian parsley
1 teaspoon minced fresh chives
1 teaspoon minced fresh dill, tarragon, or other fresh herb
Lemon or lime wedges for serving

1. Spray the baking dish with nonstick olive oil spray. Place the fillets side by side and rub both sides with the olive oil.

2. In a small bowl, stir together the mayonnaise, parsley, chives, and dill. With a small spatula, divide the sauce between the two fillets, slathering the top surface with a thick coating like icing.

3. Cover with waxed paper. Microcook on HIGH for 3 to 4 minutes, or until the fish loses its translucency and flakes when gently lifted with a fork. Allow to stand, covered, for 2 minutes to finish cooking. Serve immediately with lemon or lime wedges.

Homemade Seafood Condiments

This chapter would not be complete without a recipe for a great tartar sauce. Tartar sauce can be bought in jars from the supermarket; however, making your own sauce from scratch tastes so much better, and it can be made in minutes.

Vary your Steamed Shrimp (page 212) by offering different dipping sauces, which can be whipped up from your pantry supplies in minutes. The Wasabi Mayonnaise and Chipotle-Orange Cocktail Sauce are so delicious that you will want to use them in place of tartar sauce on other microcooked fish.

Salsa, the little salad-like condiment that has become America's favorite, can be made with tomatoes, beans, fruit, avocados, or vegetables, and it has become a common addition to meats, fish, eggs, and sandwiches. Included here is one of my all-time favorites, papaya salsa, which tastes great with all types of simple microcooked fish.

Tartar Sauce ○ Makes about 1½ cups

1 cup mayonnaise
¼ cup plain yogurt (preferably Greek-style)
2 tablespoons dill pickle relish
2 tablespoons minced onion, scallion, or chopped fresh chives
2 teaspoons freshly squeezed lemon or lime juice
Freshly ground black pepper to taste

1. Combine the mayonnaise, yogurt, relish, and onion in a small mixing bowl, stirring well. Add the lemon juice and pepper.

2. Cover the bowl with plastic wrap and place in the refrigerator for at least 1 hour before serving. You can store the prepared tartar sauce in an airtight jar in the refrigerator for up to 1 week.

Chipotle-Orange Cocktail Sauce ○ Makes 1 cup

1 cup mayonnaise
3 to 4 teaspoons ground chipotle chile powder
¼ cup freshly squeezed orange juice
Zest of 1 orange, or ½ teaspoon orange oil

Place all of the ingredients in a small bowl and whisk to combine. Cover and refrigerate until serving time. The sauce can be stored in an airtight container in the refrigerator for up to 1 week.

Homemade Seafood Condiments

Wasabi Mayonnaise ○ Makes 1 cup

4 teaspoons wasabi powder
4 teaspoons water
1 cup mayonnaise
Hot chili oil

Mix the wasabi and water in a small bowl with a fork; mash to evenly blend and moisten. Add the mayonnaise and mash to combine. Add a few drops of chili oil. Cover and refrigerate until serving time. You can store the mayonnaise in an airtight container in the refrigerator for up to 1 week.

Papaya Salsa ○ Makes about 2¾ cups

2 cups firm but ripe papaya, cut into ½-inch chunks
½ cup diced red, yellow, or green bell pepper, or a combination
⅓ cup minced red onion
⅓ cup chopped fresh cilantro leaves
Minced fresh jalapeño or serrano chile, or red pepper flakes, to taste
1 tablespoon extra-virgin olive oil
3 tablespoons freshly squeezed lime juice, or more to taste
Salt to taste

1. Place all of the ingredients in a medium-size bowl and stir gently to evenly combine. Let sit for about 5 minutes, then taste and adjust the seasoning, adding more minced chile, lime juice, or salt, as needed.

2. Serve immediately or refrigerate, covered, for up to 8 hours. (Bring to room temperature before serving.) This is best served the day it is made.

Steamed Catfish with Ginger

WILD CATFISH IS A SPECIALTY from southern United States rivers, especially the Mississippi. It has been farmed for more than four decades. It has been so integral to Cajun cuisine that the area is known as "catfish country." Today all North American channel catfish you can buy is commercially raised in freshwater farms, and they have adapted to being surface-feeders fed with pellets of soy and corn, which contribute to their mild flavor. Microcooking catfish is a much healthier and just-as-tasty way to prepare catfish as the more traditional frying. I suggest you rinse and dry this fish before cooking, because catfish is a fattier fish. ○ *Serves 2*

MICROWAVE COOKWARE: 11 × 7-inch Pyrex or microwave-safe ceramic baking dish
MICROWAVE WATTAGE: 1,100 to 1,300
MICROWAVE COOK TIME: 3 to 6 minutes
STANDING TIME: 5 minutes

Two 6- to 8-ounce catfish fillets, rinsed and patted dry
Juice of ½ lemon
2 tablespoons light olive oil or peanut oil
2 tablespoons low-sodium soy sauce
1 tablespoon dry sherry
Pinch of sugar
1½-inch piece of fresh ginger, peeled and grated
3 scallions, cut into ½-inch sections and halved lengthwise
1 to 2 teaspoons toasted sesame oil

1. Arrange the fillets in one layer in the baking dish, and squeeze the lemon juice over them.

2. In a small bowl, combine the olive oil, soy sauce, sherry, sugar, and ginger. Pour over the catfish. Sprinkle with the scallions.

3. Cover with a domed lid, piece of parchment paper, or plastic wrap. Microcook on HIGH for 3 to 6 minutes, until the thickest part of the fish is opaque and just cooked through. Uncover carefully and drizzle with the sesame oil. Let stand for 5 minutes to finish cooking. Serve immediately.

Petrale Sole Amandine

FILLET OF SOLE WITH A BUTTER SAUCE is the first meal that the late Julia Child ate when she moved to France in November 1948, and she immortalized it in her book *My Life in France* (Knopf, 2006). Petrale sole, which has larger fillets than Dover sole, is a flatfish that is a member of the flounder family, and it is most often served with a creamy butter and lemon sauce of some type. It is a fish that is delicate and mild flavored, so it is very popular. You will serve 8 ounces of fish per portion in this recipe. ○ *Serves 2*

MICROWAVE COOKWARE: 9-inch square or 11 × 7-inch Pyrex or microwave-safe ceramic baking dish
MICROWAVE WATTAGE: 1,100 to 1,300
MICROWAVE COOK TIME: 3 to 4 minutes
STANDING TIME: 2 minutes

5 tablespoons unsalted butter, cut into 5 pieces
¼ cup sliced almonds
Juice of 1 large lemon
1 pound petrale sole fillets

1. Place the butter pieces and almonds in the baking dish. Microcook on HIGH, uncovered, for 1 minute to melt the butter. Stir in the lemon juice.

2. Arrange the sole fillets in a single layer in the baking dish. If they are thin, fold them over; if the ends are thin, tuck them under to make an even layer. Spoon the butter-almond sauce up and over the fillets. Partially cover with plastic wrap. Microcook on HIGH for 2 to 3 minutes, depending on how thick the fillets are, until the fish loses its translucency. Let stand for 2 minutes, then serve immediately.

Poached Sole with Hollandaise

FILLET OF SOLE WITH A REAL HOLLANDAISE SAUCE is among the requested fare for any of my catering jobs for private clients. Hollandaise is a rich and creamy sauce with just a dash of tang from the lemon juice. It is one of the most popular of the elemental French emulsion butter sauces and often a challenge to make. But thanks to the microwave, your own fabulous hollandaise is minutes away. Instead of melting the butter and beating that into the yolks, you toss in pieces of butter. Be careful not to overheat the sauce. You definitely need the wire whisk and white pepper in lieu of black. If you want to make the sauce before the fish, do so and let it stand on the counter while you cook the fish. Reheat it in the microwave on LOW (10 percent power) or DEFROST for 30 seconds, then stir and serve. **o** *Serves 2*

MICROWAVE COOKWARE: 9-inch square or 11 × 7-inch Pyrex or microwave-safe ceramic baking dish; 1-quart Pyrex measuring cup

MICROWAVE WATTAGE: 1,100 to 1,300

MICROWAVE COOK TIME: 2 to 2½ minutes for the fish, 1 to 1½ minutes for the sauce

STANDING TIME: 5 minutes

1 pound petrale sole fillets
2 tablespoons water
2 tablespoons dry white wine
Salt and freshly ground black pepper to taste

HOLLANDAISE SAUCE:
3 large egg yolks
2 tablespoons freshly squeezed lemon juice
½ cup (1 stick) unsalted butter, at room temperature, cut into 3 equal pieces
Salt and freshly ground white pepper

1. Butter the baking dish and arrange the fillets side by side. If they are thin, fold them over; if the ends are thin, tuck them under to make an even layer. Add the water and white wine. Sprinkle the fish with some black pepper. Cover the baking dish with a layer of paper towels.

2. Microcook on HIGH for 2 to 2^1/$_2$ minutes, depending on how thick the fillets are, until the fish loses its translucency. Let stand for 5 minutes while making the hollandaise.

3. To make the sauce, place the egg yolks and lemon juice in the measuring cup; whisk lightly to combine. Add 1 piece of the butter. Microcook on MEDIUM (50 percent power), uncovered, for 20 to 30 seconds. Remove from the oven and whisk vigorously to incorporate the melted butter and eggs. Don't worry if it is a bit lumpy.

4. Drop in the second piece of butter and microcook on MEDIUM, uncovered, for 20 to 30 seconds. Remove from the oven and whisk vigorously to incorporate.

5. Drop in the third piece of butter and microcook on MEDIUM, uncovered, for 20 to 30 seconds. Whisk lightly and season with salt and white pepper.

6. Season the sole with salt and pepper and use a slotted spatula to transfer the fillets to warm dinner plates. Spoon a few tablespoons or more of the hollandaise, as you like it, over the top of the fish. Serve immediately.

Salmon with Crème Fraîche and Dill in Parchment

COOKING FISH IN PARCHMENT is so simple that you can assemble the packets in a few minutes once you have your ingredients. The edges are folded to create a little cooking envelope, which becomes an airtight steaming pouch. It is one of the fastest methods for cooking fish with the least amount of cleanup. You want a full ¼ cup of each vegetable for each packet. In this recipe, the salmon and vegetables will be in their own creamy sauce. You will cook 2 packages at a time. ● *Serves 4*

MICROWAVE COOKWARE: 10-inch Pyrex pie plate or microwave-safe ceramic plate
MICROWAVE WATTAGE: 1,100 to 1,300
MICROWAVE COOK TIME: About 6 minutes
STANDING TIME: 2 minutes

Four 12-inch-square sheets parchment paper
2 tablespoons unsalted butter, at room temperature
Four 6- to 8-ounce salmon fillets, skin on (¾ to 1 inch thick)
Salt and freshly ground black pepper to taste
8 tablespoons crème fraîche
8 teaspoons chopped fresh dill
1 cup julienned zucchini
1 cup sliced white mushrooms

1. Fold each piece of parchment in half to form a crease. Spread the butter liberally below the crease of the parchment. Place a salmon fillet on each piece of buttered parchment. Season with salt and pepper. Top each fillet with 2 tablespoons of the crème fraîche, then sprinkle each with 2 teaspoons of the dill. Divide the zucchini and mushrooms equally between the 4 packets, and season lightly again with salt and pepper.

2. Fold over the top of the parchment. Starting at the right side of the fish, fold $1/2$ inch of the edge of the parchment over in 2-inch increments, crimping the edges and making sure the previous fold is covered a bit with the next fold to securely wrap the salmon airtight. Place two packets side by side on the pie plate.

3. Microcook on HIGH for 3 minutes. Open one packet to test for doneness; the salmon will just flake at the touch of a fork. If not done, rewrap and microcook in 20-second intervals until it is cooked. Remove from the oven and transfer the packets with a spatula to individual dinner plates. Let stand while you cook the other two packets.

4. To serve, using a steak knife or scissors, let diners tear open their own packet of fragrant salmon with creamy vegetables.

Poached Salmon with Lemon Sauce

ONE OF THE MOST STRAIGHTFORWARD TECHNIQUES and most delicious ways to prepare salmon (or most any fish, for that matter) is to poach it. Poaching cooks food gently in a simmering, never boiling, liquid; you will want to see some little bubbles on the surface. This poaching liquid is especially easy to make, with some apple cider vinegar as the acidic liquid to balance the flavor of the fish, instead of lemon juice or wine. The liquid is made aromatic with a bay leaf and a slice of onion. While cooking, there will be a flavor exchange from the liquid to the fish, and the liquid will keep the fish moist as well; take care not to boil or overcook. You can use this recipe for poaching any type of fish fillets or steaks. While poached fish is certainly acceptable with just some lemon wedges, it really becomes special with a sauce. I used to love salmon with hollandaise, but here I wanted a simpler sauce. You will love this one. ❍ *Serves 4*

MICROWAVE COOKWARE: 9-inch square or 11 × 7-inch Pyrex baking dish,
2-cup and 2-quart Pyrex measuring cups
MICROWAVE WATTAGE: 1,100 to 1,300
MICROWAVE COOK TIME: About 5 minutes for the fish,
4 to 5 minutes for the poaching liquid, 1 to 1½ minutes for the sauce
STANDING TIME: 2 minutes

Four 5-ounce center-cut salmon fillets, skinned (¾ to 1 inch thick)
3 cups cold water
¼ cup apple cider vinegar
1 slice white or yellow onion
1 bay leaf
Salt and freshly ground white pepper to taste

LEMON SAUCE:
1 cup mayonnaise
Juice of 2 lemons
2 teaspoons Dijon mustard
Pinch of freshly ground white pepper

1. Arrange the fish in a single layer in the baking dish. Set aside.

2. Place the water, vinegar, onion, bay leaf, salt, and pepper in the 2-quart measuring cup. Partially cover with plastic wrap. Microcook on HIGH for 4 to 5 minutes, until the liquid reaches a high simmer/low boil.

3. Carefully pour the hot poaching liquid over the fish fillets, just to cover, leaving the solids in the cup. You may not use all of the liquid. Partially cover the salmon tightly with plastic wrap and carefully place in the oven. Microcook on MEDIUM (50 percent power) for 5 minutes ($3\frac{1}{2}$ to 4 minutes per pound), until slightly underdone. Remove from the oven and let stand in the liquid for 2 minutes.

4. Place all of the sauce ingredients in the 2-cup measuring cup. Beat with a fork to combine and loosen the mayonnaise. Microcook on LOW (10 percent power) or DEFROST for 1 to $1\frac{1}{2}$ minutes, until runny and warm. Stir.

5. Remove the fish with a slotted spatula to individual dinner plates and coat lightly with 4 to 5 tablespoons of the lemon sauce. Serve immediately.

San Francisco Cioppino

THIS MÉLANGE is one of the all-time great seafood dishes of the West. Cioppino is a fisherman's stew traditionally made from the catch of the day and a lusty tomato-wine sauce, often served over long pasta such as spaghetti. The dish is close in nature to bouillabaisse. Cioppino emerged in San Francisco in the late 1800s as a favorite meal among Italian fishermen, home cooks, sourdough bakers, and restaurateurs who settled in the North Beach area. You can go crazy putting all kinds of seafood into cioppino, but this recipe adapted for the microwave uses shrimp and crab. Be sure to crack the crab and set the table with bibs and plenty of napkins. Serve in shallow bowls for a fabulous family or company dinner.

o *Serves 2*

MICROWAVE COOKWARE: 2- or 3-quart Pyrex or microwave-safe ceramic casserole dish
MICROWAVE WATTAGE: 1,100 to 1,300
MICROWAVE COOK TIME: About 13 minutes
STANDING TIME: 5 minutes

2 tablespoons olive oil
½ large onion, chopped
½ large green bell pepper, seeded and diced
1 clove garlic, minced or crushed
One 16-ounce can stewed tomatoes, undrained
One 8-ounce can tomato sauce
½ cup white wine
½ bay leaf
¼ cup chopped fresh Italian parsley
2 teaspoons minced fresh basil
¼ teaspoon dried oregano
1 cooked Dungeness crab (about 1½ pounds), cleaned, cut in half, and cracked
8 ounces medium to large raw shrimp, shelled and deveined

1. Place the olive oil in the casserole dish. Add the onion, bell pepper, and garlic. Partially cover with plastic wrap. Microcook on HIGH for 3½ minutes, stirring once during cooking.

2. Add the tomatoes with their juice, tomato sauce, wine, bay leaf, parsley, basil, and oregano. Partially cover. Microcook on HIGH for 6 to 7 minutes, stirring halfway through cooking.

3. Add the crab and shrimp. Partially cover. Microcook on HIGH for 2 to 3½ minutes, until the shrimp turns pink and the crab is hot. Be careful not to overcook.

4. Let stand, covered, for 5 minutes, then serve immediately in shallow bowls with lots of napkins.

Baja Fish Tacos

FISH TACOS MADE IN THE MICROWAVE from start to finish? Yes, and the fish comes out perfectly, too. Use snapper, halibut, swordfish, tilapia, or salmon for the best results. You can use a small rectangular or square Pyrex dish or CorningWare SimplyLite Bakeware, which is the lightest ceramic casserole dish ever and comes with a domed glass lid with handle. The 1½-quart, 12-inch square dish is perfect for cooking two fish steaks or fillets. You will need to have your condiments ready and waiting, for once the fish is cooked, you should be ready to assemble and eat your tacos. The list of toppings here is a suggestion. You can simply have shredded lettuce and salsa and be good to go. ○ *Serves 4*

MICROWAVE COOKWARE: 11 × 7-inch Pyrex or microwave-safe ceramic baking dish
MICROWAVE WATTAGE: 1,100 to 1,300
MICROWAVE COOK TIME: About 3 minutes for the fish, 60 seconds for the tortillas
STANDING TIME: None

CONDIMENT CHOICES:
Chunky Guacamole (recipe follows)
Salsa Mexicana (recipe follows)
Chopped fresh cucumbers
Hot sauce
Sour cream
Shredded Monterey Jack cheese
Shredded iceberg lettuce
Chopped fresh cilantro or cilantro sprigs
Lime wedges

½ white onion, chopped
1 whole jalapeño chile, stemmed, seeded, and minced
3 tablespoons water or low-sodium chicken broth
1½ pounds boneless white fish fillets (1 inch thick)
1 to 2 tablespoons olive oil
¼ teaspoon salt, or to taste
Freshly ground black pepper to taste
Pure chile powder, such as ancho or New Mexican red chile, to taste (optional)
8 to 12 fresh corn tortillas

1. Prepare and assemble your taco condiments. This can be as informal as serving what you have in the refrigerator right out of plastic storage containers or as formal as setting everything out on the table in serving dishes.

2. Place the onion and chile in the casserole dish, spreading them out over the bottom of the dish. Add the water. Arrange the fish fillets in a single layer on top and rub olive oil on the top surface of the fillets. Sprinkle with salt, pepper, and a bit of chile powder. If the ends of the fillets are thin, tuck them under to make an even layer. Cover the baking dish with a layer of paper towels. Microcook on HIGH for about 3 minutes for a 1-inch thick fillet, until the fish flakes. Remove from the oven.

3. Wrap the stack of tortillas (or you can do 4 at a time to have piping-hot tortillas for each taco) in a slightly damp paper towel. Place in the microwave and microcook on HIGH for about 1 minute.

4. Portion the fish and some of the vegetables onto 4 dinner plates. For each taco, place some lettuce, if you are using it, onto a warm tortilla, then place some of the fish on top. Add a squeeze of lime, if you are using it, then top with other condiments as desired.

Chunky Guacamole

Serves 4

3 ripe avocados
1 plum tomato, diced
¼ cup finely diced red onion
½ serrano chile, stemmed, seeded, and minced
Salt and freshly ground black pepper to taste
2 limes, halved

1. Peel and pit the avocados and place in a small mixing bowl. Gently mash with a fork, leaving the avocado somewhat chunky. Leave the pits in the bowl (this is a Mexican secret to help slow the oxidation process and help the avocados stay green).

2. Fold in the tomato, onion, and chile. Season with salt and pepper. Squeeze the limes over the top. Serve immediately, or cover and refrigerate for up to 12 hours.

Salsa Mexicana

Serves 4

3 large ripe tomatoes (about 1 pound), cored, seeded, and diced into ¼-inch pieces
¼ cup finely diced red onion
2 to 3 tablespoons finely chopped fresh cilantro
1 jalapeño chile, stemmed, seeded, and finely minced
½ teaspoon salt, or to taste

Combine all of the ingredients in a small bowl. Stir well, and let stand for at least 30 minutes at room temperature before serving. The salsa can be made and refrigerated, covered, up to 1 day in advance. If you make it ahead, drain off any excess liquid and season with salt before serving.

Nut-Crusted Scallops

SEA SCALLOPS ARE ENJOYING A SURGE OF POPULARITY due to their easy availability and low fat content. Scallops are hand-caught on the ocean floor, where they are attached to undulating sea grasses, which means their harvesting doesn't destroy undersea flora or fauna like trawling does. Domestic Atlantic scallops generally come from the largest wild scallop fishery off the coast of northeastern United States and eastern Canada (there is also some scallop fishing in Alaska). The scallop population is much more abundant these days, following a century of overfishing. Left whole, sea scallops cook quickly in the microwave and come out tender. **○** *Serves 4*

MICROWAVE COOKWARE: 9- or 10-inch Pyrex pie plate
MICROWAVE WATTAGE: 1,100 to 1,300
MICROWAVE COOK TIME: About 4 minutes
STANDING TIME: 5 minutes

¼ cup unseasoned bread crumbs
¼ cup finely chopped salted macadamia nuts
⅛ teaspoon red pepper flakes
⅛ teaspoon onion powder
⅛ teaspoon ground ginger
1½ pounds sea scallops
1 to 2 tablespoons olive oil

1. In a small bowl, combine the bread crumbs, macadamias, red pepper flakes, onion powder, and ginger. Set aside.

2. Spray the pie plate with nonstick cooking spray. Place the scallops in the dish in a single layer, leaving the middle of the pie plate open, and brush each scallop with some of the olive oil. Spoon the nut mixture over the tops of the scallops.

3. Loosely cover with plastic wrap. Microcook on MEDIUM (50 percent power) for 4 minutes, until the scallops are opaque and barely firm. Be careful not to overcook or the scallops will be rubbery. Let stand, covered, for 5 minutes. Serve immediately.

Pesto Shrimp Pasta

AT THE HOME OF ONE OF MY FRIENDS, the main dish for a company dinner was often some sort of pesto pasta mounded onto a platter for easy serving. The rustic pile of spaghetti or linguine was so impressive looking and oh-so-delicious to dive into. This recipe for pesto pasta with shrimp comes from a 1980s copy of *Sunset* magazine. I was given a photocopy of the recipe by a friend, who said, "Make this for sure right away; it's fantastic," but instead it got tucked away in my file of fish recipes. Well, it has emerged, and it is one of the most delicious pasta dishes you will ever taste, topped with garlicky shrimp. It is bound together with a flavorful nut-free, lemon-spiked basil pesto. ● *Serves 2*

MICROWAVE COOKWARE: 9-inch square or 11 × 7-inch Pyrex baking dish
MICROWAVE WATTAGE: 1,100 to 1,300
MICROWAVE COOK TIME: About 4 minutes
STANDING TIME: 2 minutes

LEMON PESTO:
1 clove garlic, cut into 3 pieces
1 cup loosely packed fresh basil leaves
⅓ cup freshly grated Parmigiano-Reggiano cheese
3 tablespoons freshly squeezed lemon juice
3 tablespoons olive oil

10 ounces fresh linguine

GARLIC SHRIMP:
3 cloves garlic, crushed
1 tablespoon olive oil
2 tablespoons unsalted butter, cut into pieces
12 ounces medium-size shrimp, shelled and deveined

FOR SERVING:
2 tablespoons olive oil
½ lemon

1. Place a large saucepan filled with water and a pinch of salt on the stovetop and bring to a boil.

2. Make the Lemon Pesto. Toss the garlic clove into the work bowl of a food processor, and pulse to finely chop. Add the basil leaves, cheese, lemon juice, and olive oil; process until the mixture is a thick paste flecked with bits of basil. Set aside. (You may store the pesto in the refrigerator with a bit of olive oil poured over the top to preserve the color for up to 2 days, or freeze in a pint-size zipper-top plastic freezer bag for up to 1 month.)

3. Add the linguine to the boiling water and cook until *al dente*.

4. While the pasta is cooking, make the Garlic Shrimp. Put the garlic in the baking dish; add the olive oil and butter. Microcook on HIGH, uncovered, for 40 to 70 seconds, until the garlic is soft and the butter is melted.

5. Add the shrimp to the baking dish and stir to coat it with the garlic butter. Microcook on HIGH, uncovered, until all the shrimp are pink, $2\frac{1}{2}$ to 3 minutes, stirring every minute to bring the cooked shrimp from around the outer edges of the dish into the center for even cooking.

6. Stir the pesto into the shrimp mixture, cover with plastic wrap, and let stand for 2 minutes.

7. Drain the pasta well and toss with 2 tablespoons olive oil. Mound the pasta on a small rimmed platter. Spoon the cooked shrimp and pesto over the pasta. Toss to coat the strands of pasta with the pesto and distribute the shrimp. With a handheld grater or Microplane, grate some lemon zest over the top. Serve immediately.

Steamed Shrimp with
Not Your Mother's Cocktail Sauce

UNLESS YOU LIVE ON THE GULF COAST, in Baja California, or in Florida, the shrimp you find in your local market will be frozen, then thawed for display. If you like to eat shrimp on a regular basis or are having a large party, buy frozen shrimp in bags. Cook thawed shrimp within 24 hours and never refreeze thawed raw shrimp. To defrost shrimp, place them in a colander over a bowl in the coldest part of the refrigerator overnight. You can start peeling them when they are still semi-frozen. A little tool called a shrimper can help you; you just hold the shrimp by the tail and insert the shrimper under the shell on the headless end. Push it down the shrimp and then use your fingers to remove the shell. I prefer to leave the tails on, but you can remove them if you like. This shrimp is an appetizer favorite made simple, or a simple dinner made fabulous with steamed rice and a salad. ○ *Serves 2*

MICROWAVE COOKWARE: 9-inch Pyrex pie plate
MICROWAVE WATTAGE: 1,100 to 1,300
MICROWAVE COOK TIME: 3 to 4 minutes
STANDING TIME: 2 minutes

NOT YOUR MOTHER'S COCKTAIL SAUCE:
1 cup mayonnaise
6 tablespoons ketchup
2 tablespoons plus 2 teaspoons Grand Marnier

1 dozen large shrimp, shelled and deveined
Juice of ½ lemon

1. To make the sauce, in a small bowl, stir together the mayonnaise, ketchup, and Grand Marnier. Cover and refrigerate until serving time.

2. In the pie plate, arrange the shrimp around the edge with the tails pointing in toward the center. Drizzle with the lemon juice. Partially cover with plastic wrap.

Microcook on HIGH for 2 minutes, until the shrimp are pink and firm. Microcook on MEDIUM (50 percent power) for another 1 to 2 minutes. Remove from the oven just as each shrimp begins to curl. Allow to stand for 2 minutes to finish cooking. Drain off any accumulated liquid. Serve hot or transfer to a covered container and chill for 4 hours or overnight.

3. Serve the warm or chilled shrimp with the cocktail sauce in small individual bowls for dipping.

VARIATION

Alaska King Crab Legs with Not Your Mother's Cocktail Sauce

Serves 2 to 4

MICROWAVE COOKWARE: 10- to 12-inch Pyrex pie plate or microwave-safe platter
MICROWAVE WATTAGE: 1,100 to 1,300
MICROWAVE COOK TIME: 2 minutes
STANDING TIME: 3 minutes

4 frozen King crab legs (3 to 4 pounds), thawed and rinsed
1 recipe Not Your Mother's Cocktail Sauce (opposite page)

1. With a chef's knife on a cutting board, cut each crab leg into 4 to 6 chunks, or bend the crab leg at the "knees" into a V shape and place in the pie plate (I sometimes cook them directly on the 12-inch-diameter glass turntable) in a spoke pattern. Partially cover with plastic wrap.

2. Microcook on HIGH for 2 minutes, until the flesh is opaque. Let stand for 3 minutes. Divide the cocktail sauce equally between small shallow dishes for dipping and place on dinner plates. Divide the crab legs between the plates and let diners pick out the meat.

Chicken Curry for One

CHICKEN CURRY, with its warm bouquet of spices, is one of the dishes in Indian cuisine that has spread around the world. A curry can be mild, as it is here, or as spicy as you like it. You can conveniently use your favorite curry powder or use this combination of spices that make up the base of most commercial curry powders. Serve with some sliced fresh tomatoes, some nice chutney, and lime wedges. It's good served over steamed basmati rice. ○ *Serves 1*

MICROWAVE COOKWARE: 1-quart Pyrex casserole dish
MICROWAVE WATTAGE: 1,100 to 1,300
MICROWAVE COOK TIME: 6 ½ to 7 ½ minutes
STANDING TIME: None

1 thick slice onion, coarsely chopped
2 tablespoons light olive oil
2 thin slices peeled fresh ginger, finely chopped
¼ teaspoon curry powder of your choice, or a small pinch each of ground cumin,
    ground coriander, ground fenugreek, and black mustard seed
Pinch of chile powder or dried chile flakes, to taste
1½ teaspoons cornstarch
2 tablespoons Greek-style yogurt or other thick plain yogurt, plus more for serving
8 to 9 ounces boneless, skinless chicken breast or thigh, cut into strips
¼ cup thawed frozen petite peas
1 tablespoon golden raisins
Chopped fresh cilantro leaves for garnish

1. Put the onion in the casserole dish with the oil and toss them together. Microcook on HIGH, uncovered, for 1 minute to soften the onion, then add the ginger.

2. Microcook on HIGH for 1 minute more. Sprinkle the curry powder and chile powder over the onion and cook for another 30 seconds.

3. Sprinkle the cornstarch over the spice mixture, then stir in the yogurt until combined with the spices and cornstarch. Add the chicken.

4. Microcook on HIGH for 4 to 5 minutes, stirring at 1-minute intervals. Halfway through cooking, stir in the peas and raisins. Serve immediately topped with extra yogurt and garnished with cilantro.

Parchment-Wrapped Chicken

HERE'S A FAMILY RECIPE from Carolyn Jung, my editor when I wrote for the *San Jose Mercury News*. It was the house specialty of her father, Bob Jung, and here she has adapted his recipe for the microwave. Originally wrapped in foil and baked, the dish is considered a mystery since the filling is hidden from view until unwrapped. Many people partially freeze the chicken breast for easier slicing into bite-size pieces. Consider using homemade hoisin sauce (page 237) as an alternative to the stronger commercial product. Of course the secret of this dish is in the marinade, which caramelizes and thickens around the chicken. Serve as an appetizer or as a main dish with rice and salad. Guests can open the packets with their fingers, and eat the morsels with chopsticks, a fork, or their fingers. How many packets can one consume? Carolyn says she eats 8 to 10 herself for dinner. Be sure to serve this with plenty of napkins. **o** *Serves 4 to 5*

MICROWAVE COOKWARE: 2- or 3-quart Pyrex casserole dish with lid
MICROWAVE WATTAGE: 1,100 to 1,300
MICROWAVE COOK TIME: 5 to 6 minutes per batch (recipe makes 3 or 4 batches)
STANDING TIME: None

2 pounds boneless, skinless chicken (breast or thigh), cut into bite-size pieces
3 cloves garlic, minced
Three 1-inch chunks fresh ginger, pressed through a garlic press
½ cup plus 3 tablespoons hoisin sauce, homemade (page 237) or store-bought
6 tablespoons ketchup
5 tablespoons light soy sauce
Pinch of sugar
Dash of Asian sesame oil

1. In a medium-size bowl, combine all of the ingredients. Stir well, cover, and let marinate in the refrigerator for 2 to 3 hours.

2. From a roll of parchment paper, cut about 40 squares, each measuring 6 inches square.

3. Place a heaping teaspoon or so of the chicken mixture in the middle of one parchment square. Fold in half diagonally to create a triangle. Fold the edges of each open side of the triangle over three times to seal well. Flip back each bottom corner. You will have a little rectangle. Repeat until all the chicken is wrapped.

4. You will have to cook the parchment packages in 3 to 4 batches in the microwave. Place them two deep in the casserole dish, and cover with the lid. You can just stack the packets; they do not need to be arranged in any special way. Microcook on HIGH for 3 minutes. Shake the casserole dish to redistribute the packages.

5. Microcook, covered, on HIGH for another 2 to 3 minutes. Open one of the chicken packages to determine if the chicken is thoroughly cooked. If not, microwave in 10-second increments until the chicken is no longer pink inside. Repeat with the remaining batches of parchment packages.

6. Serve the chicken packets on a large platter. Everyone can help themselves; open each bundle by undoing the folded edges.

Chicken Breasts Diane

N THIS CLASSIC DISH that is a restaurant favorite, a luscious sauce of lemon juice, Dijon mustard, and scallions gets poured over pounded chicken breasts. The name Diane in the recipe title signifies that mustard is an ingredient. You can serve this dish with fettuccine, wild rice, or couscous. ○ *Serves 4*

MICROWAVE COOKWARE: 11 × 7-inch Pyrex casserole dish or
 oval microwave-safe ceramic baking dish; 2-cup Pyrex measuring cup
MICROWAVE WATTAGE: 1,100 to 1,300
MICROWAVE COOK TIME: 6 to 7 minutes for the chicken, 2 minutes for the sauce
STANDING TIME: 1 minute

4 boneless, skinless chicken breast halves (about 1¼ pounds total)
½ teaspoon salt
¼ teaspoon freshly ground black or white pepper
3 tablespoons unsalted butter
2 tablespoons olive oil
Juice of 1 lemon (about 2 tablespoons)
2 tablespoons brandy
2 teaspoons Dijon-style mustard
1 tablespoon finely chopped scallion
2 tablespoons chopped fresh Italian parsley
¼ cup low-sodium chicken broth
1 to 2 drops hot red pepper sauce of your choice (optional)

1. Place the chicken breasts in a gallon-size zipper-top plastic freezer bag and pound with the flat side of a meat mallet to flatten slightly. Sprinkle with the salt and pepper.

2. Place 2 tablespoons of the butter in the casserole dish. Microcook on HIGH, uncovered, for 30 to 50 seconds, to melt. Add the oil. Place the chicken breasts in the casserole dish side by side, turning to coat with the butter-oil mixture on all sides.

3. Microcook on HIGH for 3 minutes. Let rest for 1 minute. Turn the chicken over and microcook on HIGH for another 2 to 3 minutes, depending on the thickness of the chicken, until it is no longer pink in the center but still moist. Be careful not to overcook; cover with aluminum foil to keep warm and set aside while making the sauce.

4. In the measuring cup, mix together the lemon juice, brandy, Dijon mustard, scallion, and parsley. Microcook on HIGH for 1 minute. Add the juices from the cooked chicken in the baking dish and the chicken broth; stir until smooth. Add the remaining 1 tablespoon butter and the hot sauce, if you are using it. Microcook on HIGH for 1 minute more.

5. Place a chicken breast on each of 4 serving plates, drizzle the sauce over the chicken, and serve immediately.

Mini Meatloaves

EVERY COOK NEEDS AT LEAST ONE meatloaf recipe in their repertoire. This one is quick and easy to make any night of the week; cooking time is reduced by forming the meat into individual loaves, and the microwave cooks them in just a few minutes. I cook the loaves in round or oval glass custard cups, which are easy to find in the equipment section of any supermarket or in hardware stores; you will end up using them for all sorts of microwave cooking. I give you two different flavor options for the meatloaves: You can add a tangy ketchup glaze during cooking and serve the loaves right in their cups, or you can turn them out of the molds and serve with a luscious mushroom sauce. Cooking for one? Save the second meatloaf for a cold sandwich the next day. ○ *Serves 2*

MICROWAVE COOKWARE: Two 8-ounce Pyrex custard cups or
microwave-safe ceramic soufflé dishes; 1-quart Pyrex measuring cup (optional)
MICROWAVE WATTAGE: 1,100 to 1,300
MICROWAVE COOK TIME: About 4 minutes for the meatloaves;
3 to 5 minutes for the mushroom sauce
STANDING TIME: 5 to 10 minutes

1 pound ground dark-meat turkey or ground beef, or a combination
½ cup quick-cooking rolled oats
⅓ cup milk or plain yogurt
¼ cup finely chopped onion
2 tablespoons finely chopped fresh flat-leaf parsley
½ teaspoon salt
A few grinds of black pepper or a few dashes of hot pepper sauce

BROWN SUGAR–KETCHUP GLAZE:
¼ cup ketchup
2 tablespoons light or dark brown sugar
2 teaspoons cider vinegar

QUICK CREAMY MUSHROOM SAUCE:
One 13.75-ounce can condensed golden mushroom soup
½ cup milk
1 cup sour cream

1. In a large mixing bowl, combine the ground meat, oats, milk, onion, parsley, salt, and pepper. Using your hands, mix all of the ingredients together thoroughly. Divide the mixture in half and shape each portion into a slightly oval ball.

2. Coat the custard cups with nonstick cooking spray. Press each ball of meat firmly into the mold, letting it mound nice and high.

3. If using the glaze, stir together the ketchup, sugar, and vinegar in a small bowl. Top each individual meatloaf with some of the glaze, spreading it over the meat like icing. Arrange the molds on the turntable in the microwave with a few inches in between them.

4. Microcook the meatloaves on HIGH, uncovered, for about 4 minutes, until the meat is thoroughly cooked and no longer pink in the middle. Do not overcook, as it will toughen up; you want your meatloaf to be a bit juicy. An instant-read cooking thermometer should read 170°F.

5. Remove from the oven. Let stand for 5 to 10 minutes before serving.

6. If making the mushroom sauce, whisk together the soup and milk in the measuring cup. Partially cover and microcook on HIGH for 2 to 3 minutes, until heated through. Whisk in the sour cream. Microcook on HIGH for another 1 to 2 minutes, until steaming hot. Serve immediately on the side with the meatloaves.

Savory Sauces

The microwave is revolutionary in its ability to make sauces. Once you find out how easy they are to make this way, you won't ever use the stovetop again. There is no constant stirring and no sticking to the bottom of the pan. And preparation time is short. In this chapter you will find the basic sauces for savory cooking (a few sweet sauces can be found in the desserts chapter). Some sauces are microcooked uncovered so that moisture can evaporate. Others are covered to cook faster, retain

their liquid, and avoid splattering. Transform meats, fish, pasta, and vegetables with these versatile savory sauces.

With the microwave, simmering a tomato sauce all day is a thing of the past. Even though the cook time is shorter in the microwave than on the stovetop, microcooked sauces still taste like they've been cooked for hours. When tomatoes are in season, make a few batches of my basic fresh tomato sauce, Plum Tomato and Vodka Puree (page 232). After it has cooled, ladle it into zipper-top plastic freezer bags in 1- or 2-cup portions, write the date on the bags, and lay the bags flat on the freezer floor or on a cookie sheet in a single layer until they harden. You'll have slim packages that are easy to store stacked, so they take up the least amount of space in your freezer. When you warm the defrosted sauce in the microwave, you can season it with crushed garlic or an herb that goes

with the dish you're making. If your sauce is to be served over pasta, start boiling the water 15 minutes before serving, while you are making or reheating the sauce.

I've also included in this chapter a Mexican salsa and a homemade barbecue sauce, which are microcooked in the same quick manner. And check out my recipe for microwave béchamel, or white sauce, which is one of the foundation sauces of French cookery. Here it's updated with yogurt instead of milk, and it complements lots of foods in addition to pasta.

Sauces thicken evenly when microcooked and require stirring an average of just two times (in the middle and at the end of cooking). Stir with a whisk during cooking, unless otherwise directed, to prevent lumps and distribute ingredients. Flour, cornstarch, arrowroot, and tapioca all work well as thickening agents in microwave sauces.

Rich and Creamy Cheese Sauce

DESPITE TODAY'S FOCUS ON EATING LESS FAT, people have a perennial love of a thick, creamy cheese sauce for pasta, to pour over vegetables such as broccoli, or to use in casseroles such as chicken divan. This luscious recipe, which uses creamy American Neufchâtel cheese to give texture to the sauce instead of the usual heavy cream, makes enough for 1 pound of pasta. If you have some soft goat cheese in the fridge, try replacing half of the cream cheese with goat cheese. Finish any dish that includes this sauce with a few grinds of fresh black pepper, but hold the salt since the Parmesan has plenty. ○ *Makes 3 cups*

MICROWAVE COOKWARE: 2-quart deep microwave-safe casserole dish or 2-quart Pyrex measuring cup
MICROWAVE WATTAGE: 1,100 to 1,300
MICROWAVE COOK TIME: About 4 minutes
STANDING TIME: None

1½ cups milk
One 8-ounce package Neufchâtel cheese, cut into pieces
¼ cup (½ stick) unsalted butter, cut into pieces
¾ cup freshly grated Parmesan, Parmesan-Romano blend, or Asiago cheese

1. Combine the milk, cream cheese, butter, and Parmesan in the casserole dish. Cover halfway with plastic wrap to cut down on splattering.

2. Microcook on HIGH for 2½ to 3 minutes, until simmering and the cheeses are melted. (If the ingredients were very cold, you may need to microcook for another 1 to 1½ minutes.) Remove from the oven and whisk until smooth.

3. Microcook on HIGH for 1 minute longer; whisk again. Use the sauce as an ingredient in a casserole or simply pour over the pasta of your choice. Use the sauce immediately, or cover and refrigerate for up to 1 day for later use. When ready to use, microcook on DEFROST or MEDIUM (50 percent power) for 2 minutes, until warmed.

Yogurt Béchamel

THE BÉCHAMEL, OR CLASSIC FRENCH WHITE SAUCE, is one of the staples of the creative kitchen. It is very simple: butter, flour, milk, and salt. You want to use a deep measuring cup for preparing this sauce in the microwave; if you use a shallow casserole dish, it will not work. Use a medium-size wire whisk, not a spoon, to eliminate lumps. Béchamel is by nature thick and creamy, and the addition of yogurt adds a dimension of flavor. Use this in the Eggplant Moussaka recipe that follows, as well as in macaroni and cheese, lasagna, and creamed chicken, or as a sauce for open-face sandwiches, fish, or grilled chicken.

o *Makes about 1⅔ cups*

MICROWAVE COOKWARE: 2-quart Pyrex measuring cup
MICROWAVE WATTAGE: 1,100 to 1,300
MICROWAVE COOK TIME: 5 to 5½ minutes
STANDING TIME: None

3 tablespoons unsalted butter
3 tablespoons all-purpose flour or potato flour
1 cup plain yogurt, stirred until smooth
⅓ cup milk
⅓ cup low-sodium chicken broth
¼ teaspoon salt, or to taste
Pinch of freshly ground nutmeg
Pinch of freshly ground white pepper

1. Place the butter in the measuring cup. Microcook on HIGH, uncovered, for 1½ minutes, until foaming and very hot. Do not let it brown. Remove from the oven and whisk in the flour. This technique is called making a roux blanc.

2. Microcook on HIGH for 1 minute, until foamy and bubbling. It is important to cook the flour so that it will thicken the sauce properly without a strong flour taste. Remove from the oven and whisk in the yogurt, milk, and chicken broth.

3. Microcook on HIGH, uncovered, for 1½ to 2 minutes, until very hot. Remove from the oven and whisk until smooth.

4. Microcook on HIGH for 1 minute more, until thickened. Remove from the oven and whisk in the salt, nutmeg, and pepper. Use the sauce immediately, or cool and refrigerate in a covered container for up to 5 days. When ready to use, microcook on DEFROST or MEDIUM (50 percent power) for 2 minutes, until warmed.

VARIATIONS

Mustard Sauce: Omit the nutmeg. Whisk in 2 tablespoons Dijon mustard in step 4 with the salt. Microcook for 1 minute more. Serve on the side with pork tenderloin or a firm fish such as halibut.

Cheese Sauce: Add 1 cup shredded cheddar or Italian fontina, or 3 ounces soft Montrachet goat cheese, in step 4 with the salt. Microcook for 1 minute to melt the cheese. Stir in a few splashes of your favorite hot pepper sauce. Use over broccoli or a medium-size pasta like penne.

Mornay Sauce: Whisk in ⅔ cup freshly grated Parmesan cheese in step 4 and omit the salt. Microcook for 1 minute to melt the cheese. Use on poached eggs, potatoes, or fish.

Newburg Sauce: Whisk in ¼ cup dry sherry in place of the broth in step 2. Whisk in ½ teaspoon paprika and 2 teaspoons freshly grated Parmesan cheese with the salt in step 4. Use this with poached or stuffed fish.

Basil Cream Sauce: Omit the nutmeg, and whisk in 1 to 2 tablespoons basil pesto sauce in step 4 with the salt. This is great with tortellini.

Eggplant Moussaka

JUST OVER THE IONIAN AND ADRIATIC SEAS from Greece is Italy. So there has been a lot of culinary cross-pollination in that region from time immemorial. Moussaka, here a vegetarian version, is the Greek version of lasagna, replacing the noodles with layered slices of vegetables and the heavy cheese with a luscious yogurt-based white sauce. But moussaka can be made with a variety of vegetables besides eggplant. There are also versions with layered potatoes, artichokes, or zucchini. ○ *Serves 4 to 6*

MICROWAVE COOKWARE: 9-inch square Pyrex baking dish or
   1½-quart microwave-safe oval ceramic baking dish
MICROWAVE WATTAGE: 1,100 to 1,300
MICROWAVE COOK TIME: 12 minutes for the eggplant,
   8 minutes for the casserole
STANDING TIME: 15 minutes

1 medium-size eggplant (14 to 16 ounces), unpeeled, trimmed,
   and cut crosswise into ¼-inch slices
1½ teaspoons salt
1⅓ cups Tomato-Basil Sauce (page 231), with a pinch of ground cinnamon
   and a pinch of allspice added
⅓ cup dried bread crumbs
1 recipe Yogurt Béchamel (page 226)
8 ounces whole-milk mozzarella, thinly sliced

1. Place one-third of the eggplant slices in an even layer in the baking dish and sprinkle with the salt. Cover with a paper towel and microcook on HIGH for 4 minutes. Remove from the oven. Rinse the eggplant slices with warm water and pat dry; set aside on a plate. Repeat with the remaining eggplant slices in 2 more batches.

2. Rinse and dry the baking dish. Place ⅓ cup of the tomato sauce over the bottom of the baking dish. Sprinkle with the bread crumbs. Arrange one-third of the eggplant in a slightly overlapping layer to cover the bottom of the dish. Spread with another ⅓ cup of the tomato sauce, then top with ½ cup of the béchamel and one-third of the mozzarella slices. Arrange another one-third of the eggplant in a slightly overlapping layer to cover the mozzarella, then top with ⅓ cup of the tomato sauce, ½ cup of the béchamel, and one-third of the mozzarella slices. Arrange the remaining one-third of the eggplant in a slightly overlapping layer to cover the mozzarella, then top with the remaining ⅓ cup tomato sauce and spread the remaining ⅔ cup béchamel over the top. Dot the top with the remaining mozzarella slices.

3. Partially cover with plastic wrap. Microcook on HIGH for about 8 minutes, until the casserole is bubbling. Remove from the oven. Let stand for 15 minutes before serving. Moussaka is traditionally eaten warm, not hot, and can also be eaten at room temperature. Like many Greek dishes, this is even better the next day. Reheat in the microwave on HIGH, partially covered with plastic wrap, for 1 to 2 minutes depending on the portion size.

Jacquie's Favorite Easy Cooked Salsa

THIS IS LIKE THE SALSA YOU GET IN JARS, only way more fresh tasting. My friend Jacquie Higuera McMahan swears by Dixon red chile powder (www.thechileshop.com) and keeps a spring-top jar of it on the counter, she uses it so much. This is a perfect salsa to use as a sauce for huevos rancheros, to poach eggs in, to add to shredded chicken or ground beef for taco filling, or to spice up chili or a stew. It's also great warm with tortilla chips. To seed a tomato, cut the tomato in half and squeeze gently, and the seeds will spill right out.

o *Makes about 1 quart*

MICROWAVE COOKWARE: 2-quart deep microwave-safe casserole dish or 2-quart Pyrex measuring cup
MICROWAVE WATTAGE: 1,100 to 1,300
MICROWAVE COOK TIME: 6 to 8 minutes
STANDING TIME: None

One 14.5-ounce can diced tomatoes (fire-roasted is okay), undrained
4 medium-size fresh tomatoes, seeded and diced
1 cup diced onion (red, white, or yellow)
2 cloves garlic, minced
1 to 2 jalapeño chiles, seeded and minced, depending on how hot you want your sauce
⅓ cup water
1 tablespoon apple cider vinegar
1 tablespoon New Mexican chile powder
½ teaspoon kosher salt, or to taste
½ teaspoon ground cumin

1. Combine all of the ingredients in the casserole dish.

2. Microcook on HIGH, partially covered with a lid or plastic wrap, for 6 to 8 minutes to bring to a boil and blend the flavors. Taste and adjust the seasonings, if necessary. Use immediately or cool to room temperature and store in the refrigerator for up to 1 week.

Tomato-Basil Sauce

A GOOD TOMATO-BASIL SAUCE is many cooks' all-purpose, go-to sauce. You can use one recipe of Plum Tomato and Vodka Puree (page 232) in place of the canned tomatoes if you like. If you are going to freeze the sauce, add the fresh basil after defrosting but before reheating. Serve this tossed with spaghetti or linguine. ○ *Makes about 3½ cups*

MICROWAVE COOKWARE: 2-quart Pyrex measuring cup
MICROWAVE WATTAGE: 1,100 to 1,300
MICROWAVE COOK TIME: About 6 minutes
STANDING TIME: None

⅓ **cup olive oil**
10 fresh basil leaves
Pinch of red pepper flakes
One 28-ounce can diced tomatoes, undrained
1 to 2 cloves garlic, crushed
¼ **teaspoon salt, or to taste**
A few grinds of black pepper, or to taste
1 tablespoon unsalted butter

1. Put the olive oil in the measuring cup and microcook on HIGH for 1 minute to heat. Add the basil leaves and pepper flakes. Microcook on HIGH for 10 seconds to wilt the basil.

2. Add the tomatoes with their juice and the garlic; blend using a handheld immersion blender until the tomatoes are finely chopped. Microcook on HIGH, uncovered, for 5 minutes to bring to a boil and thicken a bit.

3. Remove from the oven, add the salt and pepper, and stir in the butter until it melts into the sauce. Serve immediately. Or you can store the sauce in the refrigerator for up to 1 week.

Plum Tomato and Vodka Puree
(with Three Sauces)

I F YOU ARE UNFAMILIAR with what vodka does for tomato sauce, you are in for a treat. The alcohol evaporates and the dissolved compounds in the vodka add a particular flavor accent that is not the same as the elements contributed by water, sugar, or oil. Use this puree as a substitute for canned tomatoes in other recipes or make it into a number of light, fresh pasta sauces (recipes follow).

○ *Makes 3½ to 4 cups*

MICROWAVE COOKWARE: 3-quart Pyrex casserole dish with lid
MICROWAVE WATTAGE: 1,100 to 1,300
MICROWAVE COOK TIME: About 15 minutes
STANDING TIME: None

About 4 pounds ripe plum tomatoes (16 to 18), quartered lengthwise
3 tablespoons vodka

1. Pack as many of the tomatoes as can fit into the casserole dish, pressing with your hands or a large spoon to squash the tomatoes to release some of their juice. Cover and microcook on HIGH for 3 to 4 minutes, until more juice is released. With the back of a large spoon, press the tomatoes and gradually add in some of the remaining raw tomatoes. Cover and microcook on HIGH at 3-minute intervals until all the tomatoes are in the casserole dish. Cover and microcook on HIGH for 4 minutes, until the tomatoes are nice and soft.

2. Set a food mill over a large bowl. Remove the tomatoes from the oven. Working in batches, ladle the tomatoes and juice into a food mill. Pass through the food mill fitted with a medium disc to puree. Use a rubber spatula to lift out and discard the seeds and skin after pureeing each batch.

3. Return the puree to the casserole dish (no need to wash it out) and stir in the vodka. Microcook on HIGH, uncovered, for 4 to 5 minutes, to bring to a boil and thicken a bit. If the puree is too thin, microcook at 2-minute intervals until reduced to the desired thickness. Remove from the oven. Skim off any foam, if necessary, and cool completely. Refrigerate for several hours to chill.

4. You can store the puree, tightly covered, in the refrigerator for up to 3 days. You can freeze the puree in 1-cup covered containers for up to 6 months. Defrost overnight in the refrigerator or microcook on DEFROST for 4 minutes. Proceed to make your favorite sauce (see below).

Fresh Plum Tomato Butter Sauce

Makes 2 cups

2 cups Plum Tomato and Vodka Puree
1 teaspoon salt, or to taste
2 tablespoons unsalted butter

1. Place the tomato puree and salt in a 1-quart Pyrex measuring cup.

2. Microcook on HIGH for 3 to 4 minutes, until steaming hot. Do not boil. Stir in the butter.

Tomato Cream Sauce

Makes 2½ cups

2 cups Plum Tomato and Vodka Puree
½ cup heavy cream or crème fraîche
1 teaspoon salt, or to taste

1. Place the tomato puree, cream, and salt in a 1-quart Pyrex measuring cup.

2. Microcook on HIGH for 3 to 4 minutes, until steaming hot. Do not boil. Whisk until combined.

Chunky Fresh Tomato Sauce

Makes about 2½ cups

2 tablespoons olive oil

1 small shallot or 2 cloves garlic, minced

2 tablespoons chopped celery

2 tablespoons chopped carrot

2 tablespoons chopped fresh fennel

2 cups Plum Tomato and Vodka Puree

1 plum tomato, seeded and chopped

1 tablespoon minced fresh Italian parsley

½ bay leaf

1 teaspoon salt, or to taste

Freshly ground black pepper to taste

1 tablespoon minced fresh basil

1. Place the oil, shallot, celery, carrot, and fennel in a 1½-quart Pyrex casserole dish. Cover and microcook on HIGH for 2 to 3 minutes, or until the vegetables are soft.

2. Add the tomato puree, chopped tomato, parsley, bay leaf, and salt. Microcook on HIGH for 3 to 4 minutes, until steaming hot. Do not boil. Discard the bay leaf. Season with pepper and stir in the basil.

Tomato Barbecue Sauce

ONE DAY YOU FIND OUT you don't have any barbecue sauce in the cupboard, yet you have a hankering for some barbecue chicken pronto. Here's a sauce you can make quickly in the microwave using a bit of this and that out of the fridge and pantry. Keep it on hand, as it can be stored for up to a month in the refrigerator. Then use it on Barbecue Chicken Thighs (page 236) for your quick fix. This is a great basic all-purpose barbecue sauce for use in grilling, on ribs or chicken, in baked beans, or for coating a meatloaf. If you like a smoky sauce, add ¼ teaspoon liquid smoke. ● *Makes about 1 ¾ cups*

MICROWAVE COOKWARE: 2-quart Pyrex measuring cup
MICROWAVE WATTAGE: 1,100 to 1,300
MICROWAVE COOK TIME: 4½ to 5 minutes
STANDING TIME: None

1 cup ketchup
⅓ cup packed brown sugar
¼ cup apple cider vinegar
3 tablespoons cold coffee or dry red wine
1 to 2 cloves garlic, crushed
1 tablespoon Worcestershire sauce
½ teaspoon smoked paprika
½ teaspoon chili powder
¼ teaspoon salt

1. Combine all of the ingredients in the measuring cup and stir well. Partially cover with plastic wrap.

2. Microcook on HIGH for 4½ to 5 minutes, until boiling and bubbly, stirring once halfway through cooking. At the end of the cook time, uncover and stir the sauce a few times. Use immediately, or cool, then transfer to a jar and store, covered, in the refrigerator for up to 1 month.

Barbecue Chicken Thighs

EVERYONE SHOULD KNOW HOW to make barbecue chicken in the microwave. It's instant dinner with all the fixings. Serve with coleslaw and steamed potatoes. ○ *Makes about 2 cups*

MICROWAVE COOKWARE: 11 × 7-inch shallow Pyrex baking dish or 10-inch Pyrex pie plate; 1-quart Pyrex measuring cup
MICROWAVE WATTAGE: 1,100 to 1,300
MICROWAVE COOK TIME: About 15 minutes
STANDING TIME: None

8 skinless, bone-in chicken thighs (about 3 pounds)
Salt and freshly ground black pepper to taste
¾ cup Tomato Barbecue Sauce (page 235) or store-bought barbecue sauce

1. Arrange the chicken in a single layer in the baking dish with the thick ends facing toward the outside of the dish. Sprinkle with some salt and pepper. Cover tightly with plastic wrap.

2. Microcook on HIGH for 12 to 15 minutes, turning the chicken over once with tongs at the 6-minute mark and lightly brushing with some of the barbecue sauce, until the chicken is cooked through and the juices flow clear when pierced with the tip of a knife. Drain off any chicken juices.

3. Place the remaining barbecue sauce in the measuring cup and microcook on HIGH for 2 minutes. Pour over or brush the chicken with a thick glaze of sauce. Serve immediately.

Hoisin Sauce

LOVE HOISIN SAUCE, but often commercial brands are salty and strong. With homemade hoisin, just as thick and sticky and oh so good, you can control the salt and flavor. Try it on the Hoisin Fish and Vegetables (page 238). It also can be used as an ingredient in stir-fries; as that secret touch in meatloaf, Asian marinades, or barbecue sauces; and as a glaze for chicken. This recipe originally appeared in a recipe book that accompanied new Kenmore microwave ovens years ago and was posted on RecipeZaar (www.recipezaar.com). I use the tomato paste that comes in a tube, which is convenient when you need a small amount, such as what is called for here. ○ *Makes about 2 cups*

MICROWAVE COOKWARE: 1-quart Pyrex measuring cup
MICROWAVE WATTAGE: 1,100 to 1,300
MICROWAVE COOK TIME: 3½ to 4 minutes
STANDING TIME: None

1 cup canned beef broth (not concentrated)
½ cup low-sodium soy sauce
⅓ cup dry sherry
2 tablespoons cornstarch
2 tablespoons light molasses
2 tablespoons tomato paste
1 to 2 cloves garlic, crushed
½ teaspoon ground ginger
Freshly ground black pepper to taste

1. Combine all of the ingredients in the measuring cup and stir well with a small whisk to dissolve the cornstarch. Partially cover with plastic wrap.

2. Microcook on HIGH for 3½ to 4 minutes, until bubbly and thickened. Uncover, stir a few times, and cool. You can store the sauce in an airtight container in the refrigerator for up to 2 weeks.

Hoisin Fish and Vegetables

THIS GREAT, SPLENDIDLY RESOURCEFUL RECIPE is terribly delicious. You get some thick fish fillets (whatever looks good at the market that day), cut them into wide strips, top with some fresh vegetables, and drizzle with hoisin sauce. In minutes you are feasting. ○ *Serves 2*

MICROWAVE COOKWARE: 2-quart Pyrex casserole dish
MICROWAVE WATTAGE: 1,100 to 1,300
MICROWAVE COOK TIME: 5 to 6 minutes
STANDING TIME: None

10 ounces salmon, halibut, swordfish, monkfish, or
    other firm fish fillets (1½ inches thick)
4 ounces fresh sugar snap peas
2 ounces fresh mushrooms of your choice, sliced
¼ cup coarsely shredded carrot
1 baby bok choy, root end trimmed and sliced lengthwise
3 scallions (white part and some of the green), sliced to make about ¼ cup
One 1-inch piece peeled fresh ginger, slivered
3 tablespoons hoisin sauce, homemade (page 237) or store-bought
1 tablespoon low-sodium soy sauce
1 tablespoon rice vinegar

1. Spray the casserole dish with nonstick cooking spray. Cut the fish into 1- to 1¼-inch-wide strips and place in the dish in a single layer. Sprinkle the sugar peas, mushrooms, carrot, bok choy, scallions, and ginger evenly over the fish; toss to combine.

2. Pour the hoisin sauce, soy sauce, and vinegar into a small bowl and stir to combine. Drizzle over the fish and vegetables. Cover the casserole dish with vented plastic wrap.

3. Microcook on HIGH until the fish is cooked through and the vegetables are crisp-tender, 5 to 6 minutes. Stop every 2 minutes to gently stir and reposition the fish so that the outside pieces are moved to the inside.

4. With an oversized spoon, portion the fish and vegetables onto 2 dinner plates and serve hot.

Whole Berry Cranberry Sauce

HERE IS A MICROWAVE VERSION of the from-scratch, classic recipe you see on the back of the cranberry bag (see also the flavor variations that follow). Note the use of less liquid than in stovetop preparation, since there is much less evaporation in the microwave. Peak season for fresh cranberries is September through December. Buy extra and freeze for use throughout the year. Frozen cranberries can be used in this sauce, but do not thaw them, and cook them for an additional 2 minutes. This is so easy to make that you can whip it up right before dinner.

o *Makes 2 cups*

MICROWAVE COOKWARE: 2-quart Pyrex measuring cup or 2-quart microwave-safe bowl
MICROWAVE WATTAGE: 1,100 to 1,300
MICROWAVE COOK TIME: About 5 minutes
STANDING TIME: None

One 12-ounce bag fresh cranberries, picked over, stemmed,
 and rinsed; or frozen cranberries
1 cup sugar
½ cup water

1. Combine all of the ingredients in the measuring cup. Partially cover with plastic wrap.

2. Microcook on HIGH for 2 minutes; stir.

3. Re-cover and microcook on HIGH for another 2 to 3 minutes, until the sugar dissolves, the cranberry skins burst, and the sauce thickens. Stir again. Pour into a serving bowl, cool, and serve, or cool, then transfer to a covered container and store in the refrigerator for up to 1 week. Serve at room temperature or chilled.

Juicy Cranberry Sauce: Substitute unsweetened pomegranate juice, grape juice, orange juice, tangerine juice, or cranberry juice for the water.

Rosmarie's Cranberry Sauce with Orange and Walnuts

Makes 2⅓ cups

1 recipe Whole Berry Cranberry Sauce
Grated zest of 1 orange
2 tablespoons orange liqueur
⅓ cup toasted chopped walnuts

After the final cook time in step 3 above, stir in the zest, liqueur, and walnuts. Transfer to a serving bowl or storage container and cool as directed.

Plum Chutney

THE IDEAL FRUIT CHUTNEY balances sweet, spicy, and savory all in one bite. The word *chutney* is from the Sanskrit meaning "to lick," and chutneys are an integral part of Indian cuisine. Soft fruits such as peaches, plums, and mangoes make some of the finest chutney. Plums are in the same family as apricots, cherries, and peaches, the stone fruits of the rose family. Plums are one of the most luscious of fruits to use in preserves of all types. It is difficult to find commercial plum products, so making chutney at home will give you a special product that is fresh and flavorful. Serve with chicken, fish, or any curried dish, or add to cheese sandwiches or cheese plates. This keeps for a full week in the refrigerator, or freeze it in 1-cup portions in zipper-top plastic freezer bags. ○ *Makes 3 cups*

MICROWAVE COOKWARE: 3-quart Pyrex or microwave-safe ceramic casserole dish
MICROWAVE WATTAGE: 1,100 to 1,300
MICROWAVE COOK TIME: 10 to 12 minutes
STANDING TIME: 10 minutes

½ medium-size red onion, coarsely chopped

2 medium-size shallots, sliced paper thin

¾ cup packed light brown sugar

¼ cup apple cider vinegar

1 tablespoon grated fresh ginger

8 ripe fresh plums, pitted and coarsely chopped or sliced (about 1½ pounds)

⅓ cup dried currants

2 teaspoons coarse Dijon mustard

½ teaspoon kosher salt

¼ teaspoon mustard seed

Pinch of ground cinnamon

1. In the casserole dish, combine the onion, shallots, brown sugar, vinegar, and ginger. Microcook, partially covered with plastic wrap, on HIGH for 3 minutes; stir until the sugar is dissolved.

2. Add the plums, currants, mustard, salt, mustard seed, and cinnamon. Stir to combine. Partially cover and microcook on HIGH for 7 to 9 minutes, stirring once, until the chutney is syrupy and the plums are tender. Remove from the oven. Stir occasionally for 10 minutes before ladling into storage jars, such as French glass confiture jars with plastic lids, jelly jars, or glass-topped jars with wire closures. Let stand until cool. You can store the chutney, covered, in the refrigerator for up to 1 week.

Hot and Cold Drinks

Some people love hot tea. Others splurge with hot chocolate. We offer lemonade and iced tea to guests. All of these drinks lend themselves to individual interpretation and umpteen variations.

You'll find quite a selection here, from favorite hot cocoas to milky green tea. While hot chocolate takes the lead in flavor and fashion, you can create other hot drinks from your pantry items once you get the hang of the easy technique for preparing them in the microwave. Most boxes of cocoa powder provide reliable microwave recipes, so the recipes presented here are for more adventurous variations on the theme.

Hot drinks warm you in the winter, but hot teas in particular can be enjoyed all year round as a restorative. Keep a stock of black and green teas to suit all your moods and needs. Included in this chapter is a made-from-scratch version of the popular milky chai blend that will amaze you with its flavor and ease of preparation. There's also a green tea latte, made with the exotic powdered Japanese green tea, that is a rather new invention but has become a current taste trend.

I also offer a microwave recipe for cold, old-fashioned, back-porch-style lemonade. Lemons are the most common of fruits in the citrus family, and I don't know what we would do without them. Homemade lemonade is, well, just plain fun. Tint it pink with grenadine, or add some fresh lime juice. I promise you will drain the glass.

Once you've tried these drinks, you will make them part of your repertoire, for their emphasis is on good ingredients, distinctive flavor, and easy preparation.

Mexican Breakfast Hot Chocolate

ONE OF THE TASTE SENSATIONS of modern cuisine is the combination of chocolate and chile powder. As it happens, chiles make a beautiful counterpoint to dark chocolate, accenting its natural flavors just like coffee or vanilla does. Ancho chile powder, a versatile spice made from ground dried red poblano chiles (the mild fresh green version is used for making chiles rellenos), goes beautifully with orange zest, almonds, and cloves to make a thick Mexican hot chocolate unlike any other. Look for almond milk in the section of the supermarket with the boxed soy milks. Serve with a breakfast burrito, quesadilla, muffin, or scone.

○ *Serves 2*

MICROWAVE COOKWARE: 1-quart Pyrex measuring cup
MICROWAVE WATTAGE: 1,100 to 1,300
MICROWAVE COOK TIME: About 4 minutes
STANDING TIME: None

2½ cups almond milk
1 whole clove
One 2- to 3-inch strip orange zest
4 tablespoons unsweetened cocoa powder
2 to 3 tablespoons sugar, to your taste
¼ to ½ teaspoon ancho chile powder, to your taste

1. Put the almond milk, clove, and strip of orange zest in the measuring cup. Microcook on HIGH for 2½ to 3 minutes, until just hot. Discard the clove and strip of zest.

2. Whisk in the cocoa powder, sugar, and ¼ teaspoon of the chile powder. Taste for sweetness and spiciness, adding more sugar or chile powder if desired. Microcook on HIGH for another 40 to 60 seconds. Do not boil. Stir, pour into mugs, and serve immediately.

Hot Chocolate with
Vanilla Whipped Cream for a Crowd

THIS FABULOUS RECIPE will make a hot chocolate similar to what you can get at Starbucks. Chocolate chips make for a lovely drinking chocolate without any fuss; you can use chopped chocolate bars as a substitute if you like. You can also use soy milk or rice milk instead of the regular dairy if you prefer. I like Cook's Cookie vanilla extract (www.cooksvanilla.com) for its light floral taste, which comes from Tahitian vanilla beans. Top this hot chocolate with a flourish with some homemade whipped cream, or just use some store-bought whipped topping, such as Cool Whip. You can halve this recipe and use a 2-quart measuring cup for easy pouring. Or, you can easily double this recipe and keep the double batch warm in a slow cooker. In a café, this would cost about seven bucks a cup! ○ *Serves 10*

MICROWAVE COOKWARE: 3-quart Pyrex casserole dish
MICROWAVE WATTAGE: 1,100 to 1,300
MICROWAVE COOK TIME: 6 to 9 minutes
STANDING TIME: None

VANILLA WHIPPED CREAM:
½ cup cold heavy cream
1 teaspoon confectioners' sugar
¼ teaspoon pure vanilla extract

HOT CHOCOLATE:
Two 12-ounce bags semisweet chocolate chips
5 cups whole milk
1 cup heavy cream
4½ teaspoons pure vanilla extract
Strips of orange zest, or 4½ teaspoons instant espresso powder (optional)

1. To make the whipped cream, put the cream, confectioners' sugar, and vanilla in a mixing bowl and beat with an electric mixer until soft peaks are formed. Refrigerate until ready to serve.

2. Place the chocolate chips in the casserole dish. Pour in the milk, cream, and vanilla. Add the orange zest or espresso powder, if you are using it, to flavor your chocolate.

3. Microcook on HIGH for 6 to 9 minutes, until the chocolate is melted, stopping and whisking once about halfway through the cook time to smooth the mixture. You want to see some steam, but do not let it boil. Continue to microcook on HIGH at 20-second intervals if necessary. Ladle into cups and top with some of the whipped cream. Serve very hot.

Foamy Hot Chocolate

For the ultimate foamy hot chocolate that is light and airy, froth it using a handheld immersion blender, if you do not have an espresso machine at home. You can froth a single serving of hot chocolate in a wide-mouth cup, or froth enough for a group in an oversized measuring cup or casserole dish. Holding the handle of the cup, tip the cup of chocolate while keeping the immersion wand just beneath the surface of the milk. Move the wand around as you build the chocolate foam, just as though you were making froth for a cappuccino. This takes at least a minute. Pour individual serving cups half full of liquid, and then spoon the chocolate foam on top of each cup.

Coconut Milk Hot Chocolate

THE FLAVOR COMBINATION of chocolate and coconut is a classic one. Coconut milk is an ingredient where the canned version is really an improvement on the homemade-from-scratch, crack-the-coconut version, since coconuts in the U.S. market cannot compare to those you can buy at an open-air market in the tropics. I'm mad for the canned organic coconut milk that lets the cream rise to the top, but you can use the low-fat variety if you must. Consider this a dessert. If you make it with half-and-half rather than milk, it will be really rich, like a mousse. **o** *Serves 6*

MICROWAVE COOKWARE: 1-quart and 2-quart Pyrex measuring cups
MICROWAVE WATTAGE: 1,100 to 1,300
MICROWAVE COOK TIME: About 7 minutes
STANDING TIME: None

About 3 cups canned coconut milk (not cream of coconut), shaken
5 to 6 tablespoons sugar, to your taste
3½ cups whole milk or half-and-half
18 ounces bittersweet chocolate chips

1. Combine the coconut milk and sugar in the 1-quart measuring cup; stir to dissolve the sugar. Microcook on HIGH for 3 to 3½ minutes, to heat until steaming; do not boil. Set aside.

2. Pour the milk into the 2-quart measuring cup and microcook on HIGH for about 4 minutes, or until scalding hot and steaming. Do not boil. Stir in the chocolate chips and let sit for a few minutes, until melted. Whisk until smooth.

3. Pour the hot chocolate into 6 small mugs and pour about ½ cup of the hot sweetened coconut milk on top. Serve immediately.

Hot Vanilla

MAKE NO BONES ABOUT IT: I love vanilla. I mean, I am passionate about vanilla. Vanilla ice cream, vanilla pound cake, vanilla tapioca pudding, vanilla yogurt. That aroma, that flavor. I'd take a bath in it if I could. Now we can all drink it before bed. Warm, fresh, whole milk is a most soothing, calming food, according to Ayurveda practice, and vanilla is a calming scent and flavor. Put the two together and you've got an instant, simple sleep aid that's the perfect alternative to cocoa, which can be more stimulating. Vanilla extract is the most readily available form of vanilla flavoring. Brands like McCormick-Schilling and Spice Islands (in most supermarkets), Nielsen-Massey (available through Williams-Sonoma and gourmet supermarkets), and Penzeys Spices (by online or mail order) are good choices. Bottles labeled just "vanilla extract" will have a blend of different types and grades of vanilla. Bottles from single-growing regions will be labeled from Bourbon-Madagascar, Mexico, or Tahiti. Cook's Cookie vanilla extract (www.cooksvanilla.com) is a blend of Tahitian and Bourbon, and has become my favorite vanilla for its light floral element. ○ *Serves 1*

MICROWAVE COOKWARE: 1-quart Pyrex measuring cup or large microwave-safe mug
MICROWAVE WATTAGE: 1,100 to 1,300
MICROWAVE COOK TIME: About 2 minutes
STANDING TIME: None

1 cup whole milk, soy milk, or rice milk
2 teaspoons sugar or honey, or to taste
1 teaspoon pure vanilla extract
Whipped cream or nondairy whipped topping (optional)

1. Place the milk in the measuring cup; stir in the sugar and vanilla.

2. Microcook on HIGH for $1\frac{1}{2}$ to $2\frac{1}{2}$ minutes, or until scalding hot. Do not boil. Stir before drinking. Top with whipped cream, if desired.

Amazing Chai for One

I F YOU LOVE CHAI, you will love this recipe. There is a fabulous book devoted to chai titled *Chai: The Spice Tea of India* by Diana Rosen (Storey Publishing, 1999), which has recipes along with an easy-to-read history of tea. The book contains a recipe for a simple at-home chai made with a spice concentrate you stir up and keep in the refrigerator. This is adapted from that recipe; I changed the spices slightly, which you can also do yourself to custom-mix the spice blend. It is positively addictive and tastes like one of the fancy commercial liquid chai mixes. Make sure to use fresh spices for the best flavor, or even get fancy and grind your own with a mortar and pestle. You can use any Indian or Ceylon black tea that you like. Since the spice concentrate you use for the chai makes enough for 10 cups, you can easily serve a crowd rather than just yourself. ○ *Serves 1*

MICROWAVE COOKWARE: 2-cup Pyrex measuring cup
MICROWAVE WATTAGE: 1,100 to 1,300
MICROWAVE COOK TIME: 2½ to 3 minutes
STANDING TIME: 1 to 2 minutes

SPICE CONCENTRATE:
One 14-ounce can evaporated milk
½ teaspoon ground cardamom
¼ teaspoon ground ginger
¼ teaspoon ground cloves
¼ teaspoon ground cinnamon
1 to 2 pinches finely ground black pepper

1½ cups water
1 Darjeeling or orange pekoe tea bag
Light brown sugar, Demerara sugar, turbinado sugar, or honey, to taste

1. Make the spice concentrate: Pour the can of milk into a 2-cup jar with a cover. Add all of the spices and stir well, until evenly combined with no little lumps. Cover and refrigerate. This chai spice concentrate mixture makes enough for about 10 cups of tea.

2. For each cup of tea, pour the water into the measuring cup. Microcook on HIGH for 2$\frac{1}{2}$ to 3 minutes to bring to a boil.

3. Pour the hot water into a mug and add the tea bag. Let steep for 1 to 2 minutes.

4. Remove and discard the tea bag. Add 2 to 3 tablespoons of the chai spice concentrate, to your taste. Stir and add sweetener as desired. Drink immediately.

Masala Chai

MASALA MEANS A MIXTURE OF SPICES, while *chai* is the word used in India for tea. Ergo, *masala chai* is a black tea with spices added to it. The British brought the tea ritual to Indian culture, and, just as they made Indian cuisine a staple of British eating, they took the Indian practice of adding spices to tea back home to England. The exact spices and proportions added may vary from cook to cook. While typically served hot with milk in India, many Americans enjoy masala chai iced. Either way, it's fantastic. ○ *Serves 4*

MICROWAVE COOKWARE: 2-quart Pyrex measuring cup
MICROWAVE WATTAGE: 1,100 to 1,300
MICROWAVE COOK TIME: 4 minutes
STANDING TIME: 4 minutes

2½ cups water
2 whole cloves
1 white cardamom pod, cracked
5 whole black peppercorns
One 1-inch cinnamon stick, broken
1½ cups half-and-half, milk, soy milk, or rice milk
4 Darjeeling or orange pekoe tea bags
2 fresh basil leaves
4 teaspoons sugar or honey, or to taste

1. Place the water, cloves, cardamom pod, peppercorns, and cinnamon in the measuring cup. Microcook on HIGH for 2 minutes. Let steep for 2 minutes.

2. Add the half-and-half, tea bags, basil leaves, and sugar. Microcook on HIGH for another 2 minutes.

3. Let stand for 2 minutes. Strain through a fine-mesh strainer into cups and serve.

Ginger Tea

SIMPLE AND DELICIOUS, and a favorite in southeast Asia and India, ginger tea can be served with or without milk and sugar, and it can be served hot or iced with a slice of lemon. Hot ginger tea is considered a good digestive aid.

o *Serves 4*

MICROWAVE COOKWARE: 2-quart Pyrex measuring cup
MICROWAVE WATTAGE: 1,100 to 1,300
MICROWAVE COOK TIME: About 6 minutes
STANDING TIME: 10 minutes

One 3-inch piece fresh ginger, peeled and sliced
2½ cups water
1½ cups milk or half-and-half
2 tablespoons light brown sugar, or to taste

1. Place the sliced ginger and water in the measuring cup. Partially cover and microcook on HIGH for 3½ to 4 minutes, to bring just to a simmer.

2. Remove from the oven. Let steep for about 10 minutes.

3. Add the milk and sugar, and microcook on HIGH for an additional 2 minutes. Pour through a fine-mesh strainer into cups and serve.

The Best Summertime Iced Tea

ICED TEA WAS FIRST SERVED at the St. Louis World's Fair in 1904. It has become second only to cola in popularity among cold drinks in the United States. Orange pekoe tea is not really a single-leaf tea like Darjeeling or Lapsang Souchong, but rather a grade of black tea blend that can be from any country, most probably Ceylon. "Orange" is a reference to the color of the leaf tips, and *pekoe* is the Chinese word for "leaf." Through brands like Lipton and Twinings, orange pekoe has become a house-hold name in tea. If you like iced tea, you will love this refreshing version with citrus juices and steeped fresh mint. You can use decaffeinated tea if you wish.

o *Makes 2 quarts*

MICROWAVE COOKWARE: 1- and 2-quart Pyrex measuring cups
MICROWAVE WATTAGE: 1,100 to 1,300
MICROWAVE COOK TIME: About 8 minutes
STANDING TIME: 30 minutes

8 cups water
8 orange pekoe tea bags
½ small bunch fresh mint
1 cup freshly squeezed orange juice
½ cup freshly squeezed lime juice

SUGAR SYRUP:
1 cup sugar
1 cup water
A few strips of orange zest and lime zest

1. Place the water in the 2-quart measuring cup. Microcook on HIGH for 5 to 6 minutes, to bring to a boil.

2. Place the tea bags and mint in a deep, heatproof bowl. Add the boiling water and let steep for 30 minutes.

3. Add the juices, stir, then pour through a strainer into a large serving pitcher. Discard the tea bags and mint. Cover the pitcher and refrigerate for at least 4 hours.

4. Make the sugar syrup: In the 1-quart measuring cup, combine the sugar and water. Add the zests. Microcook on HIGH for 2½ minutes, until the water is hot and the sugar is dissolved. Stir to completely dissolve the sugar. Discard the zests. Cool and transfer to a jar, cover, and refrigerate.

5. Serve the iced tea over ice cubes in a tall glass, with a small pitcher of sugar syrup on the side to sweeten as desired.

Green Tea Latte

STARBUCKS CAME UP WITH THE GREEN TEA LATTE as an alternative to coffee drinks. Powdered green tea, the real thing, hence became mainstream, which is great because green tea is great for your health and has tons of antioxidant power. The powdered Japanese teas sencha and matcha are used in Japanese tea ceremonies. There is a harmonious blend in sencha of fresh sweetness and slightly bitter-sharp flavor, from the tannins developed by growing it in full sunlight. Matcha is grown in the shade under reed screens and has a lower astringency, making it a dash easier to drink. Do not confuse the concentrated powders with the tea leaves or tea bags; powder is needed for this recipe. Never store green tea in a glass jar, as it begins to lose its flavor when exposed to natural or artificial lighting. Find powdered green tea in ethnic markets or online.

o *Serves 1*

MICROWAVE COOKWARE: Microwave-safe mug
MICROWAVE WATTAGE: 1,100 to 1,300
MICROWAVE COOK TIME: About 2 minutes
STANDING TIME: None

1 cup milk
¼ teaspoon sugar, or to taste
¼ teaspoon good-quality sencha or matcha green tea powder

Combine the milk, sugar, and green tea powder in the mug. Microcook on HIGH for 2 to 2½ minutes, until steaming hot and beginning to foam up but not boiling. Green tea tastes best at a slightly lower-than-boiling temperature, so stop microcooking as soon as you see the foaming begin. Drink immediately.

The Best Lemonade

THERE ARE NOT TOO MANY PEOPLE who will turn down a glass of home-made lemonade, which is a special treat these days. Even though today's supermarkets offer a wide variety of commercial lemonade products made from reconstituted lemon juice (as well as powdered versions), you will see that the taste can't come close to homemade. The pinch of salt, a technique borrowed from Indian cooking, is used to cut the natural bitterness of lemons. Heating the lemons in the microwave before juicing will give you a remarkable amount of juice if your lemons are very firm; you may need more lemons, if they are not juicy, to get the full cup of juice you need for the recipe. Half lemonade and half cold orange pekoe tea is one of my all-time favorite drinks, called an Arnold Palmer.

Makes about 2 quarts, serving 6 to 8

MICROWAVE COOKWARE: 2-quart Pyrex measuring cup
MICROWAVE WATTAGE: 1,100 to 1,300
MICROWAVE COOK TIME: 5 to 6 minutes, plus 3 to 4 minutes for the lemons
STANDING TIME: 1 hour to overnight

6 cups water
1 cup sugar
2 pinches fine sea salt
1 cup freshly squeezed lemon juice (from 6 to 8 lemons)

1. In a 2-quart measuring cup, combine the water and sugar; stir. Microcook on HIGH for 5 to 6 minutes, until the water is steaming hot and the sugar is dissolved. Stir to fully dissolve the sugar, then add the salt. Cool and refrigerate for at least 1 hour.

2. When ready to make the lemonade, roll the lemons very firmly between your hands on the counter, then poke several holes in each lemon with the tip of a knife. Place two at a time in the microwave and microcook on HIGH for 1 minute, pausing at the 30-second mark for a few seconds, and then restarting the oven for the final 30 seconds. Cut the lemons in half and juice them.

3. In a large pitcher, mix the chilled sugar water and lemon juice together. Add more water or sugar, if desired. Chill before serving, or serve immediately over ice.

(continued)

Pink Lemonade: *Grenadine* comes from the French word meaning "pomegranate," and grenadine is a popular nonalcoholic syrup. The lovely pinkish-red color tints anything you add it to. The characteristic flavor comes from a combination of pomegranate juice, cherry juice, and sugar. It provides the pink color in the "kiddie cocktail" drink known as a Shirley Temple. To make pink lemonade, add 1 to 2 tablespoons grenadine syrup, depending on how pink you want it, to the sugar water and lemon juice in step 3.

Lemon-Limeade: This is an excellent base for daiquiris, but on its own it makes the best of summertime thirst-quenchers for the wee folk. Increase the amount of sugar in the syrup to 1¼ cups. Substitute a combination of ¾ cup freshly squeezed lemon juice and ¾ cup freshly squeezed lime juice for the 1 cup lemon juice in step 3.

Sweet Treats

Sweets are the real comfort food. A beautiful dessert is a source of pride to the home cook, and to watch everyone eat it up is just the icing on the cake. While the microwave performs any number of tasks in dessert preparation, here I introduce you to some of the desserts the microwave handles best: puddings, custards, poached fruit, and bar cookies.

Puddings may be humble looking, depending on the serving bowl, but the ingredients are fresh and unadulterated. The result is a satisfying,

delicious dessert with that ever-so-smooth texture and 100 percent comfort appeal.

If you do not have time to whip up a pie, use the microwave to make a seasonal fruit crisp, the deep-dish pie without a bottom crust. But the simplest way to serve fruit, beyond serving it raw in a bowl, is by poaching. The best poached fruit is never mushy, but tastes refreshing and has a very straightforward visual appeal. Fruit can be poached with just a simple sugar syrup, or with an exotic ingredient added to tease the palate. Micro-Roasted Pears with Balsamic Raspberry Sauce (page 276) is sweet, tart, and hot all in one. Poached fruit can be made a few hours ahead of serving or a full day ahead and kept in its syrup in the refrigerator.

Bar cookies are the best cookies for microwave baking. In this chapter you'll find recipes for brownies (the ultimate bar cookie), butterscotch bars, and coconut shortbread. The unbaked dough is usually stiff and must be spread or patted into the pan. After baking, the bars should have a thin, delicate crust and a moist crumb.

Look to see if the cookies are done when set on the bottom and glossy on the surface. The tops may look moist just out of the oven, but a standing time will complete the baking process. Over-mixing produces a hard and crusty top; over-baking results in a dry and crumbly cookie.

How many cooks who love to bake have ventured to make candy? It's thought of as messy work with lots of cleanup. Enter the microwave, which makes perfect fudge, brittle, bark, and truffles. You will be amazed at the ease of making candy in the microwave.

Likewise, making delicious homemade jams requires only one special tool: the microwave oven. The microwave is excellent for small-batch jam making, 2 cups at a time, because the sugar will not easily scorch or boil over, as it tends to do on the stovetop. Just remember to stir as the recipe instructs so that the jam will not burn around the edges during the final stage of cooking. With the small amounts, you can forget about the time-consuming canning and sterilizing procedure. Just make the jam and keep it in the fridge or freezer. There isn't a lot of evaporation during cooking as with stovetop methods, so there are certain jams, citrus marmalade, and chutneys that will thicken to a spreadable consistency without any gelling. The best containers in which to microcook jams have tall straight sides, such as an oversized Pyrex measuring cup with a handle for easy gripping. The glass can take the high cooking temperatures of the boiling fruit. You want to use a container with about five times the capacity of the amount of raw ingredients for most efficient cooking. After cooking always remember to open any lid away from you to allow for the ultra-hot steam to escape and prevent burns.

Last but not least, the sweet sauces here are the crowning touch to ice cream and other desserts. Whether chocolate, butterscotch, or blueberry, these sauces are simple but special.

Double Chocolate Pudding with Jasmine Green Tea Whipped Cream

REMEMBER THE FIRST TIME I made a chocolate pudding from scratch and the amazement that I felt when I realized how very simple it was. Chocolate pudding is the quintessential childhood dessert that is also comfort food for adults. Though not made from a box, this extra-thick and smooth-on-the-tongue dark chocolate pudding is still instant when made in the microwave. The chocolate flavor of the pudding depends on the cocoa powder you use. Consider high-end brands like Guittard or Scharffen Berger, or else use good old Baker's or Hershey's. To vary the accent flavor of the pudding, substitute orange oil or almond extract for the vanilla. I especially like this recipe since it contains no eggs. If you want a nondairy pudding, substitute soy milk or rice milk for the milk. For an extra-special treat, be sure to make the green tea whipped cream, which really complements the chocolate. ◑ *Serves 4*

MICROWAVE COOKWARE: 1- or 2-quart Pyrex measuring cup,
2-cup Pyrex measuring cup
MICROWAVE WATTAGE: 1,100 to 1,300
MICROWAVE COOK TIME: About 4 minutes for the pudding,
about 3 minutes for the whipped cream
STANDING TIME: 2 to 4 hours for the pudding,
at least 1 hour for the whipped cream

½ cup sugar

2 tablespoons unsweetened cocoa powder

3 tablespoons cornstarch

Pinch of sea salt

2¾ cups whole milk or half-and-half

2 teaspoons pure vanilla extract

1¼ cups (8 ounces) semisweet or bittersweet chocolate chips

JASMINE GREEN TEA WHIPPED CREAM:

1 cup heavy whipping cream

2 teaspoons jasmine pearl green tea

2 tablespoons sugar

1. In the 1-quart measuring cup, use a medium-size wire whisk to stir together the sugar, cocoa powder, cornstarch, and salt. Whisk in the milk until smooth.

2. Microcook on HIGH, uncovered, for 4 minutes, stirring once with the whisk halfway through cooking, just until it comes to a low boil, then becomes thick and smooth. Whisk in the vanilla and chocolate chips until dissolved into the mixture. You can microcook on HIGH for another 30 seconds to melt if needed.

3. Pour the pudding into four individual soufflé dishes or small dessert bowls, or one large bowl. Let stand for 15 to 20 minutes to cool, and then serve soft and warm. Or if you like your pudding firm and chilled, tightly cover the dishes with plastic wrap and refrigerate for 2 to 4 hours.

4. To make the green tea whipped cream, place the whipping cream in the 2-cup measuring cup and microcook on HIGH, uncovered, until steaming hot, 2 to 3 minutes. Remove from the oven and stir in the green tea (you can use a mesh tea ball if you like). Cover loosely and let steep for 3 to 5 minutes. Taste the cream; if left too long, the cream will have a bitter edge. When the cream has the proper flavor to your palate, pour the cream through a fine-mesh strainer (if you did not use a tea ball), and chill for at least 1 hour and up to overnight. When ready to serve, pour the cream into a mixing bowl and add the sugar; whip with an electric mixer until soft peaks form. Serve immediately, or cover and chill for up to 1 hour until ready to use.

Butterscotch Pudding

BUTTERSCOTCH PUDDING is true comfort food, but getting that clean butterscotch flavor can be a challenge. Instead of brown sugar alone, which I find cloying, this recipe uses butterscotch chips and just a bit of sugar. I love the caramel, toffee-like flavor of butterscotch chips so much that I am always looking for ways to use them. This is adapted from an egg-free recipe by food writer and innovative baker Mani Niall. Serve it with graham crackers or crisp butter wafers on the side or pushed down into the pudding itself. **o** *Serves 4*

MICROWAVE COOKWARE: Two 1-quart Pyrex measuring cups or batter bowls
MICROWAVE WATTAGE: 1,100 to 1,300
MICROWAVE COOK TIME: About 5 minutes
STANDING TIME: 3 to 4 hours

1½ cups whole milk or soy milk
2 tablespoons dark brown sugar
2 tablespoons cornstarch
One 8-ounce package cream cheese or Neufchâtel cheese (do not use fat-free),
    cut into about a dozen chunks
1¼ cups butterscotch chips
1 teaspoon pure vanilla extract

1. Use a wire whisk to stir together the milk, sugar, and cornstarch in one of the measuring cups until smooth. Microcook on HIGH, uncovered, for 2 minutes, then remove from the oven and whisk vigorously. Microcook on HIGH in 30- to 45-second intervals for another 1½ to 2 minutes, whisking twice, until the mixture thickens to the consistency of a thin gravy or sauce.

2. Place the cream cheese in the other measuring cup. Microcook on HIGH, uncovered, for 30 seconds, then remove from the oven and mash with a fork. Add ¼ cup of the hot cornstarch mixture to the cream cheese, mash together, and microcook on HIGH for an additional 20 to 30 seconds. Whisk until smooth.

3. Add the hot cream cheese mixture to the remaining cornstarch mixture, scraping the sides of the measuring cup with a heatproof spatula, and whisk constantly until thick and smooth. Whisk in the butterscotch chips and vanilla; stir until the chips are melted. Microcook on HIGH for another 20 seconds if you need to melt the chips further.

4. Divide the pudding between four custard cups or small individual serving dishes. Refrigerate for 3 to 4 hours, until chilled and firmed up. If refrigerating overnight, cover the dishes with plastic wrap.

Sweet Crumb Crusts

Scoop one of the puddings in this chapter into a crumb crust, chill, and serve with whipped cream for an easy and refreshing hot-weather dessert. Cookie and graham-cracker crumb crusts come out beautifully when baked in the microwave, and you don't have to heat up the entire stove for just a few minutes of cooking. ❍ Makes one 9-inch crumb crust

5 tablespoons unsalted butter, cut into pieces
1½ cups crushed graham crackers, biscotti, vanilla wafer cookies, chocolate wafer cookies,
    gingersnaps, or zwieback
2 tablespoons sugar (omit if using wafer cookies)
¾ teaspoon ground cinnamon (optional)

Place the butter in a 9-inch Pyrex or microwave-safe ceramic pie plate. Microcook, uncovered, on HIGH for 30 to 45 seconds to melt the butter. Add the crumbs, sugar, and cinnamon, if you are using it. Stir the crumbs and butter together with a fork until clumpy, then use your fingers to press the mixture firmly into an even layer onto the sides and bottom of the pie plate. Set the pie plate on top of an inverted 9-inch Pyrex pie plate. Microcook on HIGH, uncovered, for 1½ to 2 minutes, until set. Do not overbake or the crust will burn. Cool on a heatproof surface to room temperature before adding a filling. The crust will become firm as it cools.

Soy Milk Rice Pudding
with Dried Cranberries

WANT SOME RICE PUDDING IMMEDIATELY? This delicious, quick, and easy-to-prepare recipe calls for leftover cooked rice, something most of us have in the refrigerator. You can use any long-grain rice—converted, white, basmati, Carolina, or brown. The pudding comes together so easily that you can make it right after dinner while you are doing the dishes and refrigerate it overnight for the next day. It is even better with soft, freshly made rice rather than refrigerated rice, but if your rice is cold, don't let that stop you. You can use vanilla rice milk instead of the soy if you like. ○ *Serves 4*

MICROWAVE COOKWARE: 2-quart Pyrex measuring cup or microwave-safe casserole dish
MICROWAVE WATTAGE: 1,100 to 1,300
MICROWAVE COOK TIME: 8 minutes
STANDING TIME: 5 minutes

1½ cups vanilla soy milk
3 large egg yolks
¼ cup sugar
3 tablespoons cornstarch
1½ teaspoons pure vanilla extract
2 cups cooked long-grain white or brown rice,
    warmed in the microwave for 2 minutes if cold
½ cup dried cranberries

1. In the measuring cup, whisk together the soy milk, egg yolks, sugar, cornstarch, and vanilla until well combined.

2. Microcook, uncovered, on HIGH for 8 minutes, stopping and stirring every 2 minutes to smooth the pudding with a whisk, until boiling and thickened.

3. Remove from the microwave and immediately stir in the rice and cranberries. Cover and let stand for 5 minutes before serving. Serve warm, or place in the refrigerator for at least 6 hours and serve chilled.

Raspberry Trifle with Cream Sherry

TRIFLE IS A QUINTESSENTIAL winter holiday dessert and positively addictive. My mother is known for her trifle, a cold dessert with layers of dense-textured plain cake soaked with cream sherry and a vanilla English custard, which she has made every Christmas for decades, ever since she got her first microwave. While many people make trifle using a package of Bird's custard mix because homemade custard is too time-consuming, here is a microwave recipe that will give you perfect custard in minutes. Be sure to check for doneness at the minimum time specified in the recipe, as seconds can make a difference here. Trifle is typically layered in a glass bowl so that from the side, its layers can be seen. The bowl should have a flat bottom and straight sides and not be too deep. Special trifle bowls often have a pedestal. You could also compose individual trifles in small footed glass bowls. ○ *Serves 8 to 10*

MICROWAVE COOKWARE: 2-quart Pyrex measuring cup
MICROWAVE WATTAGE: 1,100 to 1,300
MICROWAVE COOK TIME: 5 to 8 minutes
STANDING TIME: About 2 hours

½ cup sugar
½ teaspoon salt
2 tablespoons cornstarch
2½ cups cold whole milk
4 large egg yolks
2 teaspoons pure vanilla extract
1 pound cake (store-bought or homemade), cut into ½-inch slices and air-dried at room
  temperature for a few hours
½ cup cream sherry
2 cups fresh raspberries, or one 12-ounce package unsweetened frozen raspberries

FOR SERVING:
1 cup cold heavy cream
3 tablespoons sugar
½ cup coarsely broken amaretti cookies
½ cup toasted slivered almonds (page 26)

1. In the measuring cup, combine the sugar, salt, and cornstarch. Pour in the milk in a stream, whisking to prevent lumps. Microcook on MEDIUM (50 percent power), uncovered, for 4 to 6 minutes, stirring with a whisk every 1½ to 2 minutes, until very hot, smooth, thickened, and clear. Do not boil and do not try to rush the process.

2. Beat the egg yolks in a small bowl and quickly stir in a small amount of the hot custard. Pour the tempered egg yolks into the measuring cup, whisking continuously.

3. Microcook on MEDIUM, uncovered, for 1 to 2 minutes, stirring once after 30 seconds, until smooth and thick. The custard will have a soft center area about the size of a quarter; it will set upon standing. Remove from the oven and whisk in the vanilla. Whisk briskly to cool the custard down. Pour into a bowl; place plastic wrap directly on the surface of the custard (this will prevent a skin from forming) and refrigerate until cool, about 2 hours.

4. Cut the pound cake into 1¼-inch-thick fingers; use one-third of the cake fingers to line the bottom of a deep glass bowl, fitting the cake in a single layer so there are no large spaces. Drizzle with ¼ cup of the sherry and top with 1 cup of the berries. Repeat with a second layer of cake, sherry, and berries, and end with a layer of cake. Press down gently on the top of the layered ingredients.

5. Pour the cooled custard over the layers of cake and berries; it will soak into the cake and down the sides of the bowl. Cover and refrigerate until well chilled, 6 hours or up to overnight.

6. Before serving, whip the cream with the sugar until soft peaks form. Cover the top of the trifle with a thick layer of the whipped cream and sprinkle with the cookies and toasted almonds. Cover the dish with plastic wrap and refrigerate until serving, no longer than a few hours.

Egg-Free English Custard

Here is an eggless version of English custard to use in making trifle. Because there are no eggs, the mixture can boil and cook at a higher temperature. For a chocolate custard, add ½ cup unsweetened cocoa powder along with the cornstarch.

○ Makes about 3½ cups

MICROWAVE COOKWARE: 2-quart Pyrex measuring cup or batter bowl
MICROWAVE WATTAGE: 1,100 to 1,300
MICROWAVE COOK TIME: 6 to 8 minutes
STANDING TIME: About 2 hours

¾ **cup sugar**
¼ **cup cornstarch**
¼ **teaspoon salt**
3½ **cups cold whole milk**
4 teaspoons pure vanilla extract

1. In the measuring cup, combine the sugar, cornstarch, and salt. Pour in the milk in a stream, whisking to prevent lumps. Microcook on HIGH, uncovered, for 3 minutes, stirring with a whisk after 1½ minutes, until very hot. Stir again.

2. Microcook on HIGH, uncovered, for 3 to 5 minutes, stirring every 60 seconds, until boiling, smooth, and thickened. Remove from the microwave and whisk in the vanilla. Whisk briskly for 5 seconds. Pour the custard into a bowl; place plastic wrap directly on the surface of the custard (this will prevent a skin from forming) and refrigerate until cool, about 2 hours.

Lemon Panna Cotta

PANNA COTTA, WHICH TRANSLATES TO "COOKED CREAM," is a northern Italian dessert traditionally made by simmering together cream and sugar, then mixing with gelatin and letting it cool in individual custard cups until set. When chilled, you have a silky smooth eggless custard dessert that goes especially well with berries. There are a lot of variations on this theme. Buttermilk, whole milk, and/or sour cream may be substituted for some of the half-and-half. Here is a microwave version made with mascarpone cheese, yogurt, and lots of delectable lemon curd; the recipe is adapted from one in a Better Homes and Gardens recipe contest many years ago. Serve with the fresh strawberries moistened with balsamic vinegar as in the recipe, or with Sweet Blueberry Sauce (page 305). ● *Serves 8*

MICROWAVE COOKWARE: 2-cup Pyrex measuring cup
MICROWAVE WATTAGE: 1,100 to 1,300
MICROWAVE COOK TIME: 60 to 90 seconds
STANDING TIME: 4 to 24 hours in the refrigerator

1¼ cups half-and-half
1 envelope unflavored gelatin
Two 6-ounce cartons thick lemon yogurt (such as Yoplait Thick & Creamy)
One 10-ounce jar lemon curd
One 8-ounce carton mascarpone cheese

BALSAMIC STRAWBERRIES:
1 pint strawberries, hulled and thinly sliced
2 teaspoons sugar
4½ teaspoons balsamic vinegar

1. Coat eight 6-ounce round or oval Pyrex or ceramic custard cups with nonstick cooking spray. Set aside. Place ½ cup of the half-and-half in the measuring cup. Sprinkle with the gelatin and let stand for 5 minutes. Microcook on MEDIUM (50 percent power), uncovered, for 60 to 90 seconds, stirring every 30 seconds, until the gelatin is dissolved. Set aside.

2. In a medium-size mixing bowl, whisk together the yogurt, lemon curd, and mascarpone. Beat until smooth. Whisk in the remaining ¾ cup half-and-half until incorporated. Slowly pour in the gelatin mixture, whisking continuously.

3. Spoon the panna cotta cream in the prepared custard cups, filling each cup about three-quarters full. Place the filled cups on a small tray and cover with plastic wrap; chill for 4 to 24 hours, until firm.

4. Place the strawberries in a medium-size bowl. Sprinkle with the sugar, then drizzle with the balsamic vinegar; stir to coat the berries. Let stand for 30 minutes, tossing occasionally. If not using immediately, cover and refrigerate.

5. To serve, run a small rubber spatula around the inside edges of the custard cups. Place a shallow small bowl of warm water on the counter and dip each cup in the water for a few seconds. Gently invert each cup onto a plate to release the panna cotta. Spoon strawberries over and around the panna cotta and serve immediately.

Apple-Almond Crisp for One

MY BAKING MENTOR USED TO MAKE small individual apple crisps using one apple. Why hadn't I ever thought of that? While larger crisps take a while to cook and the topping can get gluey, an individual crisp has a topping that comes out of the oven soft but becomes crunchy after cooling. When I worked in a restaurant, we made an apple crisp every single day as one of the fruit dessert offerings. We would eat any leftovers warmed up for breakfast the next morning before our shift. Basically a crustless pie with a buttery crumb topping, apple crisp is a quick-to-prepare, homey fruit dessert that can switch right over and dress up for company. Some people make their crisps with unpeeled apples, but I always peel them. Use firm, tart baking apples for the best crisp. This recipe features a thick crumble topping; you can use half the amount if you prefer a lighter topping. I usually make my apple crisp in a soufflé dish, but you could also use a microwave-safe coffee cup or even a French onion soup bowl, which usually has a capacity of 8 ounces. Serve this yummy dessert with whipped cream, ice cream, or a dollop of plain thick yogurt. ❍ *Serves 1*

MICROWAVE COOKWARE: 4-inch diameter, 1½-inch deep individual round soufflé dish
MICROWAVE WATTAGE: 1,100 to 1,300
MICROWAVE COOK TIME: 4 to 4½ minutes
STANDING TIME: 10 minutes

¼ cup packed light brown sugar
3 tablespoons all-purpose flour, whole-wheat pastry flour, or
    gluten-free flour blend (such as Bob's Red Mill brand)
⅛ teaspoon ground cinnamon
2 tablespoons cold unsalted butter, cut into pieces
1 tablespoon slivered almonds, chopped or left whole
1 large tart cooking apple, peeled or unpeeled as desired, cored and
    sliced ¼ inch thick (about 1 cup sliced apple)
1 tablespoon water or apple juice

1. Place the sugar, flour, and cinnamon in a small bowl. Cut in the butter pieces with your fingers or a fork or pulse in a mini food processor until the mixture just holds together and looks crumbly. Toss in the nuts. Set aside or refrigerate in a tightly covered container. (The crumble topping can be made up to 1 day ahead. You can also double or triple the ingredients to make a larger batch of the topping, store it in the freezer in a pint-size zipper-top plastic freezer bag, and portion it out as you need it.)

2. Arrange the sliced apple in the soufflé dish, filling to the rim. Have the slices lay flat and fill any spaces on the side by pushing slices in. Add the water. Pile the topping on, covering the fruit.

3. Microcook on HIGH, uncovered, for 4 to 4½ minutes, until the apples are tender and can easily be pierced with the tip of a knife. If the apples are not soft, microcook on HIGH in 30-second intervals until cooked. Do not overcook or the nuts will burn.

4. Remove the crisp from the oven and allow to stand on a wire rack or folded kitchen towel for 10 minutes to cool slightly. The apples will collapse. Serve warm, at room temperature, or chilled.

VARIATION

To serve four people, multiply the topping ingredients by four (1 cup light brown sugar, ¾ cup flour, ½ teaspoon ground cinnamon, 1 stick cold unsalted butter, and ¼ cup slivered almonds). Use 4 large apples and place the sliced apples in an 8-inch square glass baking dish. Microcook on HIGH, uncovered, for 10 to 12 minutes, until tender.

Micro-Roasted Pears with Balsamic Raspberry Sauce

THIS IS ADAPTED FROM a lovely microwave recipe I found printed on the inside of an envelope from The Good Cook book club a few years ago. It is from the book *Wine, Food & Friends* by Karen MacNeil (Oxmoor House, 2006). Bosc pears, known more as a cooking pear than an eating pear, are very firm and hold their shape well while poaching. They weigh anywhere from 8 to 12 ounces; here we are using the 8-ounce size. This dish is equally delicious served warm or chilled. You need to make the sauce before micro-roasting the pears, so you may need to do it the day before you are serving the pears. ◦ *Serves 8*

MICROWAVE COOKWARE: 2-quart microwave-safe casserole dish or ceramic soufflé dish
MICROWAVE WATTAGE: 1,100 to 1,300
MICROWAVE COOK TIME: 8 minutes
STANDING TIME: None

Two 12-ounce bags frozen unsweetened raspberries
2 tablespoons sugar
2 teaspoons balsamic vinegar
⅛ teaspoon freshly ground black pepper
8 firm Bosc pears, peeled
2 tablespoons freshly squeezed lemon juice

1. Place the raspberries in a bowl and sprinkle with the sugar. Cover with plastic wrap and let stand for a few hours until thawed. Press the raspberries through a fine-mesh sieve set over a bowl; discard the seeds. Add the vinegar and pepper to the berries. Refrigerate, covered, until serving.

2. Peel the pears, keeping the stems intact, and rub with the lemon juice. You can core out the base by a few inches with a small knife, if you wish. Lay 4 of the pears on their sides in the casserole dish with the thick ends facing toward the outer edge of the dish. Cover with a lid or plastic wrap pierced a few times. Microcook on HIGH for 4 minutes, or until the pears are tender. Turn the pears over halfway through cooking. Immediately and gently remove them from the casserole dish with a slotted spoon (if you leave them in the hot dish, they will continue to cook) and place on individual dessert plates or on a large plate to chill in the refrigerator before serving. Repeat to cook the remaining 4 pears.

3. To serve, stand 1 pear on each dessert plate and drizzle 2 tablespoons of the raspberry sauce over the top of the pear, letting it drip down.

Chunky Stewed Rhubarb over Crystallized Ginger Ice Cream

THIS IS AN UNBELIEVABLY DELICIOUS poached summer fruit to make when fresh rhubarb is in season. Rhubarb is one of the fruits that gets the least attention. It has a pucker-y sour quality, so it needs plenty of sugar to taste good. It is a fibrous fruit, so it must be fully covered to cook properly. Remember that only the stalks should be eaten, as the leaves contain oxalic acid, which is toxic, and must be discarded. You will not believe how luscious and simple-to-make the ice cream is and how tasty the combination of the ginger and rhubarb is. The stewed rhubarb is also good served over rice pudding, pound cake, or cheesecake.

Serves 6

MICROWAVE COOKWARE: 2- or 3-quart Pyrex or microwave-safe ceramic casserole dish
MICROWAVE WATTAGE: 1,100 to 1,300
MICROWAVE COOK TIME: 7 minutes
STANDING TIME: 5 minutes, plus overnight to chill the stewed rhubarb

STEWED RHUBARB:
1½ pounds fresh rhubarb, trimmed of all leaves and bottom stalk cut off, washed, and sliced into ½-inch diagonal chunks
1 cup sugar
⅓ cup water or orange juice
2 teaspoons freshly squeezed lemon juice

CRYSTALLIZED GINGER ICE CREAM:
1 quart vanilla ice cream
⅓ cup finely chopped crystallized ginger

1. Place the rhubarb in the casserole dish. Toss with the sugar, then pour in the water and lemon juice.

2. Cover tightly and microcook on HIGH for 4 minutes; gently stir.

3. Re-cover and microcook on HIGH for another 3 minutes, until the rhubarb is tender but still holds its shape. Let stand, covered, for 5 minutes; gently stir. Let stand to come to room temperature, then refrigerate overnight, covered, to chill in its pink syrup. The rhubarb will keep for up to 5 days in the refrigerator.

4. Make the ice cream: Let the ice cream soften slightly at room temperature for 10 to 15 minutes. Transfer to a mixing bowl. With an electric mixer, beat on low speed until just creamy (do not let melt). Sprinkle in the crystallized ginger and mix on low speed until just evenly distributed. Working quickly, scrape the ice cream back into the carton with a large spatula. Refreeze for at least 6 hours.

5. To serve, scoop the ginger ice cream into chilled bowls and top with the stewed rhubarb and pink syrup.

Rich Microwave Brownies with Nuts

NOTHING BEATS BROWNIES, the bar cookie divine, made in a conventional oven. Or so you might have thought. These from-scratch brownies rival those produced by the time-honored oven-baking method, and you will probably be surprised by the moist and delicious results. They have ultra-rich chocolate flavor from plenty of unsweetened cocoa powder, which eliminates the extra step of melting bar chocolate. ○ *Makes one 8-inch brownie cake*

MICROWAVE COOKWARE: 8-inch round Pyrex, microwave-safe ceramic, or silicone cake pan

MICROWAVE WATTAGE: 1,100 to 1,300

MICROWAVE COOK TIME: 4 to 5 minutes

STANDING TIME: About 15 minutes

2 large eggs

1 cup sugar

½ cup (1 stick) unsalted butter, softened

2 teaspoons pure vanilla extract

1 teaspoon chocolate extract (optional)

1 cup all-purpose flour

½ cup unsweetened cocoa powder

½ teaspoon baking powder

¼ teaspoon salt

½ cup coarsely chopped walnuts

1. In the bowl of a food processor, combine the eggs, sugar, butter, and extracts until creamy, 30 seconds. Add the flour, cocoa, baking powder, and salt; pulse 10 times until mixed thoroughly and the batter is smooth.

2. Add the nuts and pulse a few times, just until mixed in.

3. If you are using a glass or ceramic cake pan, line it with parchment paper and coat with nonstick cooking spray. If using a silicone pan, coat it lightly with nonstick cooking spray. Scrape the batter into the pan and spread it evenly in the pan.

4. Microcook on HIGH for 4 to 5 minutes, until a cake tester inserted into the center comes out clean and the top of the cake is springy; do not overbake or the brownies will be dry. The few moist spots on top will dry as the brownies cool. Remove from the microwave and allow the brownies to cool completely in the pan on a wire rack, about 15 minutes.

5. Cut into 6 or 8 equal-size pie-shaped wedges and serve. You can store the brownies in the pan, covered, at room temperature or in the refrigerator for up to 4 days, or in the freezer for up to 1 month.

VARIATION

Rich Microwave Brownies with Chips: Omit the nuts. Stir 1 cup of your favorite chips (semisweet, milk chocolate, Guittard vanilla milk, peanut butter, butterscotch, or mint) into the batter in step 2. Proceed as directed.

Butterscotch Blondies

BROWNIES WITHOUT CHOCOLATE translate into blondies, the brownie for people who love caramel, butter-pecan flavor, and butterscotch. Blondies are so easy to prepare, they can be made well by both beginning and professional bakers. But I think that blondies are more versatile than brownies—you can serve them for brunch like a coffeecake or as an afternoon tea snack. If you like your blondies warmed, they are best reheated in a toaster oven to retain their firmness. If you reheat them in the microwave, do so for no more than 15 seconds or else they will soften too much. ● *Makes 12 to 16 bars*

MICROWAVE COOKWARE: 8-inch square Pyrex, microwave-safe ceramic, or silicone cake pan

MICROWAVE WATTAGE: 1,100 to 1,300

MICROWAVE COOK TIME: 4½ to 5 minutes

STANDING TIME: At least 20 minutes

¾ cup packed light brown sugar

6 tablespoons (¾ stick) unsalted butter, softened

1 large egg

1 tablespoon water

1½ teaspoons pure vanilla extract

1 cup all-purpose flour

1 teaspoon baking powder (I use Rumford aluminum-free)

Pinch of salt

1 cup butterscotch chips

½ cup chopped pecans

1. Coat the cake pan with nonstick cooking spray. You can line the bottom with parchment paper that overhangs the pan on two sides if you are superstitious (it always helps when removing blondies from the pan after cooling). If using the parchment paper, coat it with nonstick cooking spray.

2. In a bowl, use an electric mixer on medium speed to beat together the sugar, butter, egg, water, and vanilla until the mixture is smooth and light.

3. Combine the flour, baking powder, and salt in a bowl, and add the mixture by the spoonful to the butter mixture, with the mixer on low speed. Beat until just combined. With a spatula, stir in the butterscotch chips and nuts until just evenly distributed in the batter. The batter will be stiff; spread it in the pan with your fingers (dipped in water) or with a spatula. (I use both.)

4. Microcook on HIGH for $4\frac{1}{2}$ to 5 minutes, until a cake tester inserted in the center comes out clean. If moist crumbs are attached, microcook on HIGH for another minute and test again.

5. Remove from the oven and set on a wire rack. Cool for 20 minutes in the pan, then turn out the blondies by inverting the pan over a plate or cutting board; peel off the parchment paper if you used it. Or let the blondies cool in the pan and serve from there. Cut with a sharp knife into 12 medium-size or 16 small bars. You can store the blondies at room temperature or in the refrigerator in an airtight container for up to 5 days, or in the freezer for up to 2 months.

VARIATIONS

o   Substitute semisweet chocolate chips for the butterscotch chips.

o   Substitute $\frac{2}{3}$ cup white chocolate chips and $\frac{1}{4}$ cup coarsely chopped Heath Bar for the butterscotch chips.

Coconut-Macadamia Shortbread

BUTTER SHORTBREAD IS CONSIDERED the jewel in the crown of Scottish baking. It is famous in the baking world and has been part of the cooking of the British Isles for hundreds of years. It turns out to be one of the best dessert items to bake in the microwave, retaining its texture and pale color to perfection. The "short" in "shortbread" means a high percentage of butter to flour, which creates the fabulous melt-in-your-mouth crumbly texture. Use the very best butter you can find; if there is one recipe that will showcase butter in all its glory, this is it. Modern bakers have gone crazy with shortbread, adding all sorts of flavors such as white chocolate chips, dried cranberries, brown sugar, and one of my favorites, coconut with macadamia nuts. I use a 9-inch ceramic pie pan from Tufty Ceramics (www.tuftyceramics.com) when making this recipe. Alternatively, you can use a round Pyrex pie plate. You will be cutting the shortbread into triangles, poetically known as "petticoat tails" in the shortbread lexicon. You score the dough before baking, which will act as your cutting guideline, and later use a serrated or chef's knife to cut all the way through into clean wedges along the marks.

o *Makes 8 wedges*

MICROWAVE COOKWARE: 8- or 9-inch round Pyrex pie plate
MICROWAVE WATTAGE: 1,100 to 1,300
MICROWAVE COOK TIME: About 5 minutes
STANDING TIME: About 1 hour

½ cup sweetened shredded coconut
6 tablespoons (¾ stick) unsalted butter, softened
⅓ cup confectioners' sugar
1 teaspoon pure vanilla extract
¾ cup all-purpose flour
¼ cup cornstarch
½ teaspoon baking powder
Pinch of salt
⅓ cup salted macadamia nuts

1. Line the pie plate with parchment paper. Dab a bit of butter underneath to hold the liner in place. Spread the coconut evenly in the pie plate and microcook on HIGH for 1 minute, stopping to stir once, until the coconut is lightly golden. Set aside.

2. In the bowl of a food processor, cream together the butter, sugar, and vanilla until fluffy. Add the flour, cornstarch, baking powder, salt, macadamia nuts, and ¼ cup of the coconut and pulse a few times until it is the consistency of a coarse meal; the nuts will be finely chopped.

3. Spread a sheet of parchment paper on your countertop or a large cutting board and sprinkle lightly with flour. Invert the bowl of the food processor onto the paper. With your fingers dipped in flour, pat the crumbly dough into a solid 7-inch round patty, then lift and invert onto the lined pie plate. Sprinkle the remaining coconut over the top. Press and pat the dough firmly into the pie plate, filling to the edges in an even layer and pressing the coconut into the surface.

4. Prick the dough all over with a fork to release steam as it bakes. With a paring knife, gently score into eight sections. Microcook on HIGH, uncovered, for about 4 minutes, or until the dough is set. The shortbread will not brown.

5. Remove from the oven to a wire rack. While the shortbread is still warm, loosen the edges from the pie plate with a small knife and cut along the score lines into 8 wedges. Let the shortbread cool completely in the pan, about 1 hour. Carefully slip the shortbread out of the pan and transfer to a small platter. You can store the shortbread in an airtight container at room temperature for up to 1 week.

VARIATION

White Chocolate–Cranberry Shortbread: In place of the coconut and macadamia nuts, add ⅓ cup sweetened dried cranberries and 2 tablespoons white chocolate chips to the flour mixture in step 2. Shape and bake as directed.

Orange–Milk Chocolate Bars

THIS RECIPE ESSENTIALLY TAKES chocolate chip cookie dough flavored with orange zest and orange liqueur, presses it into a square pan, bakes it in the microwave, then cuts it into bars. Chocolate chips are specially made to retain their shape during baking, which is why they are not often used in other recipes calling for chocolate. They are squeezed through a nozzle and immediately set up into the pert, pointed morsel shape that is like a miniature Hershey's Kiss. They are available in about eight varieties: semisweet, bittersweet (also called double or dark chocolate), white chocolate, milk chocolate, mint, peanut butter, butterscotch, and sugar-free, and in sizes ranging from ½-inch discs (also called cookie chips, made by Guittard) down to ⅛-inch-diameter mini-morsels. Stock up on bags of white, semisweet, and milk chocolate chips, especially if they are on sale. You can find the lesser-known Tropical Source chips, made with tofu powder for creaminess and no refined sugar, and organic brands like Dagoba at Whole Foods Market and other natural foods stores. Before you poo-poo these brands, consider that Tropical Source ranked first in a blind tasting of chocolate chips by *Cook's Illustrated* magazine. ○ *Makes 18 bars*

MICROWAVE COOKWARE: 8- or 9-inch square Pyrex or silicone cake pan
MICROWAVE WATTAGE: 1,100 to 1,300
MICROWAVE COOK TIME: 4 to 6 minutes
STANDING TIME: 15 minutes

½ cup (1 stick) unsalted butter, softened
½ cup granulated sugar
¼ cup packed light brown sugar
1 tablespoon freshly grated orange zest
1 teaspoon pure vanilla extract
1 teaspoon orange-flavored liqueur, such as Grand Marnier, or orange juice
½ teaspoon baking soda
⅛ teaspoon salt
1 large egg
1 cup plus 2 tablespoons all-purpose flour
½ cup (2 ounces) coarsely chopped pecans, walnuts, or macadamia nuts
6 ounces coarsely chopped milk chocolate bars or 1 cup milk chocolate chips

1. In a large bowl with a wooden spoon or in a stand mixer, cream the butter with the sugars until fluffy.

2. With the mixer running, add the orange zest, vanilla, liqueur, baking soda, and salt, then add the egg. Slowly, on the lowest speed, add the flour and then the pecans and chopped chocolate.

3. If you are using a glass cake pan, line it with waxed paper or parchment paper and spray lightly with nonstick cooking spray. If using silicone, spray the pan lightly with nonstick cooking spray. Pour in the batter and spread it evenly in the pan. Cover the baking dish and refrigerate until firm, 1 hour to overnight.

4. Microcook on HIGH, uncovered, for 4 to 6 minutes, until set on the bottom and glossy on the top surface. (The cooking time will vary by 60 to 90 seconds according to the size and shape of pan you have chosen, plus the degree of chilling.) Remove from the microwave and allow the bars to cool for about 15 minutes, then invert the pan onto a plate. The bars will release easily. Cut into 9 equal sections, then cut 2 bars from each section. You can store the bars in an airtight container or cookie jar at room temperature for up to 5 days, or freeze for up to 2 months.

Black and White Fudge

FOR A LITTLE CHANGE OF PACE, why not try a two-tone fudge? A layer of dark chocolate is topped with a layer of white chocolate flavored with a hint of vanilla, coconut, or orange. It is so attractive and dramatic looking, and the taste is splendid. Using chocolate chips makes this recipe a snap to prepare.

o *Makes about 2 pounds*

MICROWAVE COOKWARE: Two 2-quart Pyrex measuring cups or batter bowls
MICROWAVE WATTAGE: 1,100 to 1,300
MICROWAVE COOK TIME: 4 minutes
STANDING TIME: About 1½ hours

1 pound semisweet chocolate chips
¼ cup (½ stick) unsalted butter
One 14-ounce can sweetened condensed milk
1 cup chopped walnuts
1 pound white chocolate chips
1 teaspoon vanilla, coconut, or orange extract

1. In one of the measuring cups, combine the semisweet chocolate chips, 2 tablespoons of the butter, and ¾ cup of the milk.

2. Microcook on HIGH, uncovered, for 2 minutes; stir. The chips will not appear to be melted until you stir them.

3. Stir in ½ cup of the nuts; mix well. Using an offset spatula, spread the mixture into an aluminum foil–lined 8-inch square pan (leave foil overhanging the edges so you can easily pull it out) and cool in the refrigerator until firm, about 30 minutes.

4. In the other measuring cup, combine the white chocolate chips, remaining 2 tablespoons butter, and remaining milk. Microcook on HIGH, uncovered, for 2 minutes. Stir in the remaining ½ cup nuts and the extract. With an offset spatula, spread the mixture evenly over the semisweet chocolate layer.

5. Refrigerate the fudge until firm, about 1 hour. With a paring knife, cut into pieces of desired size. (You may wish to rinse the knife under hot running water between cuts to ensure that it cuts easily through the cold fudge.) You can store the fudge in an airtight container or zipper-top plastic bag in the refrigerator for up to 1 month or in the freezer for up to 2 months. Place parchment paper between the layers to prevent sticking.

Peppermint Bark

THIS BARK IS SIMPLE, but the flavors harmonize so perfectly. Gourmet shops sell out peppermint bark early in the holiday season, so having a recipe on hand is a good way to be sure you get your holiday quota and have some to give as gifts. And what a great way to use up all those Christmas candy canes no one eats! To crush the peppermint candy canes for the topping, simply place them in a zipper-top plastic bag and smash the pieces with a rolling pin or hammer. Peppermint extract is easy to find in the spice section of your supermarket.

○ *Makes about 1 pound*

MICROWAVE COOKWARE: 1- or 2-quart Pyrex measuring cup
MICROWAVE WATTAGE: 1,100 to 1,300
MICROWAVE COOK TIME: About 2 minutes
STANDING TIME: 10 minutes to 1 hour

12 ounces semisweet or bittersweet dark chocolate chips or white chocolate chips
2 teaspoons vegetable oil
½ teaspoon peppermint extract
4 regular-size candy canes, crushed into small pieces

1. Line a baking sheet with parchment paper.

2. Place the chocolate chips and oil in the measuring cup. Microcook on HIGH, uncovered, for about 2 minutes to melt the chips (the chips will not look melted until you stir them). Remove from the oven and stir in the peppermint extract.

3. With a heatproof spatula, quickly scrape the mixture onto the prepared baking sheet. Using an offset spatula, spread to a thickness of ³/₄ to 1 inch, depending upon your desired thickness. Immediately sprinkle the crushed candy over the top of the chocolate while it is still warm and press in with your fingers.

4. Refrigerate for 1 hour or freeze for 10 minutes, until the bark is solid and hard. Cut or break into 3 × 1-inch pieces to serve. You can store the bark in an airtight container in the refrigerator for up to 3 days, or freeze in a zipper-top plastic freezer bag for up to 1 month.

VARIATIONS

Aztec Chocolate Bark: Melt the chocolate and in step 2, stir in ¹/₂ teaspoon ground cinnamon, ¹/₂ teaspoon ancho chile powder, and ¹/₈ teaspoon cayenne pepper or New Mexico red chile powder instead of the peppermint extract. In step 3, sprinkle with ¹/₂ cup chopped pistachios or toasted pumpkin seeds instead of the candy canes.

Chocolate Fruit Bark: Melt the chocolate and in step 2, stir in 1 teaspoon orange oil or ¹/₂ teaspoon orange extract instead of the peppermint extract. In step 3, sprinkle with ¹/₂ cup finely chopped dried apricots and ¹/₂ cup dried cranberries instead of the candy canes.

Dark Chocolate Truffles

CHOCOLATE TRUFFLES are the easiest and most elegant candy you can make. Making truffles by hand is messy work, but the end product is so delicious that it's worth the cleanup. You might want to wear disposable plastic gloves to keep your hands clean, just like they do in the chocolate shops. You can easily make truffles weeks before you will need them, and they store perfectly in the freezer. You can also make your truffles any size you like. I prefer my truffles to be about 1-inch-diameter size rather than a big bonbon. Use excellent-quality chocolate and organic heavy cream for the tastiest results. ◦ *Makes 24 to 30 truffles*

MICROWAVE COOKWARE: 1-quart Pyrex measuring cup
MICROWAVE WATTAGE: 1,100 to 1,300
MICROWAVE COOK TIME: About 1 minute
STANDING TIME: 3½ hours to overnight

9 ounces bittersweet or semisweet chocolate (such as Lindt, Ghirardelli, or Callebaut; 62% cacao or higher), chopped into small pieces

½ cup heavy cream

4½ teaspoons unsalted butter

2 tablespoons amaretto or other liqueur of your choice

2 teaspoons pure vanilla extract

¾ to 1 cup unsweetened cocoa powder, finely chopped walnuts, or finely chopped almonds

1. Cover a large baking sheet with parchment paper. Set aside. Place the chocolate, heavy cream, and butter in the measuring cup.

2. Microcook on HIGH, uncovered, for about 1 minute, until the cream is hot and the butter is melted. The chips will not appear to be melted. Remove from the oven and whisk the mixture until melted and smooth; stir in the liqueur and vanilla. (This is called a ganache.)

3. Transfer the mixture to a small bowl. Cover with a piece of plastic wrap and press it directly on the surface of the chocolate. Refrigerate until firm, about 3 hours or up to overnight.

4. With a teaspoon, portion out some of the ganache. Roll between the palms of your hands quickly (it will melt from the heat of your hands) to shape into imperfect balls. Place on the prepared baking sheet. Refrigerate for 30 minutes.

5. Place the cocoa powder in a shallow bowl. Dip the balls into the cocoa to coat. Serve immediately. You can store the truffles, well wrapped or in an airtight container, in the refrigerator for up to 1 week, or in the freezer for up to 1 month. If necessary, redust the truffles in cocoa before serving, which I usually do since it tends to get absorbed during storage. Let stand at room temperature for 1 hour before serving for the truffles to soften a bit.

VARIATIONS

Raspberry Dark Chocolate Truffles: Add 2 tablespoons seedless raspberry jam in step 1 and use a raspberry liqueur, such as Chambord, instead of the amaretto. Proceed as directed for chilling, shaping, and coating. Coat with chopped walnuts instead of the cocoa powder.

Rum Raisin Dark Chocolate Truffles: Combine 2 tablespoons rum and 4½ teaspoons chopped dark raisins in a small bowl. Let macerate for at least 1 hour at room temperature. Omit the amaretto. Stir the rum-raisin mixture in with the vanilla in step 2. Proceed as directed for chilling, shaping, and coating. Coat with cocoa powder.

Nut and Seed Brittle

HAVE A CAN OF FANCY NUTS left over from your last party? One of the great ways to use them up is to make a nut brittle. Brittle is the quintessential American candy, our modern version born and bred in Colonial kitchens. The microwave turns a job that used to require lots of stovetop stirring and a candy thermometer into a snap. The timing is crucial to getting the caramel just right. Don't keep fiddling with the mixture in the microwave just to "check it." It has to stay really hot to cook to the hard crack stage, which will make the cooled candy harden properly. Don't worry about your brittle looking perfect, since it will be broken up into uneven chunks. You can use salted nuts, but if so, omit the salt in the recipe. If you like your brittle fancied up with a layer of chocolate, sprinkle the top of the still-warm mixture on the baking sheet with some semisweet chocolate chips, which will begin to melt, and immediately spread them into a thin layer with a small metal spatula. With chocolate or without, this makes an exceptionally great gift for holidays and birthdays. Do not double this recipe; just make multiple batches. ○ *Makes about 1 pound*

MICROWAVE COOKWARE: 1- or 2-quart Pyrex measuring cup
MICROWAVE WATTAGE: 1,100 to 1,300
MICROWAVE COOK TIME: 5 to 6 minutes
STANDING TIME: At least 2 hours

1 cup sugar
½ cup light corn syrup
2 tablespoons water
One to two pinches of salt
1 cup unsalted dry-roasted peanuts
3 tablespoons white or unhulled sesame seeds
2 tablespoons unsalted butter, softened
Heaping ½ teaspoon baking soda

1. Line a baking sheet with parchment paper, a silicone baking liner, or aluminum foil, and coat with nonstick cooking spray. (You can also use a marble slab if you have it.) Spray the insides and spout of the measuring cup and a heatproof spatula with nonstick cooking spray. Measure out all of the ingredients, including the baking soda, and set aside. Have your oven mitts close by. This goes very quickly.

2. In the measuring cup, stir together the sugar, corn syrup, water, and salt. Microcook on HIGH, uncovered, for 2 to 2¼ minutes. The mixture will bubble vigorously when it comes to a boil. When the bubbling stops, use a heatproof spatula to fold in the peanuts and sesame seeds. Microcook on HIGH for another 2 to 2¼ minutes. Do not overcook the nuts.

3. Stir in the butter, and microcook on HIGH for 1 to 1½ minutes, until the brittle reaches your desired degree of golden; longer and it will turn a dark, toasty amber-brown, which some people prefer. Each microwave will be a bit different, so watch carefully when you make this for the first time.

4. Remove from the microwave and quickly stir in the baking soda. The mixture will foam up and create the brittle's light, airy texture.

5. Working quickly, immediately pour the hot mixture onto the prepared baking sheet, and shake to level it out or use the back of a spatula or wooden spoon coated with nonstick cooking spray to spread it to the desired thickness. While it is warm and slightly pliable, you can press and stretch it out before it hardens. Allow the brittle to cool at room temperature, uncovered, until cold and hard, at least 2 hours. (If your brittle becomes too hard as you are pouring it out, you cooked it too long, and if it is soft like taffy, you undercooked it.)

6. When the brittle has hardened, break it into uneven pieces with your hands or by hitting it with a small rolling pin. You can store the brittle in a zipper-top plastic bag at room temperature, or in an airtight container in the freezer, for up to 1 month.

VARIATIONS

Almond-Coconut Brittle: Use 1 cup coarsely chopped roasted salted almonds and ½ cup unsweetened shredded coconut in place of the peanuts, sesame seeds, and salt.

Cashew Brittle: Use 1 cup coarsely chopped roasted salted cashews in place of the peanuts, sesame seeds, and salt. If you use unsalted dry-roasted cashews, leave in the salt.

Pumpkin Seed Brittle: Use 1 cup toasted pumpkin seeds in place of the peanuts and sesame seeds. Look for pumpkin seeds, often labeled "pepitas," in Mexican markets.

Fresh Strawberry Jam

EXCEPTIONAL, CHUNKY, FRESH-FRUIT JAMS are easily made within half an hour in the microwave. Homemade jams are less sweet than commercial jams and much more exciting in flavor, texture, and color. Every spring when the first strawberries hit the market, my mother makes her strawberry jam in the microwave. This jam is a bit loose, even drippy, compared to the solid jelled texture of commercial jams. Use overripe as well as underripe berries; it's best to make the jam from just-bought berries rather than refrigerated berries, as their flavor dulls with refrigeration. Because they absorb water quickly, never float berries in water to clean them. When ready to use, rinse briefly with cold running water, then hull them. Pectin is important for thickening microwave jams, as the fruit's juice does not evaporate during cooking, resulting in a greater yield per batch than on the stovetop. You may substitute raspberries, blackberries, or blueberries for the strawberries, but definitely taste the jam while adding the sugar and adjust the sweetness as desired. ○ *Makes 4 cups (2 pint jars)*

MICROWAVE COOKWARE: 1½- to 2-quart deep, straight-sided microwave-safe glass or ceramic casserole dish (that can hold about three times the volume of the fruit), preferably with a pouring spout
MICROWAVE WATTAGE: 1,100 to 1,300
MICROWAVE COOK TIME: 11 to 13 minutes
STANDING TIME: 10 minutes

1 quart (4 cups) fresh strawberries, washed, drained, and hulled
Half of a 1.75- to 2-ounce box powdered pectin
2½ cups sugar, or to taste

1. Coarsely crush the berries by hand or in a food processor, leaving a few whole berries or chunks, as desired, to make 2 to 2½ cups. Place in the casserole dish, sprinkle with the pectin. Let stand at room temperature for 10 minutes.

2. Microcook on HIGH, uncovered, to bring to a rolling boil that cannot be stirred down, about 6 minutes. Add the sugar and stir well.

3. Microcook on HIGH, uncovered, for 5 to 7 minutes, stirring twice. Skim off the white foam with a large metal spoon. Remove from the oven. Let cool for 10 minutes, stirring occasionally, before ladling into storage jars such as glass French confiture jars with plastic lids, jelly jars, or glass-topped jars with wire closures. Let stand until cool. Store, covered, in the refrigerator for up to 2 months, if it lasts that long.

Orange Marmalade

MARMALADE USUALLY REFERS TO a preserve derived from a citrus fruit, the most common being tart oranges. Marmalade can also be made from lemons, limes, grapefruits, or a combination. Marmalade recipes include sliced or chopped fruit peel, which is simmered first in fruit juice and water until soft before adding the pulp and pectin; it can take hours to make traditional marmalade. No more. Here is a lovely microwave recipe based on one created by Jane Trittipo, a microwave-cooking teacher, who ran the recipe as Marvelous Microwave Marmalade in *Bon Appétit* magazine in the 1980s and self-published a book called *The Everyday Gourmet: Fast and Fabulous Microwave Recipes* (1988). Instead of stripping the peel and cooking it separately, the entire fruit is ground. Your finished product won't have the strips of zest, but it will still be incredibly delicious and do your morning toast proud. ○ *Makes about ¾ cup*

MICROWAVE COOKWARE: 2-quart Pyrex measuring cup
MICROWAVE WATTAGE: 1,100 to 1,300
MICROWAVE COOK TIME: 5 to 6 minutes
STANDING TIME: At least 1 hour

1 navel orange (preferably organic), unpeeled, scrubbed, and quartered
Sugar
Light corn syrup

1. Place the orange quarters in the work bowl of a food processor fitted with the metal blade. Pulse until reduced to ¼-inch pieces.

2. Transfer to the measuring cup. Note the amount and add an equal amount of sugar; stir. Note the amount and add 1 tablespoon corn syrup, which will prevent crystallization during cooling, per cup of orange-sugar mixture.

3. Microcook, uncovered, on HIGH for 2 minutes. Microcook on LOW (10 percent power) or DEFROST for 3 to 4 minutes, until the mixture is slightly thickened and the peel is tender. Be careful not to overcook. The mixture should fall from a spoon in thick drops.

4. Transfer to a storage jar. Let stand to cool to room temperature; the mixture will continue to thicken as it cools. You can store the marmalade in a tightly covered jar in the refrigerator for up to 2 months.

VARIATION

Two-Citrus Marmalade: Combine 2 medium-size Meyer lemons, washed, cut into sixteenths, and seeded, with the orange in the food processor in step 1. Continue to add the sugar and corn syrup in the appropriate proportions as directed, and microcook as directed, adding 50 to 60 seconds to the cook time. This makes about 1 cup.

The Best Nondairy Cocoa-Chocolate Sauce

THIS SMOOTH, SHINY SAUCE is adapted from a recipe by David Lebovitz, who is like a chocolate guru here in the San Francisco Bay area. It is delectable, and you certainly won't miss the butter and cream. Since chocolate and cocoa are the dominant flavors, be sure to use high-quality products. Unsweetened cocoa can be thought of as bitter, but when sugar and vanilla are added, get ready for a flavor that can only be described as heavenly. Good cocoa brands are Scharffen Berger, Lindt, Callebaut, and Guittard. This is a rather thin sauce after cooking, but it will thicken as it cools. You can pour this sauce over ice cream or dip strawberries into it. ○ *Makes about 2½ cups*

MICROWAVE COOKWARE: 2-quart Pyrex measuring cup
MICROWAVE WATTAGE: 1,100 to 1,300
MICROWAVE COOK TIME: 2 to 3 minutes
STANDING TIME: A few hours

1 cup water
¾ cup unsweetened cocoa powder (preferably Dutch-processed)
½ cup sugar
½ cup light corn syrup
2 ounces bittersweet or semisweet chocolate, finely chopped
1½ teaspoons pure vanilla extract

1. Place the water, cocoa, sugar, and corn syrup into the measuring cup. Whisk to combine.

2. Microcook on HIGH, uncovered, for 2 minutes, and then at 30-second intervals as needed, to simmer and just bring to a boil.

3. Remove from the oven and stir in the chopped chocolate and vanilla; stir until melted. Let stand at room temperature for a few hours to thicken. You can store the chocolate sauce in an airtight container in the refrigerator for up to 10 days. Rewarm in the microwave for about 30 seconds on HIGH before serving. (The amount of time will vary according to the volume of sauce and the size of the container used for reheating.)

Robert's Adult Fantasy Chocolate Sauce

ROBERT IS ROBERT LAMBERT, who is a whiz in the kitchen. He knows his stuff about chocolate, having been a private dessert chef making designer-style, lip-smacking-good fantasy chocolate desserts for the likes of Joan Collins and Lily Tomlin in his cooking-in-Hollywood days. He wrote a book based on this chapter of his life called *Fantasy Chocolate Desserts* (Chronicle Books, 1988). Now he has a business creating his own line of artisan condiments that are so personalized that he often goes out and picks the fruit himself, in addition to preparing and canning hundreds of jars. The sauce recipe he generously shares here is similar to the Dark Chocolate Cognac Sauce in his new line (www.robertlambert.com). Serve on ice cream, drizzle over composed desserts or pound cake, use as a cake or brownie icing glaze, top profiteroles, or make hot chocolate by adding 3 tablespoons to a mug of hot milk heated in the microwave. You can substitute coconut milk for the regular milk. ● *Makes 1¼ cups*

MICROWAVE COOKWARE: 1-quart Pyrex measuring cup
MICROWAVE WATTAGE: 1,100 to 1,300
MICROWAVE COOK TIME: 2 to 4 minutes
STANDING TIME: 10 minutes

8 ounces semisweet chocolate of your choice (Robert uses 72% cacao)
½ cup milk
2 tablespoons light corn syrup
2 tablespoons brandy, cognac, eau de vie (try pear-flavored), or liqueur such
as Chambord, Grand Marnier, or Cherry Marnier

1. Chop or break the chocolate into pieces and place in the measuring cup. Pour in the milk and corn syrup.

2. Microcook on HIGH, uncovered, in 2-minutes intervals, just until the mixture can be whisked smooth. Do not overheat or allow to boil. Stir in the liqueur. Let stand for 10 minutes if using right away. The sauce should be just above room temperature to pour, and it will become firm when refrigerated. You can store the sauce, tightly covered, in the refrigerator for up to 3 weeks. Microcook on HIGH for 10 to 15 seconds to rewarm refrigerated chocolate sauce.

Butterscotch Sauce

BUTTERSCOTCH SAUCE is something you make when you want to impress guests. Authentic butterscotch sauce isn't like the thick stuff you buy in the jar; it is silky and pourable and not cloyingly sweet. Surprisingly, the flavor of the butterscotch blooms when there is both vanilla and salt added, and there is no Scotch whisky involved (the "scotch" in the title refers to a technique used in making hard butterscotch candy). Use dark brown sugar, as light brown sugar doesn't give a deep enough flavor. Don't skip the corn syrup, as it keeps the sugar from recrystallizing as it cools. Serve this sauce over ice cream, as it accents all sorts of flavors from coffee to chocolate (not to mention vanilla), and bring out the toasted, salted nuts (almonds, cashews, macadamias). Chop some up and sprinkle on top of your sundae, for the flavor combination of salt and caramel is one of the dynamic classics of the food world. This sauce is also good over gingerbread, cheese-cake, poached pears, sliced bananas, or steamed pudding. For a slightly thicker sauce, you can use heavy whipping cream (not ultra-pasteurized, please) in place of the half-and-half. ○ *Makes about 1⅓ cups*

MICROWAVE COOKWARE: 2-quart Pyrex measuring cup
MICROWAVE WATTAGE: 1,100 to 1,300
MICROWAVE COOK TIME: 3 to 4 minutes
STANDING TIME: None

¼ cup (½ stick) unsalted butter, at room temperature, cut into pieces
1¼ cups packed dark brown sugar
½ cup half-and-half
2 tablespoons dark corn syrup
⅛ teaspoon salt
1 teaspoon pure vanilla extract
1 teaspoon brandy

1. Put the butter in the measuring cup. Microcook on HIGH for 1 minute to melt.

2. Stir in the brown sugar, half-and-half, corn syrup, and salt. Stir with a wooden spoon to break up any lumps in the sugar. Cover with a piece of parchment paper. Microcook on HIGH for 3 to 4 minutes, stirring once with the handle of a wooden spoon until thickened and the sugar is dissolved. The mixture will come to a full boil.

3. Remove from the oven and immediately stir in the vanilla and brandy until smooth and well blended. Serve warm. If not using immediately, cool completely, then pour into a glass jar and cover. This sauce will keep in the refrigerator for up to 1 month (it will thicken as it chills). You might find yourself eating it with a spoon out of the jar. To reheat, place the sauce in a glass bowl, and microcook on DEFROST for 1 to 2 minutes. (The amount of time will vary according to the volume of sauce and the size of the container used for reheating.)

Coffee Sauce for Ice Cream

F YOU HAVE EVER poured a cup of cold coffee over a scoop of vanilla ice cream, you know what coffee can do as a dessert sauce. The flavors sing. You can substitute a cup of strong brewed coffee for the water and instant coffee mixture. To make a coffee-walnut sauce, stir in ½ cup chopped toasted or untoasted walnuts at the very end of cooking. ○ *Makes about 1⅔ cups*

MICROWAVE COOKWARE: 2-quart Pyrex measuring cup
MICROWAVE WATTAGE: 1,100 to 1,300
MICROWAVE COOK TIME: About 4 minutes
STANDING TIME: None

1 cup water
2 tablespoons instant espresso powder
3 teaspoons cornstarch
1 cup sugar (or half sugar and half honey)
2 tablespoons brandy (optional)

1. Combine the water, espresso powder, and cornstarch in the measuring cup. Whisk to combine and to dissolve the cornstarch. Add the sugar and the brandy, if you are using it.

2. Microcook on HIGH, uncovered, for 2 minutes, until very hot. Stir with a whisk to dissolve the sugar.

3. Microcook on HIGH for another 2 minutes, pausing at 30-second intervals and stirring once halfway through, to simmer and just bring to a boil. The sauce will thicken slightly and become clear. Cool to room temperature and store in a covered container in the refrigerator for up to 10 days. Serve cold.

Sweet Blueberry Sauce

NOW THAT BLUEBERRIES are considered a "superfood" with all kinds of health benefits, you can find lots of blueberries in the grocery store year round. When they are in season and the price is right, freeze fresh berries by placing them in a single layer on a cookie sheet in the freezer. When frozen, put the berries in zipper-top plastic freezer bags. It is best to rinse blueberries before using them, but not before freezing them. Pour this delicious sauce over ice cream, yogurt, pancakes or waffles, or pound cake. It is also good over a fresh fruit cup or sliced fresh oranges. ○ *Makes about 2 cups*

MICROWAVE COOKWARE: 2-quart Pyrex measuring cup
MICROWAVE WATTAGE: 1,100 to 1,300
MICROWAVE COOK TIME: About 4 minutes
STANDING TIME: None

1 pint fresh blueberries, or 2 cups unsweetened frozen blueberries
¼ cup sugar
2 teaspoons cornstarch
¼ cup orange juice
Zest of 1 orange
½ teaspoon grated fresh ginger

1. In the measuring cup, combine the blueberries, sugar, and cornstarch; toss to coat the berries. Add the orange juice.

2. Microcook on HIGH, uncovered, for 4 minutes, until the berries are hot and soft and the sauce is thickened and clear (frozen berries will take an extra minute). Stir in the zest and the ginger. Let stand until ready to serve. This sauce can be served warm or cold. You can store it in the refrigerator, covered, for up to 5 days.

Measurement Equivalents

Please note that all conversions are approximate.

Liquid Conversions

U.S.	Metric	U.S.	Metric
1 tsp	5 ml	1 cup	240 ml
1 tbs	15 ml	1 cup + 2 tbs	275 ml
2 tbs	30 ml	1¼ cups	300 ml
3 tbs	45 ml	1⅓ cups	325 ml
¼ cup	60 ml	1½ cups	350 ml
⅓ cup	75 ml	1⅔ cups	375 ml
⅓ cup + 1 tbs	90 ml	1¾ cups	400 ml
⅓ cup + 2 tbs	100 ml	1¾ cups + 2 tbs	450 ml
½ cup	120 ml	2 cups (1 pint)	475 ml
⅔ cup	150 ml	2½ cups	600 ml
¾ cup	180 ml	3 cups	720 ml
¾ cup + 2 tbs	200 ml	4 cups (1 quart)	945 ml
			(1,000 ml is 1 liter)

Weight Conversions

U.S. / U.K.	Metric	U.S. / U.K.	Metric
$1/2$ oz	14 g	7 oz	200 g
1 oz	28 g	8 oz	227 g
$1^{1}/2$ oz	43 g	9 oz	255 g
2 oz	57 g	10 oz	284 g
$2^{1}/2$ oz	71 g	11 oz	312 g
3 oz	85 g	12 oz	340 g
$3^{1}/2$ oz	100 g	13 oz	368 g
4 oz	113 g	14 oz	400 g
5 oz	142 g	15 oz	425 g
6 oz	170 g	1 lb	454 g

Oven Temperature Conversions

°F	Gas Mark	°C
250	$1/2$	120
275	1	140
300	2	150
325	3	165
350	4	180
375	5	190
400	6	200
425	7	220
450	8	230
475	9	240
500	10	260
550	Broil	290

Index

F

Feta
  -Artichoke Dip, 37
  Minted Peas with, 161
Fish. *See also* Shellfish
  Baked Beets with Anchovy
    Vinaigrette, 142–43
  Fillets with Buttered Crumb
    Coating, 191
  Halibut with Lemon and
    Parsley, 192
  homemade condiments for,
    194–95
  microwaving times, 190
  My Mom's Halibut with
    Garden Herbs, 193
  Open-Faced Tuna Melts,
    85–86
  Petrale Sole Amandine, 197
  Poached Salmon with
    Lemon Sauce, 202–3
  Poached Sole with Hollanda-
    ise, 198–99
  Salmon with Crème Fraîche
    and Dill in Parchment,
    200–201
  Steamed Catfish with
    Ginger, 196
  Tacos, Baja, 206–7
  and Vegetables, Hoisin,
    238–39
Florentine Oatmeal, 101
Fontina cheese
  Cheese Sauce, 227
  Mixed Vegetable Risotto
    with, 120
  Oatmeal Lorraine, 101
  Pesto Potatoes in Their
    Jackets, 183
  and Tomato Sauce, Polenta
    Casserole with, 124–25
Food safety considerations,
  14–15
Frittatas
  Cereal Bowl Vegetable, 60
  Huevos Rancheros for One,
    61
Fruit. *See also specific fruits*
  Bark, Chocolate, 291
  citrus, juicing, 30
  dried, rehydrating, 28

Fudge, Black and White,
  288–89

G

Garlic Toasts, 72–73
Ginger
  Crystallized, Ice Cream,
    Chunky Stewed Rhubarb
    Over, 278–79
  Fresh, Napa Cabbage with,
    145
  Steamed Catfish with, 196
  Tea, 255
Goat Cheese
  Cheese Sauce, 227
  Individual Veggie Tortilla
    Pizzas, 89
  Melted, in Marinara, 43
  Provençal Oatmeal, 101
Grains. *See also* Rice
  Barley Pilaf with Sun-Dried
    Tomatoes and Scallions,
    114–15
  Breakfast Steel-Cut Oats,
    102–3
  Bulgur Cracked Wheat, 121
  Cooked Wheat Berries, 93
  Exotic Oatmeal, 101
  Family-Style Creamy
    Maple-Cranberry Oat-
    meal, 99
  Florentine Oatmeal, 101
  Mediterranean Oatmeal,
    101
  Microwave Wild Rice,
    104–5
  Oatmeal Lorraine, 101
  Old-Fashioned Apple-Raisin
    Oatmeal, 97
  Old-Fashioned Cranberry
    Oatmeal, 97
  Old-Fashioned Creamy Oat-
    meal, 97
  Old-Fashioned Oatmeal,
    96–97
  Old-Fashioned Oatmeal and
    Wheat Berries, 98
  Old-Fashioned Oatmeal with
    White Chocolate, 97
  Olive Oil Granola with
    Golden Raisins, 94–95

Orient Express Oatmeal, 101
Perfect Quinoa, 122–23
Polenta Casserole with Fon-
  tina and Tomato Sauce,
  124–25
Provençal Oatmeal, 101
Savory Oatmeal, 100–101
Granola
  Berry Parfaits, 95
  Olive Oil, with Golden Rai-
    sins, 94–95
Grapefruit zest, drying, 30
Gratin, Gold and White
  Potato, 177
Greek Spinach Rice (*Spanako-
  rizo*), 112–13
Green Beans and Garlic
  Toasts, Quickest Mine-
  strone with, 72–73
Greens. *See also* Spinach
  Beet, and Scallions, 165
  Braised Escarole alla Ro-
    mana, 160
  Braised Escarole and Can-
    nellini Beans, 160
  Buttered Cabbage Wedges
    with Caraway, 150
  Coconut Chicken Soup with
    Bok Choy, 76–77
  Florentine Oatmeal, 101
  Hoisin Fish and Vegetables,
    238–39
  Napa Cabbage with Fresh
    Ginger, 145
  Olive Oil–Braised Escarole,
    159–60
  Watercress Soup, 64
Green Tea, Jasmine, Whipped
  Cream, 264–65
Green Tea Latte, 258
Grenadine syrup, 260
Grilling, parcooking foods for,
  29
Guacamole, Chunky, 207

H

Halibut
  with Garden Herbs, My
    Mom's, 193
  Hoisin Fish and Vegetables,
    238–39